Beyond Burning Bras

BEYOND BURNING BRAS

Feminist Activism for Everyone

Laura Finley and Emily Reynolds Stringer

 PRAEGER

AN IMPRINT OF ABC-CLIO, LLC
Santa Barbara, California • Denver, Colorado • Oxford, England

3/7/11
Lan
$44.95

Library of Congress Cataloging-in-Publication Data

Finley, Laura L.
  Beyond burning bras : feminist activism for everyone / Laura Finley and
  Emily Reynolds Stringer.
      p. cm.
  Includes bibliographical references and index.
  ISBN 978–0–313–36580–5 (hard copy : alk. paper) — ISBN 978–0–313–36581–2 (ebook)
1. Feminism—United States—History. 2. Women's rights—United States—History. 3. Sex discrimination—United States—History. I. Stringer, Emily Reynolds. II. Title.
HQ1426.F56   2010
305.420973—dc22   2009053890

ISBN: 978–0–313–36580–5
EISBN: 978–0–313–36581–2

14 13 12 11 10   1 2 3 4 5

This book is also available on the World Wide Web as an eBook.
Visit www.abc-clio.com for details.

Praeger
An Imprint of ABC-CLIO, LLC

ABC-CLIO, LLC
130 Cremona Drive, P.O. Box 1911
Santa Barbara, California 93116-1911

This book is printed on acid-free paper (∞)

Manufactured in the United States of America

Contents

Preface

We can save the world as we commute. Okay, maybe not, but we sure can cook up some great plans! This book was generated from just such a conversation. In fall 2006, I (Laura Finley) met Emily Reynolds when a friend invited me to a women's book club Emily was organizing. We soon discovered that we were both commuting to the same college—Emily as a graduate student and me as a professor. So we decided to take turns driving. Through those drives, we learned about each other—our passions, our political views, our personal baggage, and our dreams. We often discussed what can be lumped together as "women's issues": things like mothering (I was one at the time, Emily was engaged), inequalities in the workplace, and making changes to end gender inequalities. We discussed the fact that people do things all the time that are amazing, and that help forward human rights for everyone, women included. Yet, too often these people receive little recognition.

I had already authored some books on various sociology topics, and would occasionally speak about them. Emily one day shared her idea that we should capture the stories of all the amazing people we knew that we would call "everyday" feminist activists. It would couple history with current issues, political with personal, cerebral with creative, and above all, inspire people that they too can be activists for social change. This is that book, of course. After a year of dedication to soliciting friends, acquaintances, and absolute strangers to contribute, countless hours of researching and organizing materials, and who-knows-how-many phone conversations, emails, and texts to exchange ideas, we give you *Beyond Burning Bras: Feminist Activism for Everyone*.

The book is an eclectic compilation. It begins with a review of the history of feminist activism. The timeline at the front of the book provides readers with a chronology of key events. Then Chapters One, Two, and Three describe the first, second, and third waves of women's rights and feminist activity, respectively. These are written in a more traditional fashion and will allow readers to see the progress and continued concerns of feminist activists. We do not intend that this be an exhaustive account of the women's rights movement or feminist activism throughout all of human history. Those books do exist and can provide interested persons with a critical understanding of history. Rather, we include this brief compilation of background information in order to provide a framework for the individual entries from activists.

The remainder of the book is organized thematically. It presents the stories of "everyday" people who think, say, and do things that help advance the rights of women and decrease gender inequalities. It is not all there is to feminist activism, but these entries certainly show how diverse it can be and how action to help the environment and impoverished women, as well as that by artists, for instance, also helps women. Unlike the first portion of the book, these are written in the first person, although each chapter has an introduction that provides a brief overview of the issue. Although we hope they educate readers, more importantly, we want readers to see that no one has to burn a bra in protest, organize a large scale march, or tie themselves to a tree to be a feminist activist. Further, we hope that these stories help readers to realize that neither feminism nor activism is a dirty word. Emily perhaps said it best, when she responded to a young man who questioned what a feminist activist was, "Would it make you feel better if I said I am an equalist?" This book is intended to illustrate that, rather than chalking feminism up to the sole domain of man-hating lesbians or crazy spinsters, we all can and should be activists for gender equality. We edited these entries only for grammatical and typographical errors, as it is our intent to present each author's unique voice and style.

Again, we do not pretend that these entries encapsulate all there is to feminist activism. We included as many and as diverse a group of contributions as we could compile, but surely there are many more individuals and groups doing wonderful work that is not included. Perhaps a follow-up volume will be the result! Or an inspired reader may see some gap in our coverage and take it upon himself or herself to share with the world that specific perspective.

At the end of the book, readers will find several additional items. An appendix with tips for feminist activism is included so that readers can begin immediately to take action. The Resources list provides recommended books, journals, and Web sites for more information. Please enjoy these tools, and more importantly, use them!

Chronology: Milestones of Feminist Activism in American History

1607	First European women arrive at Jamestown colony.
1638	Anne Hutchinson is expelled from the Massachusetts Bay colony.
1650	Anne Bradstreet, earliest American poet, publishes her first poem.
1692	Salem witch trials.
1773	Phillis Wheatley's poetry becomes the first book by a Black American.
1776	Abigail Adams ι ᵉr husband John to "remember the ladies."
1783	New Jersey woɪ under their state statute.
1792	Mary Wollstonε *A Vindication of the Rights of Women* is published in the United States.
1818	Emma Willard asks for taxpayer support for females' education.
1826	The American Society for the Promotion of Temperance is founded.
1829	The first book advocating birth control is published in the United States.
1833	Oberlin is founded as the first coeducational college in the United States.
	The Female Anti-Slavery Society of Philadelphia is founded.
	The first National Temperance Convention is held.
	Lydia Maria Child published the first antislavery book in the United States
1834	Lowell mill girls go on strike.
	The American Female Moral Reform Society is founded.
1837	Mary Lyon founds Mount Holyoke Seminary, the first women's college.

Angelina and Sarah Grimke lecture to mixed-sex audiences about abolitionism.

1840 Women are divided over abolition.

Georgia Female College grants the first bachelor's degrees to women.

Lucretia Mott is denied a seat at the World Anti-Slavery Conference.

1843 Dorothea Dix exposes the poor treatment given the mentally ill in Massachusetts hospitals.

1848 The first women's rights convention is held in Seneca Falls, NY.

1849 Elizabeth Blackwell is the first modern woman to graduate from medical school.

1850 Amelia Bloomer introduced bloomers.

First National Women's Rights Convention in Worcester, MA.

The Woman's Medical College in Pennsylvania is founded by Philadelphia Quakers.

Harriet Tubman leads first slaves to freedom.

1851 Sojourner Truth addresses women's rights convention in Akron, OH.

1852 Harriet Beecher Stowe writes *Uncle Tom's Cabin*.

Emily Dickinson's first poem is published.

1853 Antoinette Blackwell is first ordained female minister in the United States.

1859 The American Medical Association (AMA) opposes abortion.

1863 The National Women's Loyal League supports emancipation.

1869 The Knights of Labor is founded and includes women workers.

Susan B. Anthony and Elizabeth Cady Stanton form the National Woman Suffrage Association.

Lucy Stone, Henry Blackwell, and others form the American Woman Suffrage Association.

1872 Virginia Woodhull runs for president of the United States.

1873 Congress passes the Comstock Law.

1878 A woman suffrage movement is first introduced to Congress.

1879 Mary Baker Eddy founds the Christian Science movement.

The first woman practices before the U.S. Supreme Court.

1881 Clara Barton founds the American Red Cross.

1883 *Ladies Home Journal* begins publication.

1885 Annie Oakley joins Buffalo Bill's Wild West Show.

1889 Jane Addams founds Hull House in Chicago.

1890 Suffragists unite under the banner of the National American Woman Suffrage Association (NAWSA).

1892 Illinois becomes the first state to limit work hours for women.

1893 Colorado is the first state to adopt an amendment granting women the right to vote.

1895 The first American Women's Amateur Golf championship held at same time as the first men's championship.

1896 Formation of the National Association of Colored Women.

1898 Charlotte Perkins Gilman publishes *Women and Economics*.

1903 Foundation of National Women's Trade Union.

Mother Jones leads a caravan of children to the president's Oyster Bay home.

1908 The American Home Economics Association is founded.

1911 Dr. Alice Hamilton publishes the first study of occupational disease.

The Triangle Shirtwaist fire kills many young women.

Kansas City, MI, passes the nation's first Mother's Pension Law.

1912 Juliette Gordon Low founds the Girl Scouts of America.

Alice Paul leads a protest at Woodrow Wilson's inauguration.

The U.S. Children's Bureau is founded.

1913 Alice Paul and Lucy Burns form the Congressional Union to work toward the passage of the federal amendment to give women the right to vote. The group was later named the National Women's Party.

1915 The Woman's Peace Party is started.

1916 Jeanette Rankin becomes the first woman elected to U.S. Congress.

Margaret Sanger starts the first birth control clinic in Brooklyn, NY.

1917 The American Women's Hospitals Service helps female physicians serve in World War I.

1919 Formation of the League of Women Voters.

Congress passes the Nineteenth Amendment.

The National Federation of Business and Professional Women's Clubs is formed.

1920 Formation of the Women's Bureau of the Department of Labor.

1921   Margaret Sanger forms American Birth Control League, which becomes Planned Parenthood Federation in 1942.

First appearance of Betty Crocker.

1922   Ida Husted completes the six-volume *History of Woman Suffrage.*

Emily Post publishes *Etiquette.*

1925   Florence Sabin is elected to the National Academy of Sciences.

1928   Margaret Mead publishes *Coming of Age in Somoa.*

1929   Female pilots organize the Ninety-Nines, Inc.

1930   Formation of the Association of Southern Women for the Prevention of Lynching.

1931   Jane Addams wins Nobel Peace Prize.

1932   Amelia Earhart flies solo over the Atlantic Ocean.

Frances Perkins is first female cabinet member.

1935   Mary McLeod Bethune accepts position as Minority Affairs Advisor.

Formation of the National Council of Negro Women.

Congress enacts the Social Security Act.

1936   Margaret Mitchell publishes *Gone with the Wind.*

Eleanor Roosevelt is a transformational first lady.

1938   Pearl Buck wins Nobel Prize for Literature.

1939   Freud student Karen Horney publishes *New Ways in Psychoanalysis.*

Grandma Moses's paintings are displayed at the Museum of Modern Art.

1941   Women are accepted into the armed forces in roles other than nursing.

1945   Eleanor Roosevelt joins the U.S. delegation to the United Nations.

1946   Emily Greene Balch is given Nobel Peace Prize.

United Nations establishes the Commission on the Status of Women.

1949   Babe Dickinson Zaharias is named female athlete of the century.

1950   Althea Gibson breaks the color barrier in women's tennis.

1952   Marilyn Monroe achieves stardom in *Gentlemen Prefer Blondes.*

1955   Rosa Parks refuses to give up her seat to a white passenger on Montgomery, AL, bus.

The Daughters of Bilitis (DOB), the nation's first lesbian organization, is founded.

1956 Foundation of La Leche League.

1960 "The Pill" is approved by FDA.

1961 President John F. Kennedy establishes the President's Commission on the Status of Women and appoints Eleanor Roosevelt as chairwoman.

1962 Dolores Huerta helps form the United Farm Workers Union.

Rachel Carson's *Silent Spring* alerts the public to the dangers of pesticides.

1963 Mary Kay Cosmetics Co. is founded.

Congress passes Equal Pay Act.

Betty Friedan's *The Feminine Mystique* is published.

1964 The Civil Rights Act prohibits sex discrimination in employment.

1965 Helen Gurley Brown takes over as editor of *Cosmopolitan*.

Griswold v. Connecticut strikes down last law prohibiting use of birth control by married couples.

1966 Foundation of National Organization of Women (NOW).

1967 Executive Order 11372 broadens affirmative action to cover gender.

1968 Shirley Chisholm Brown is first African American female congressperson.

1969 First women's studies BA program started at San Diego State.

Formation of National Association for the Repeal of Abortion Laws (NARAL).

California is first state to adopt "no-fault" divorce law.

1970 Annie Mae McCabe Hays is first female general in the U.S. Army.

1971 Foundation of *Ms.* Magazine.

Gloria Steinem cofounds the National Women's Political Caucus as well as the Women's Action Alliance.

1972 Shirley Chisholm is first African American female to run for president.

Title IX prohibits discrimination on the basis of gender in federally funded education programs.

Congress passed Equal Rights Amendment.

1973 Billie Jean King defeats Bobby Riggs in tennis "Battle of the Sexes."

Roe v. Wade strikes down abortion laws.

1976 First law prohibiting marital rape passes in Nebraska.

1977 A Year of the Woman Conference held in Houston.

1978 Pregnancy Discrimination Act passes.

1979 UN General Assembly adopts the Convention on the Elimination of All Forms of Discrimination Against Women (CEDAW).

1981 Sandra Day O'Connor is first female Supreme Court justice.

First child conceived from in vitro fertilization.

1982 Unveiling of Maya Lin's Vietnam Veterans Memorial.

1983 Sally Ride is first American woman to travel in space.

Barbara McClintock wins Nobel Prize in Physiology or Medicine.

1984 Geraldine Ferraro accepts Democratic vice-presidential candidacy.

1985 Wilma Mankiller becomes Principal Chief of the Cherokee Nation.

1987 Opening of the National Museum of Women in the Arts in Washington, D.C.

1991 Anita Hill testifies at Clarence Thomas confirmation hearings.

American Association of University Women (AAUW) reports on sex bias in U.S. schools.

1992 Mae Jemison is first woman of color in space.

Bosnian Serbs systematically rape and kill women in an effort to exterminate Muslims.

1993 African American Toni Morrison wins Nobel Prize for Literature.

UN World Conference on Human Rights.

Ruth Bader Ginsburg is second woman on Supreme Court.

President Bill Clinton signs Family Medical Leave Act (FMLA).

Maya Angelou reads an original poem at President Clinton's inauguration.

1994 Violence Against Women Act is passed.

1995 World Health Organization establishes working group on female genital mutilation (FGM).

1996 Supreme Court mandates that all-male Virginia Military Institute admit women.

1997 Madeline Albright becomes first female secretary of state.

2002 California becomes first state to require paid parental leave.

2005 Senate confirms John Roberts as chief justice of the U.S. Supreme Court, against opposition by pro-choice groups

2006 U.S. Supreme Court upholds ban on partial-birth abortion.

Samuel Alito is confirmed as U.S. Supreme Court justice, against opposition by pro-choice groups.

South Dakota bans abortions, first since *Roe v. Wade.*

2007 Nancy Pelosi becomes first female Speaker of the House.

2009 President Obama signs Lilly Ledbetter Fair Pay Restoration Act.

Sonia Sotomayor is confirmed as first Hispanic Supreme Court justice.

Chapter One

The First Wave

Before examining the history of feminist activism, it is important to have a clear idea of what is meant by the term "feminist" and where it came from. "Feminism" is a relatively new word in the political sense. It was first used in this way in France in the 1880s. At that time, the word was *feminismé*, a combination of the French word for women's, *féminin*, and *-isme*, meaning a social movement or political ideology. It spread through Europe in the 1890s and to North and South America by 1910. From the beginning, the name was controversial. Even proponents of the movement disagreed about the term. Many women supported emancipation but rejected the label. Some women believed that middle-class demands for suffrage and property rights did not necessarily speak to working women's needs, which were more about homes, jobs, and wages. Middle-class women also hesitated because they were concerned about it diminishing their roles as mothers. Further, the "radical" idea that there should be a social movement for and about women was highly inflammatory. In the United States, the term is still controversial. In the 1800s, activism for gender equality was generally lumped under the umbrella term, "the women's movement."[1] Clearly, the major limitation of that term is that it focuses only on women, suggesting male activists are neither needed nor wanted.

Historian Estelle Freedman has defined feminism as "a belief that women and men are inherently of equal worth. Because most societies privilege men as a group, social movements are necessary to achieve equality between women and men, with the understanding that gender always intersects with other social hierarchies."[2] Sociologist Michael Kimmel further explained feminism, saying,

> Feminism dares to posit that the choice between bitches and babes is a false choice, and dares to imagine that women can be whole people, embracing and expressing ambition and kindness, competence and compassion. And feminism also dares to expect

more from men. Feminism expects a man to be ethical, emotionally present, and accountable to his values in his actions with women—as well as with other men. Feminism loves men enough to expect them to act more honorably and actually believes them capable of doing so. Feminism is a vision that expects men to go from being "just guys," accepting whatever they might happen to do, to being *just* guys—capable of autonomy and authenticity, inspired by justice. That is, feminism believes that guys can become men.[3]

Most feminists are critical of patriarchal, or male-dominated, societies. Above all, patriarchy divides or compartmentalizes humans. It divides qualities or characteristics into "male" and "female." It disconnects emotion from intellect, thought from action, science from art. It is "human beings categorized; by sex, age, race, ethnicity, sexual preference, height, weight, class, religion, physical ability, *ad nauseum*. The personal isolated from the political. Sex divorced from love. The material ruptured from the spiritual. The past parted from the present disjoined from the future. Law detached from justice. Vision dissociated from reality."[4]

Part of the reason patriarchy is sustained is that the Western world is very individualistic. We tend to believe that when bad things happen, it is because the individuals themselves are somehow bad or flawed. For instance, racism is due to individual white bigots. Women are oppressed because individual men feel superior to them and wish to dominate. An individual focus also blames the victims of oppression for their own plight, pointing out that it must be their personal flaws that keep them apart. This thinking ignores the fact that we operate institutions and systems that go well beyond any one individual. We participate actively in the system of patriarchy. We occupy positions in a patriarchal system by the simple fact that we are female or male. We therefore cannot control whether we participate in a patriarchy, only how we choose to do so.[5] The individualistic model does not offer us a chance to change patriarchal systems, but a more sociological, collective view does.

Some feminists attempt to reconnect that which has been compartmentalized. Feminists point out that there are indeed other models of relations. Prehistoric artifacts demonstrate that women have at some times shared spiritual prestige with men. Women have also held important social positions. There were female queens in ancient Egypt and female Emperors in ancient Japan.[6] In her groundbreaking book *The Chalice and the Blade*, historian Riane Eisler chronicled women's contributions and maintained that there are important historical precursors for a world focused on partnership, not domination.[7]

In the United States, the feminist movement is said to have occurred in three waves. The first wave began roughly in the mid-1800s and lasted until the mid-1950s. The second wave began in the mid-1950s and lasted until approximately the late 1970s. The third wave began in the 1980s and continues today.

HISTORICAL PRECURSORS TO THE FIRST WAVE

Freedman argued that there are two historical transitions that spawned feminist activism. These are the rise in capitalism and new political theories on individual rights and a representative government. Capitalism began to replace older relationships—both in society as well as in families. Men were economically advantaged by the emphasis on labor outside the home. Factories replaced home-based, artisanal production, creating wider gaps between men's largely paid and women's generally unpaid domestic labor. Consequently, men also came to be viewed as the head of the household, as women were more economically dependent on them due to their fewer opportunities. At the same time, new political ideas about free will and individual rights and responsibilities benefitted men, who were viewed as rational thinkers to women's supposed irrationality. "In response, feminist movements named these disparities as unjust, insisting on the value of women's economic contributions and the justice of political rights for women."[8]

THE COLONIAL ERA

Anne Hutchinson was one of the most famous colonial women. She and her husband, William, were Puritans who arrived in Boston in 1634 seeking religious freedom. Although Anne's views were accepted by Governor Henry Vane and her favorite minister, John Cotton, her belief that people are saved through faith alone was not accepted by all. She soon opened her home on Sunday evenings to women who wanted to hear more about her beliefs. As word spread, up to 80 women would turn out to hear her discussion. Some men attended as well. But Puritan women were not allowed to preach or to teach religion, so Hutchinson was warned by Governor John Winthrop for stepping out of her place. She was arrested in late 1638 and tried for her "traducing the ministers" and for heresy. At the time, she was 46 years old and pregnant with her fifteenth baby. She was imprisoned for four months, then forced to leave the Massachusetts Bay Colony.[9]

As Hutchinson's case illustrates, women in the early American colonies lacked many basic rights that are taken for granted today. A particularly glaring example of this can be seen in the Salem Witch Trials, in which more than 300 women in New England were accused of witchcraft. Estimates are that close to 50 were executed. Although there were some men accused, the belief was that women were more likely to be witches because it was easier for the devil to corrupt their "weaker souls."[10]

Perhaps the most important characteristic of colonial life was hard work. Everyone, including women, worked like demons. Even the wives of wealthy men were responsible for helping shelter the rest of the community when threatened by Indian attacks. It was the household, however, that was the one place where a colonial housewife was often in charge. She was "the chief executive and artisan of a little factory producing the items the family needed to survive."[11] Because most women in the colonial era could not do all the requisite "housewifely" tasks well, or, for that matter, even have time to do them all, women often exchanged goods and services. Women created an informal barter economy and built a network of community assistance and support.[12]

There were some groups that offered more opportunities for women outside of the home. In New Amsterdam, colonists followed their Dutch heritage and encouraged female entrepreneurs, allowing women to maintain a civil identity after marriage, to buy and sell goods and property, to contract debt, and to determine who would inherit their property. All these rights were eroded when New Amsterdam became New York in 1664.[13]

As women were losing control of the household in terms of producing food, owing to a growing capitalist economy, they were gaining respect for their role as mothers. Seventeenth-century writers rarely focused on child-rearing, and when they did, they generally discussed it as a father's role. Women were less intelligent and lacked the self-control to be taken seriously by their sons.[14]

Popular books promoted the division of roles, including *Advice to a Daughter*, a best seller from London in 1688. Few women remained single as single women had few opportunities to make money. Those who did typically had to care for relatives' children, with whom they generally lived. Because they spent so much time spinning wool they came to be known as "spinsters." Once they married, women had no legal right to any money they may have earned. If a woman's husband got into debt, his creditors could seize the wife's belongings and the children were considered his property. Many have asserted a "rule of thumb," in which men were allegedly allowed to physically "discipline" their wives with whips no thicker than their thumbs. Historians have not been able to find evidence of such laws, and in fact have found that numerous statutes and sermons condemned wife-beating. The practice surely occurred, however.[15]

In some of the middle colonies, Quakers gave women an active role in church affairs, although it was generally limited to interactions involving other women. A Quaker woman, then, unlike other women, could rise in the community's esteem through her ability to represent the church. If a colonial Euro-American woman wasn't a Quaker and she wanted a public voice, she pretty much had to head to the frontier.[16]

Native American women generally enjoyed far greater rights than did their white counterparts. The Iroquois League of Nations, for instance, authorized children as the property of their mother's clan, not their father's. Elder women controlled the sale of land, and they selected the clan's new chiefs.[17]

One colony even allowed women to vote after the Revolutionary War. New Jersey granted women suffrage, perhaps due to pressure from the Quakers. It was awarded to all free inhabitants who owned a certain amount of property. In 1797, about 75 women turned out to vote in Essex County. More turned up in 1800, and then the fear set in. What if women did not follow their husbands' lead, but instead voted on their personal beliefs? The legislature voted to end women's voting in 1807 in the same act that disenfranchised free blacks, a political trade-off between the Republican northern counties with a higher proportion of free blacks and the Federalist southern counties with a higher proportion of Quaker women.

Barring the few areas that offered women some opportunities for income, poverty was a major issue in Colonial America. The number of very poor people grew throughout the eighteenth century, and the most disadvantaged, like today, were single women with children. Most were widows whose husbands had been killed during the British wars against the French. Few organized resources existed for impoverished women. A few colonies had rudimentary welfare systems. For instance, in parts of Pennsylvania a woman "on the dole" had to wear a red P, for pauper, on her sleeve. Massachusetts had an almshouse for the indigent, but it was open only for those in the most dire circumstances, generally the very ill. Those institutionalized at the almshouse received only bread and water and were required to work at the looms.[18]

Women found ways to experience more equality in this era. Despite the fact that custom forbade women to join the fight against the British during the Revolutionary War, a few women joined regardless. Deborah Sampson Gannett disguised herself by cutting her hair and wearing men's clothing. Her identity was discovered and she was dismissed. She enlisted again, this time under the name of Robert Shurtleff, and she spent the next three years fighting next to her male counterparts. When she caught a musket bullet in her thigh, she removed it herself rather than having surgery that would have revealed her identity. After the war, her exploits became known, and her church expelled her for her "unchristian" behavior.[19] In an unusual move, her husband was later granted a pension as the widower of a Revolutionary soldier. More common was the woman who traveled with her soldier husband, taking care of the cooking, washing, and mending. Occasionally, these women replaced their husbands on the lines. The most legendary of these women is Molly Pitcher, who took her wounded husband's place loading a cannon at a critical moment during the Battle of Monmouth. Colonial records suggest she may have actually been a camp follower named Mary Ludwig Hays McCauley.[20]

Colonial women also lobbied politicians for change, although there is little to suggest it was an organized movement. "By the time of the American Revolution, the enlightenment emphasis on progress, benevolence, and education had undercut authoritarianism generally, yet older ideas about household authority persisted."[21] Perhaps the most famous example is Abigail Adams's famous request that her husband, John Adams, "remember the ladies" while drafting the Declaration of Independence in 1776. "Do not put such unlimited power into the hands of the husbands," she wrote. She intended to invoke the same criticism of absolute power the founding fathers had used to justify rebellion against British rule. "Remember, all Men would be tyrants if they could," she cautioned. Unfortunately, John did not listen to his wife, and women were not considered in the Declaration of Independence.[22] "The same men who declared that all men were created equal wrote slavery into the Constitution. Nor did most show any inclination to question the authority of husbands and fathers in the family."[23] Even slaves were considered above women. Although they had no right to vote, they were at least included (albeit in the bizarre three-fifths taxation rule). "For women, there was neither express inclusion, nor exclusion. Rather, there was silence . . . "[24]

A pivotal moment occurred in September 1791, when the antislavery playwright Olympe de Gouges authored a revised version of the French Declaration of the Rights of Man and Citizen. In her Declaration of the Rights of Woman, she insisted that "Woman is born free and remains equal to man in rights" [Article 1]. "All citizenesses and citizens, being equal in its [the law's] eyes, should be equally admissible to all public dignities, offices, and employments, according to their ability, and with no other distinction than that of their virtues and talents" [Article 6]. Her Declaration and her inversion of the language of the official 1789 Declaration may not shock us today, but it certainly shocked at the time. She was deemed a revolutionary and was sent to the guillotine. Her revamping of the French Declaration created a model for early U.S. feminists. In England, Mary Wollstonecraft followed in de Gouges footsteps, writing with great passion and at far greater length about the ways education and tradition had stunted women's minds. In *A Vindication of the Rights of Women*, published in 1792, she was one of the first to clearly link the emancipation of women to other forms of hierarchy in society. Wollstonecraft avoided the guillotine, but like de Gouges, she was publicly vilified.[25]

Once these path-breaking women got the movement started in Europe, others joined in. Between 1791 and 1793, women set up political clubs in Paris and at least 50 other provincial towns and cities. Women's rights were debated in the clubs, in newspapers, and in pamphlets.[26] It was in the early 1800s that women in the United States began to get more organized to fight for gender equality.

THE 1800s

Early on, great thinkers like French writer Jean Jacques Rousseau justified women's exclusion from education. They argued that education was essential to a representative government, as it ensured the citizenry would be reasonable, and independent thinking. Women, however, were not citizens and were thus not required to be independent thinkers. Drawing on ancient Greek medical notions that women were ruled by their bodily functions while men were ruled by their minds, Rousseau maintained that women were equal parts irrational and manipulative.[27] The paradox is indeed striking.

During the 1800s, the notion that there should be separate spheres for men and women generally intensified. "Man for the field and woman for hearth . . . Man to command woman to obey; all else confusion" was how Alfred Lord Tennyson characterized the British point of view in an 1849 poem. It was the mark of middle-class status for a wife in the United States or England to stay in the home while her husband earned money in trade, commerce, or another profession. "In contrast to this private ideal, a woman who turned to prostitution became a 'public woman,' stigmatized for her fall from chastity. Although working-class women had to help support their families, the domestic ideal shaped the occupations available to them—mostly servant or seamstress—and their low wages."[28]

As noted above, after the French Revolution, feminists like Mary Wollstonecraft, Harriet Taylor, and John Stuart Mill challenged these ideas and advocated for property and voting rights for women. During the nineteenth century, some of these activists put their ideas into practice, creating academies for girls in England and later the United States. Yet these early feminists wrote almost exclusively for middle-class women. Benjamin Rush, a well-known physician, led a small group in the 1800s arguing that providing a broader education for women would help create a stronger democracy. In 1821, Emma Willard followed Rush's lead and established the Troy Female Seminary in Troy, New York. Rather than education for its own sake, both argued that education would improve women's effectiveness as mothers.[29]

While Wollstonecraft sought to obtain both educational and political rights for women, not all feminists agreed suffrage was appropriate. In the United States, for example, Catharine Beecher devoted her life to establishing schools to train women teachers. But, because she believed that it was not politics but the home that was woman's "proper sphere," Beecher opposed suffrage.[30]

In the nineteenth century, new scientific ideas reinforced earlier notions of women's dependence on men. According to Charles Darwin's evolutionary theory of sexual selection, different reproductive strategies created vastly different male and female natures, with males much stronger than females. Darwin proposed that, in order to compete for mates, male animals had to have more variations and thus were more advanced than females. For instance, the vibrant color of the male peacock is intended to draw mates, while the plain-colored female peacock is not. Darwin's views helped justify male privilege. In the United States, G. Stanley Hall, the preeminent scholar of child-rearing, cautioned that women would be unfit for motherhood if they taxed their brains too much. Social Darwinists believed that, through natural selection, Europeans, specifically, Anglo-Saxons, had been endowed with greater mental and moral capacity than "primitive" peoples. This attitude justified horrific oppression of people of color, most notably Native Americans.[31]

Women were gradually offered more opportunities to work, but only because men no longer needed or wanted certain jobs. When there stopped being enough men to staff public schools, women began to be offered the positions, at far lower wages. In 1838 in Connecticut, male teachers earned $14.50 per month, while female teachers earned $5.75. By 1870, more than half of the primary and secondary school teachers in the United States were female.[32]

Perhaps one of the reasons it was difficult for women to organize around common pursuits was because it seemed in pre-civil war America that women were always ill. Historian Gail Collins explained that many women suffered serious damage during childbirth that their physicians could neither diagnose nor treat. Midwives who thought they were removing the afterbirth were said to sometimes drag out a woman's entire uterus. Prolapsed uterus was so common that plugs and other devices were available to allegedly hold the womb in place. Some women suffered from vesicovaginal fistula. The wall between their vagina and the bladder or rectum ripped during childbirth, leaving them unable to control the leakage of urine or feces through the vagina. "Nervousness" was a so-called feminine malady. Hysterical women needed anything that could calm their crazy nerves, and pretty much anything was what was provided. Doctors injected water, milk, and linseed into the uterus. They cauterized infections with silver nitrate, or sometimes with a hot iron. They put leeches on the vagina and on the rectum.[33]

Around 1830, literature about birth control began to be disseminated around the country. The most widely recommended tactic, suggested in Robert Dale Owen's well-read *Moral Physiology*, was *coitus interruptus*, or withdrawal. Women were also urged to douche, or to wash their private parts right after intercourse with water and a spermicide like alcohol or vinegar. Women received information via mail about birth control, thanks to the increasingly efficient postal system. They could also order diaphragms and sponges, condoms, spermicides, and pills that would allegedly induce abortion. Urban newspapers advertised condoms, cures for venereal diseases, aphrodisiacs, and abortion services. Agents even distributed ads for birth control devices on street corners and mailed them to newlyweds, although sometimes they were named discretely. " 'French' was a code word for contraceptive, and 'Portuguese' for something that induced abortion."[34]

The pre-civil war era was one of many in which "young women were at war with their bodies ... girls starved themselves to win the ultimate compliment of 'fairylike.' Warm clothing was not fairylike, and fashionable women wore only shawls for protection in the winter."[35] Girls were taught at a very young age that they were to restrain themselves from anything physically taxing. Further, their delicate nerves could not take too much emotional strain. "A story in *Godey's Lady's Book* told about a tomboy named Ellen, who insisted on playing rough sports outdoors. When Ellen refused to heed her aunts' warning about appropriate womanly behavior, she was thrown from her horse and crippled for life. It was a familiar plot theme, including the paralysis, and the happy ending always came when the immobilized heroine realized this was God's way of teaching her how to act like a lady."[36] Essentially, the term "tomboy" was applied to any little girl who showed the slightest tendency to think or act for herself.

Consequently, there were few women in the United States who stepped outside of their assigned gender roles and became public figures. An important public figure was Dorothea Dix. At one point she was called on by an overseer of a poorhouse in Lancaster, Pennsylvania, to write an article for the local paper because she was so widely known throughout the state. Dix was a spinster living in Massachusetts. In 1841, a friend asked her to teach a Sunday school class for female inmates in a local jail. There she was disturbed by the number of mentally ill women who had been locked up in the cold, dank cells. Dix became obsessed with the plight of these forgotten people and of the poor in general. Eventually, she visited every state but California looking for the often hidden locations where local officials kept the helpless people they called "lunatics." Dix authored shocking reports about what she saw, lobbying state legislators to build modern mental hospitals.[37]

Women were central to the growing abolition movement. In 1833, Lydia Maria Child wrote *An Appeal in Favor of That Class of Americans Called Africans*, one of the first antislavery books to be published and one of the boldest, arguing that the races should be allowed to freely mix. Eventually, the abolition movement became heavily reliant on the monies raised by women. Women made scarves and doilies with antislavery messages and sold them, among other things. It was *Uncle Tom's Cabin*, though, by Harriet Beecher Stowe, that really mobilized the northern critique of slavery. Even women like Dix and Beecher Stowe were careful to behave "like discreet housewives in public." When Harriet Beecher Stowe toured England after the publication of *Uncle Tom's Cabin*, she "sat silently in the 'women's gallery' of the crowded auditoriums, while her husband read her speech from the stage."[38]

CIVIL WAR ERA AND BEYOND

For women in the South, the Civil War offered a new opportunity to get involved in public affairs. It was no longer considered unfeminine to get involved during the crisis, as everyone was needed for the war effort. An estimated 400 women disguised themselves as men and fought in the war. Amy Clarke enlisted so she could stay with her husband when he joined the confederate army. Some women served as spies. Women also served in important background roles, including piecework sewing clothing and clerical positions. Until mid-century, nursing had been a job for men and lower-class women. But Florence Nightingale made the profession acceptable for ladies. She became an international heroine when she reorganized the nursing care during England's Crimean War, prompting a "mania" to act like Florence Nightingale. Another influential nurse was Clara Barton, whose work distributing supplies and offering medical care to wounded soldiers earned her the title "The Angel of the Battlefield." She later got involved in suffrage efforts and founded the American Red Cross in 1881.[39]

Politically, the antislavery movement in the United States was also the birthplace of feminism. Northern women were moved to advocate abolition for many reasons. Some white women opposed the system because of the ways slave families were broken up. For others, it was the rape of female slaves that was most offensive. It was both religious principles and their adherence to the belief that females are morally superior to males that inspired northern women to form dozens of local Female Anti-Slavery Society chapters in the 1830s. They distributed pamphlets and gave talks that called on women to exercise their indirect political influence by praying to convert Americans to antislavery. Sojourner Truth, a former slave who could neither read nor write, traveled the country lecturing to thousands of people about both slavery and women's rights.[40]

It was women who gathered the bulk of the signatures asking legislators to abolish slavery. In 1863, Susan B. Anthony and Elizabeth Cady Stanton founded the National Woman's Loyal League, the first national women's political organization, which petitioned Congress to free all slaves. Some women took more direct action. Those who supported the Underground Railroad hung special quilts on their clotheslines to mark safe houses for fugitives from slavery. This opposition to slavery did not necessarily translate into a belief in racial equality, however. Interestingly, some antislavery societies admitted only white women.[41]

Elizabeth Cady married abolitionist Henry Stanton in 1840, and then traveled to London with her new husband for the World Anti-Slavery Convention. She was not allowed to participate, however, as females were required to sit behind a curtain and could not speak or vote. She and another delegate, Lucretia Mott, decided to create a women's convention when they returned to the United States. After a few years of exchanging letters, the two ladies, with more than 200 women, met on July 19, 1848, in Seneca Falls, New York. The women at the meeting drafted the Declaration of Sentiments, modeled after the Declaration of Independence, calling for full rights under the law. Many people there, including Henry Stanton, thought the call for suffrage would not be well received. But Frederick Douglass, a free black man, spoke up and he swayed just enough people that the convention barely adopted the suffrage resolution.[42]

Interesting, Elizabeth Stanton had, should she have been aware of it, a model for her Declaration that was being used just a few dozen miles from her Seneca Falls home. In the year of the convention, the Seneca Nation formed a constitution that granted both men and women voting rights. "Unaware of the alternative histories around her, she failed to ask how a patriarchal world had emerged, given the more egalitarian potential of human cultures."[43]

After the Civil War and the emancipation of slaves, Sojourner Truth explained that if colored women did not get the same rights as did colored men, the men would simply become masters of the women and things would be as bad as before. In 1869, Douglass, with Lucy Stone and others, formed the American Woman Suffrage Association which supported black women's suffrage. Elizabeth Cady Stanton and Anthony formed the National Woman Suffrage Association (NWSA) to push for black and women suffrage, but in 1870, the Fifteenth Amendment granted only black men the right to vote. Despite their disappointment, the early suffragists pressed on, many times enduring great suffering, including fines, jail time, and discrimination.

Women's rights conventions met locally throughout the northern states during the 1850s. Through speeches, reform newspapers, and petitions to legislatures they demanded, in Elizabeth Cady Stanton's words, "the equal station to which they are entitled." These early feminists were attacked by hostile journalists, who still insisted women had no place in political life. Political cartoons commonly portrayed them as unfeminine, at best. Yet the activists persisted and helped attain new educational opportunities as well as revised laws allowing married women the right to own their own property and to control their own wages.[44]

Post-Civil War Americans, especially those who did not travel west, were fascinated by stories of cowboys and Indians. They read western romances and adventure novels, and flocked to wild west shows. Generally, women were portrayed as victims in need of rescue, but gradually the cowgirl was introduced. The most famous of these wild west women were Hurricane Nell, Wild Edna, Annie Oakley, and Calamity Jane. As Americans explored the west, the labor shortage also helped erase some of the most traditional gender roles. Women worked as doctors, lawyers, and real estate agents not so much because attitudes were more progressive but because there were nowhere near enough men for the job.[45]

Wyoming actually granted women the right to vote well before the passage of the Nineteenth Amendment, in 1869. Historian Collins explained that, although a progressive move in one sense, it was less radical than it sounds. With few women around, there was really little danger that female voters would make a dramatic difference.[46] Not long after Wyoming granted women the right to vote, Esther Morris was appointed to fill a vacated seat as a justice of the peace, making her the first female judge in the country. In 1872, Victoria Woodhull ran for U.S. president on the Equal Rights Party ticket. Perhaps more importantly, she argued that women had the right to control their own sexuality.[47] This would become a major issue for second wave feminists.

Women in this era also broke barriers in education, which helped them to obtain work in nontraditional fields. In 1833, Oberlin College became the first in the nation to admit women. Antoinette Brown ignored her parents and headed to Oberlin College, where she planned to become the nation's first ordained minister. The faculty assured her this would not happen, but did allow her to enroll in theology classes. Although she did not graduate, she found a progressive parish in New York that ordained her and made her pastor. In 1837, Mount Holyoke Seminary was founded as the first college for women in the United States. In *Bradwell v. Illinois*, the U.S. Supreme Court refused to address whether the State of Illinois could prohibit women from obtaining licenses to practice law. Instead, they ruled on a complex legal issue relevant to standing before the court. But in writing about the case, Justice Joseph P. Bradley made clear his view that women did not have the right to engage in any profession they might choose. He wrote that this was due to "the natural and proper timidity and delicacy which belongs to the female sex . . . [that] evidently unfits it for many of the occupations of civil life."[48] Elizabeth Blackwell was the first woman to graduate from an American medical college. She was prompted to do so when she saw a friend die of uterine cancer because she had been unable to discuss her symptoms freely with her male physician.[49] In her 1898 book *Women and Economics*, Charlotte Perkins Gilman explained that women, regardless of their marital or work status, needed economic dependence.[50]

Many women worked for change within the paradigm of the home. In 1829, Child pulled together a collection of household tips ad recipes, which were published as *The American Frugal Housewife*. The book was full of tips on how to economize in the home, and it soon became the publishing phenomenon of the nineteenth century. In 1841, Catharine Beecher's *A Treatise on Domestic Economy* took over as the next biggest thing.[51]

Despite some of these advances, women grappled with the image of themselves as frail and hysterical. A popular image during the mid-1800s was that of the virtuous, sexless woman. Although this was progress from being considered the morally unreliable descendants of Eve, it was still very restrictive. Popular novelists portrayed "true women" as timid, doubtful, and dependent.[52]

During the Gilded Age (roughly 1878–1889), the image of women shifted to a healthier one, both physically and emotionally. "The rejection of the small, thin, and retiring female image came at a time when women were, in every way, becoming more visible. Wives completely took over the family shopping; the ones who had enough money turned that chore into a social pastime. And they were beginning to go out by themselves for amusement—to have lunch with friends or see a play at a theater."[53] An example of female resistance to prescribed gender roles was in 1851 when Elizabeth Cady Stanton designed some baggy, ankle-length trousers—the first pants designed for women. Amelia Bloomer, editor for the women's newspaper *The Lily*, advertised the pants, and they came to be known as bloomers. Similarly, Anthony resisted the fashion of elaborate hairdos that took hours to create, instead chopping her hair short.[54]

Part of the explanation is that the Gilded Age was about celebrating all things outrageous, splashy, and outspoken. Women, too, were granted permission to attract attention to themselves in ways that were previously viewed as unacceptable.[55] For example, Nellie Bly, a reporter for the *New York World*, was on the front page regularly during the 1880s with what the papers then called "stunt journalism," a forerunner of today's investigative reporting. In fact, the excesses of the era led to numerous problems. In the late nineteenth century, there were somewhere between 200,000 and 400,000 drug addicts, owing to the lack of regulation and the overprescription of drugs. The typical addict was a middle-class white woman who had been introduced to the habit by her doctor.[56]

Most women, however, stayed out of the newspapers and devoted themselves to their families. But they also sought experiences outside of the household. In an apparently spontaneous movement, women's study clubs started popping up all over the country.[57] The first was likely Sorosis, formed in New York City in 1868 by Jane Cunningham Croly, a journalist. By the turn of the century, there were 5,000 local organizations listed by the General Federation of Women's Clubs.

The fight for suffrage continued after the Civil War. In 1872, Anthony cast a ballot in Rochester, New York. She was promptly arrested. The judge declared her guilty and assigned her a $100 fine, which she refused to pay. The event made the front page of the newspapers, gaining movement for women's rights efforts. In 1871, Abigail Scott Duniway began publishing a women's rights newspaper called *The New Northwest*. She also joined Anthony in touring around the country campaigning for suffrage.[58]

In 1876, the United States celebrated its centennial with a gala event in Philadelphia. The NWSA used the event to further their mission.

Susan B. Anthony, Elizabeth Cady Stanton, and several others set up a temporary headquarters in a Philadelphia hotel. Anthony had to rent the room, since she was the only single woman in the group and married women were prohibited from doing so. On July 4, immediately after a speaker read the Declaration of Independence in front of a large crowd, Anthony and four others walked to the stage and handed him the Declaration of Sentiments. They also distributed copies in the crowd.[59]

At the start of the twentieth century, America saw a falling white birth rate. In 1800, each American-born white woman gave birth, on average, to seven children. By 1900, that number had declined by approximately one half. One of the main factors, according to some historians, was the use of contraceptives or abstinence, although few still talked openly about those things.[60]

Many, but not all, of the women's rights advocates got involved in the temperance movement. Some were simply teetotalers. Some felt it was an issue of morality that women should lead. Others maintained that it was drunken husbands who were responsible for the violence women endured in the home, and thus temperance would help women. Some women marched into saloons, destroyed the liquor supply, and began preaching to men on the streets. They even convinced some saloon owners to close their businesses. By 1900, millions of women had mobilized to oppose men's drinking. The Women's Christian Temperance Union (WCTU) became the largest women's organization in the United States.[61] Carrie Nation was one of the most outspoken and colorful leaders of the temperance movement. She led women in raids on Kansas saloons, ransacking them if they were not licensed or legal. In the winter of 1873–1874, more than 60,000 women crusaded through the streets of Ohio and Michigan for the cause. Primarily middle-class women joined the WCTU. The WCTU's goals were not just to restrict alcohol but also to improve education for children, to help conditions for prisoners, and to support other social causes.[62]

In the years leading up to the right to vote, women were also involved in "The Purity Campaign." According to Historian Gail Collins, like temperance, "its bottom line was forcing men to behave."[63] The WCTU started a campaign to get men to wear white ribbons, showing they had taken a pledge to be sexually pure until marriage and faithful thereafter. They also created a panic about white slavery, scaring people that their wives, daughters, and sisters might be lured away from their homes and kept by pimps as slaves.[64]

Women were also leaders in the labor movement. Mary Harris Jones was one of the most important leaders of the labor movement. When she was widowed in 1867, the Irish immigrant moved to Chicago and joined the Knights of Labor, a group trying to organize for better wages and improved working conditions. She became known as "Mother Jones" because she devoted the next 50 years of her life to organizing industrial workers. Mother Jones was not a supporter of the suffrage movement, however. She argued that "you don't need a vote to raise hell!"[65]

EARLY 1900s

One of the best symbols of the transformation that was occurring in women's lives at the turn of the century was the bicycle. Women who had previously been forced to endure constricting corsets and heavy skirts were now far freer. Better yet, it was not only considered in style to ride a bicycle, it was actually respectable.[66]

In 1911, Socialists began to observe March 8 as a day to honor the women who had walked out on strike for better working conditions as part of the earlier labor movements. International Working Women's Day became a national holiday in socialist countries, although Western nations generally did not celebrate it. Liberal and socialist feminists in the West revived it in the 1960s under the name International Women's Day by staging marches and demonstrations for women's rights. In the United States, Congress declared March to be women's history month.[67]

Women were also making progress in controlling their own bodies. Although Margaret Sanger is most associated with the issue of birth control in the United States, even earlier feminist activists wrote and spoke about the importance of allowing women to prevent pregnancy. Sarah Grimke published a pamphlet containing advice on contraception in 1837.[68]

Sanger became an activist for birth control partly due to her own mother's experience. Although contraceptives were available in New York at the time, her mother, Ann Purcell, refused to use them. As such, she was pregnant for virtually all of the two decades immediately after she married. When she was in her twenties, Sanger worked part-time as a nurse in the immigrant districts of New York's Lower East Side. She described her time there: "Pregnancy was a chronic condition among the women of this class."[69] So-called prevention techniques includes herbal teas, turpentine, steaming, rolling downstairs, inserting slipper elm, knitting needles, and shoe hooks. Since most of these techniques did not work, women lined up in huge groups, sometimes numbering 100, outside the offices where someone could offer a $5 abortion. Sanger began to lecture about birth control as early as 1911, but watching a young mother die from a self-induced abortion in 1912 turned her into a crusader. At the time, her work was not only controversial but illegal. The 1873 Comstock Act made it a federal crime to send any obscene, lewd, or lascivious materials through the mail. It also banned the distribution of educational information about abortion. Twenty-four states passed similar prohibitions. In 1915 her husband, William Sanger, was charged with violating the law and in 1918, Margaret was charged. Her conviction was overturned on appeal.[70]

Although women were now afforded some opportunities to work outside of the home, few made significant wages. Ida Tarbell was one of the few women who had a lucrative career at the turn of the century. She was the star investigative reporter for *McClure's Magazine*, and she helped to expose corporate greed and collusion, especially in the Standard Oil Company. Other women became successful in the beauty industry, with the most famous being Madam C. J. Walker, who was the first female to become a millionaire.[71]

Another change for women at the turn of the century was child-rearing. Before, it was viewed as something women innately knew because of their gender. In the twentieth century, it became a scientific production. Experts told women to follow a strict schedule and never to give in to their infants' demand. Although this gave women more authority in the home, it also took up more of their time, and opened women up to the criticism of being "unsuccessful" mothers.

Clearly, one of the major events of the early twentieth century was World War I (WWI). Although women's involvement in World War II (WWII) has received a great deal of attention, most people know very little about women's involvement in WWI. Long before the United States entered the war in 1917, women were volunteering to serve as nurses, canteen hostesses, ambulance drivers, and switchboard operators overseas. An estimated 25,000 women crossed the ocean to help the cause. Some women were appalled by the war even if they never saw it firsthand. Jane Addams, one of the most popular reformers of the era, lost most of her popularity when she spoke out strongly against American involvement.[72]

In 1917, right after Montana granted women the right to vote but before the ratification of the Nineteenth Amendment, Jeannette Rankin was the first woman elected to the U.S. Congress. Rankin voted "no" when Congress authorized U.S. entry into the fighting. She had been elected on a peace platform in a year when most politicians, including U.S. President Woodrow Wilson, were vowing to stay out of the conflict, a brave move by a minority in Congress. In the years after the passage of the Nineteenth Amendment, more women were elected to government positions. In 1925, Nellie Tayloe Ross because the first female state governor in Wyoming and in 1926, citizens of Seattle elected the first female mayor, Bertha Knight Landes.[73]

Legendary activist Alice Paul, founder of the National Women's Party, organized a demonstration of 10,000 at the 1913 inauguration of President Wilson, protesting his opposition to women's rights. Three years later, after Wilson was reelected, she picketed outside the White House and was arrested. She staged a jail-based hunger strike and, upon her release, began to picket again. Many credit her dedicated actions for the momentum that lead to the passage of the Nineteenth Amendment in 1920.

POST SUFFRAGE

American women were visibly transformed after the war in ways that seemed to parallel changes occurring in the country. The United States had changed from a developing industrial state to a world power and a vibrant economy that relied on its citizens to borrow money and to buy both needed and luxury items. After suffrage, the popularity of the progressive and serious settlement house worker was replaced by the jazz-crazed, fun-loving flapper. Essentially, anything that had something to do with consumption was in style. This included drinking, smoking, and sex, even for women. Women were given more control of their bodies in 1921, with the sale of the first successful sanitary napkins. Historian Collins has called this "the most important unheralded moments in the history of American women."[74]

Smoking was considered by some younger women to be an example of "freedom" and women's right to enjoy the same pleasures as men. Of course, advertisements helped encourage this connection, and they also implored weight-conscious flappers to "reach for a lucky instead of a sweet." Essentially, cigarettes became a method of weight control in an era of skinny women.[75] Tanned skin became fashionable for the first time in the 1920s, as it represented that you were wealthy enough to have the leisure for outdoor sports. Conversely, "anything that reeked of 'reform' was out."[76] This was the initial era in which feminism was denounced, by men but also by many women. Flappers were thin, flat-chested, and happy, not driven by causes. The movies of the 1920s stressed plots that appealed to women—romances and melodramas. These were not critical of gender inequalities but tended to reinforce gender roles. Many of the most successful screenwriters were women as well.[77] Since women had won the right to vote, many felt nothing further was needed.

The 1920s and 1930s saw the emergence of a new type of role model for women—the adventurer. One of the most famous athletes was Gertrude Ederle, an Olympic swimmer who at age 19 swam across the English Channel in 1926. Amelia Earhart, a former mechanic, barnstormer, and social worker, became the first woman to fly across the Atlantic in 1928.[78]

Not all women in this age were carefree flappers, however. In 1923, the National Woman's Party, led by Alice Paul, proposed an Equal Rights Amendment, as they saw that, despite the right to vote, women were still treated inequitably in many ways. The League of Women Voters, the nation's leading women's rights group at the time, opposed the ERA, arguing it would alienate needed supporters and that supportive legislation didn't really work.[79]

In 1927, the U.S. Supreme Court upheld involuntary sterilization of the "feebleminded" in the case of *Buck v. Bell*. Carrie Buck was a young white female who was otherwise fertile. Buck had been deemed "slow."

One of the justices declared "three generations of imbeciles is enough" in deciding that the involuntary sterilization of Buck was lawful.[80] Some estimates are that more than 70,000 women were sterilized since states passed legislation authorizing it in 1907.

Post suffrage, many women's rights advocates essentially stopped concerning themselves with some of the race issues that were once a part of the movement. Alice Paul, for instance, simply dismissed the topic. At the extreme end, some women formed the Women's Ku Klux Klan (KKK), which by 1924 claimed a membership of a quarter of a million. The men's group had revived and was at record high enrollments as well.[81] Some women were concerned with the growth of the KKK and with the shocking lynchings of black men that occurred throughout the country.

Passage of the Nineteenth Amendment did not guarantee all women had equal access to vote. Many areas instituted Jim Crow laws that required poll taxes or literacy tests in order to prevent African Americans from exercising their right to suffrage. Great leaders like Mary McLeod Bethune, president of the National Association of Colored Women worked in the 1920s to gain equal access for all women. White southerner Jessie Daniel Ames responded to pleas by black churchwomen in the 1930s and founded the Association of Southern Women for the Prevention of Lynching. "The members decided to take responsibility for preventing or exposing the murders carried out by men who claimed to be protecting the purity of white womanhood when they lynched alleged black male rapists."[82] Perhaps the most important rejection of racism and anti-Semitism was modeled by First Lady Eleanor Roosevelt. According to Historian Estelle Freedman, "the tentative connections made across race and religious lines would nurture the rebirth of feminism in the 1960s."[83]

The general frivolity of the 1920s largely came to an end with the Great Depression. An estimated 500,000 to two million people were homeless in the 1930s. Approximately 10 percent of them were women. By 1932, more than 30,000 American businesses had failed, and unemployment was almost 25 percent. One in four families was without their traditional male breadwinner.[84] Movies, however, remained a popular pastime and an escape from the drudgery of daily life. Depression-era women identified with Scarlett O'Hara, but young girls identified with Nancy Drew, the adventurous girl sleuth. During the Depression era, "Mae West was a sort of marker for the shifting attitudes toward women's sexuality in the country and in Hollywood. She was a product of the tougher side of the New York entertainment industry, where she made her name with a series of plays that she wrote and was repeatedly arrested for starring in. The first was called *sex*."[85]

Feminists' work continued throughout the Depression, albeit in different ways. A major achievement was in 1931, when Addams won the Nobel Peace Prize. Many thought the prize was long overdue based on

Addams's work founding Hull House and in assisting women in need. In 1940, Rankin was elected to her old house seat and again voted against war, the only member of the representatives to do so. Women took part in movements to improve conditions for the urban working poor. U.S. Secretary of Labor Frances Perkins, the first female cabinet member, helped gain passage of the Fair Labor Standards Act in 1938.[86]

WWII is a critical marker in U.S. history, not just because of the war but also for women's rights. During WWII, "the theory that women should only be asked to do work that was safe and relatively mundane was ignored whenever something risky or difficult actually needed to be done."[87] By the end of the fighting in 1945, women made up more than one-third of the national workforce, although largely in clerical, sales, and other pink-collar jobs. New work opportunities were opening up for women during the 1920s and 1930s, and even more opportunities were added during WWII. At the peak of the war, women constituted 27 percent of the industrial workforce, according to the Rosie the Riveter Trust, whereas in other industries they were the majority, even up to 80 percent. By 1944, five million U.S. women were working.[88]

After WWII, a survey by the U.S. Department of Labor found 80 percent of women wanted to keep their jobs, yet women's participation in the workplace fell from 36 percent in 1944 to 12 percent in 1948. Although many women lost their jobs when the war ended, the employment landscape had changed dramatically for women. By 1950, the Bureau of Labor Statistics found women were still 30 percent of the labor force. Newspaper and magazine articles at the end of the war told women they needed to return to their normal roles. "The hype seems to have worked: the number of women attending college fell from 47 percent to 35 percent between 1920 and 1958, and roughly 60 percent of women attending college or universities left school, fearing that 'too much education' would rule them out as potential wives."[89]

In sum, feminist activists in the first wave achieved many important milestones, most notably the right to vote. They also "helped change the perception of women from voiceless dependents to independent thinkers with a valid voice in shaping the country."[90] Yet the first wave also left a mixed legacy in that while they criticized the domestic realm for limiting women, they also emphasized women's moral superiority *because* of their maternal and domestic roles. Charlotte Perkins Gilman in the United States and Virginia Woolf in England both wrote passionately about the ways that women, because of their gender, had a uniquely critical perspective.[91] Further, although some feminists were active in the fight for civil rights for people of color, others paid little attention to the lives of those who were not white and middle class.

Chapter Two

The Second Wave

The second wave of feminism began in the 1950s. Critical goals of the second wave included increased gender equality in the workplace, access to reproductive health care and sexuality information, the election of more women to political offices, legalized abortions, and civil rights legislation addressing sexual and racial harassment. Although it was never enacted, the Equal Rights Amendment (ERA) was another main goal. "The personal is political," a phrase coined by Carol Hanisch (a member of the radical New York group the Redstockings), can help readers understand that second wavers were interested in making issues that were once thought of as "private"—domestic violence and reproductive choices, for instance—and emphasizing that they were indeed concerns for the broader culture to address. Rather than individual problems, gender inequalities were the result of sexist power structures.

Second wavers achieved many milestones. Women's studies scholars Susan Shaw and Janet Lee reminded us of these when they asked us to:

> Imagine a world without feminism. If you are a woman, you would not be in college. You would not be able to vote. You could not play sports. Contraception is illegal. So is abortion. You're expected to marry and raise a family. If you must work, the only jobs available to you are in cleaning, clerical services, or teaching. And you have no legal protection on the job if your boss pressures you for sex or makes lewd comments. Your husband can force you to have sex, and, if you were sexually abused as a child, most likely no one will believe you if you tell. If you are sexually attracted to women, you are considered mentally ill and may be subjected to an array of treatments for your illness.[1]

Specific second wave achievements include passage of the Equal Pay Act of 1963, the Title VII of the Civil Rights Act, which forbids workplace discrimination, and the creation of the Equal Employment Opportunity Commission (EEOC) to enforce antidiscrimination laws. Affirmative Action was extended to women in order to reverse the effects of discrimination. Title IX of the Education Amendment Act of 1972 forbade gender discrimination in schools and universities, and also addressed equity in sports.[2] At the same time, the second wave has had many critics. They point out the lack of integration of all women, the Western bias, and the alienation of male activists.

1950s: THE BEGINNING

The 1950s are generally not known for feminist activism. As has been noted of other eras, changes in women's fashion reflected changes in women's lives, and in the 1950s, this was toward domesticity. The primary feature of post–World War II fashion was discomfort, with full, mid-calf skirts held out by stiff petticoats and other itchy fabrics. Long, formfitting sheaths were equally uncomfortable and made movement a joke, especially when coupled with the four inch heels. Hair was to be set in huge rollers that one slept in, or at least tried to. As hairstyles got bigger, more chemicals and more time had to be involved (as in the movie *Hairspray*).[3] Even when the bulk of women bought into this, there were always resisters. Women who were already married with children, for instance, had trouble living up to the expectations and began to discuss this openly.[4] Even when women were told they should be in the home, they organized. Even those who were housewives could support one another by watching after each other's children, getting together to chat, and enjoying family events.[5]

Although the 1950s have generally been viewed as a sexually repressive era, change was afoot. In 1953, Alfred Kinsey published his second groundbreaking report, *Sexual Behavior in the Human Female*, which reported that about half of married white women had sex before marriage, and that a quarter committed adultery.[6] Kinsey's work helped normalize the notion that both men and women are sexual beings, although this notion really took hold in the 1960s when it coupled with the free love movements.

1960s

By some accounts, it was books that helped usher in the feminist activism most people think of when they talk about feminists. In 1962, Helen Gurley Brown's *Sex and the Single Girl* became a best seller, controversial in that it urged women to have affairs with married men.[7]

The publication of Betty Friedan's *The Feminine Mystique* in 1963 is considered to be the starting place of 1960s feminist activism. Women all over read Friedan's critique of the cult of domesticity and seriously began to question whether the home was where women needed or wanted to be. She argued women had been sold a false sense that the only way they could achieve a sense of identity was through their families. It has been included on lists of the 100 most influential books of the twentieth century. Not everyone loved the book, though. Katie O'Beirne criticized Friedan's likening of American woman trapped at homes in the suburbs to American POWs in Korea, a comparison O'Beirne found offensive.[8]

In 1964, the phrase "women's liberation" was first used in the United States. By 1968, it was used to refer to the entire women's movement. The idea was that women were not just to be liberated politically, but also from their stereotypical roles.

Women began to organize to pressure for greater opportunity and for fair treatment in the workplace. When the Civil Rights Act was passed in 1963, the airline industry was one of the first to be challenged. They were required to be carefully groomed at all times, and to retire if they gained weight, got married, or turned 32.[9] In 1964, almost half of all women worked outside the home, yet they tended to be clustered in low-paying work in the service and clerical industries. Only 7 percent of the nation's doctors were women, women were fewer than 4 percent of the nation's lawyers, and only 1 percent were federal judges. Women earned only 60 percent of the average wage a man could earn doing the same job.[10]

Certainly, the feminist movement benefitted from the other civil rights movements that occurred in the 1950s and 1960s. The Black civil rights movement helped provide a model for action and inspiration that political and social change could be achieved. Other movements like the Chicano Rights efforts, the Native American rights movement, and the gay rights movement were also influential, although some historians have argued that these movements competed for adherents and attention.

Both racial and sex discrimination were outlawed with the passage of The Civil Rights Act of 1964, which had received some support from the aging National Woman's Party. The act established the Equal Employment Opportunity Commission (EEOC) to hear complaints about discrimination based on either race or gender. When the EEOC failed to live up to the promises that it would respond to sex discrimination complaints, feminists decided they needed a political lobby akin to the National Association for the Advancement of Colored People. In 1966, 300 women created the National Organization for Women (NOW).[11]

Although progressive in regards to race, civil rights groups like the Student Nonviolent Coordinating Committee (SNCC) were not free of sex bias. In 1964, Casey Hayden and Mary King, two civil rights workers, drafted a position paper on women's contributions to the movement and distributed it to staff members of the SNCC in Mississippi. They claimed the staff at the SNCC called women "girls," assigned them only clerical and cooking work, and never allowed them to hold executive positions. Hayden and King distributed the paper to other women in the peace and freedom movements, and in December 1965, they took it to the Students for a Democratic Society (SDS) national convention at the University of Illinois. SDS sponsored days of conversation about the role of women within the movement. Other women of color took on leadership roles. Dolores Huerta cofounded the United Farm Workers of America (UFW) which, in 1960, worked with César Chávez to obtain better wages and working conditions for farm workers.

This public dialogue spurred more activism.

Enthusiasm led to action. In New York, radicals released white mice at a commercial bridal fair in Madison Square Garden. In Seattle, a frightened young student spontaneously stood against *Playboy* and its bunnies by staging a protest at a student event. At Yale Divinity School, female graduate students occupied the only toilet in the library until the school agreed to remove the sign that said "Men." The most famous demonstration occurred in Atlantic City in September 1968. A hundred women, some of whom had come from as far away as Florida, carried posters and paraded a live sheep on the boardwalk outside the Miss America pageant. The *New York Post* reported that they planned to burn their bras. But since city regulations forbade fires on the boardwalk they threw bras, girdles, eyelash curlers, home permanents, and copies of *Good Housekeeping* and *Playboy* into a "Freedom Trash Can." "Down with these shoes," said a sixty-eight year old woman as she dumped her high heels. "And down with bound feet!" yelled another.[12]

Over time, the movement splintered. The liberal branch of the second wave of U.S. feminism emphasized antidiscrimination law and supported court cases to achieve equal pay and promotion for women workers at all levels. The second group, often referred to as radical feminists, argued that legal or legislative changes could never completely address the patriarchal system. Some argued that until patriarchy was completely destroyed, women would not be equal to men. "The master's tools will never dismantle the master's house," a famous quote by poet Audre Lord, became a mantra for some feminist activists. Radical feminists began to articulate separatist politics, much like the Black Power movement.

Many of these feminists, such as Shulamith Firestone, believed racial equality would only occur after gender equality. Predominately white women's groups formed, such as the Redstockings, the Feminists, the Furies, and the Radical Women. Through direct action, radical feminists challenged cherished beliefs about women's place. They gained publicity for women's liberation when they demonstrated against the Miss America pageant, occupied the offices of the *Ladies Home Journal*, and held speak-outs about once unmentionable topics such as abortion, rape, and prostitution. They created women-only spaces to heal from the daily wounds of patriarchy.[13]

Radical feminists often denounced anything related to traditional gender roles, including motherhood. Backlash against the radicals prompted other forms of feminist activism, such as when Nancy Hawley began offering workshops on women's bodies in New England after she was appalled at hearing a radical feminist dismiss pregnancy as "barbaric." Hawley had just given birth to her second child and felt that pregnancy and childbirth were beautiful and natural, not barbaric. By December 1970, she and her friends had borrowed $1,500 and published a 136-page self-help booklet that provided factual information as well as told personal stories. It was called *Women and Their Bodies*. "When it came time to print a second edition, somebody shouted, 'Hey, it isn't women and *their* bodies—it's us and our bodies.' By 1980, the Simon and Schuster edition of *Our Bodies, Ourselves* had earned over half a million dollars in royalties for their nonprofit organization."[14]

Within the movement, black feminists accused the predominately white groups of racism. Socialist feminists, who saw the root of gender inequality in capitalism, expressed disdain at the notion that legal changes would really help and found the consciousness-raising activities to exemplify elitism. Some groups accused others of hogging the media attention and trying to speak as if there was one feminist voice. While many applauded the new *Ms.* magazine, first published in 1971, conservative Phyllis Schlafly condemned it as "a series of sharp-tongued, high-pitched, whining complaints by unmarried women." Some, like the radical New York group Redstockings, claimed *Ms.* magazine was actually setting back the women's liberation movement, as it generally promoted liberal feminism.[15]

NOW was dealing with another difficult issue at the time. A riot at the Stonewall Inn after a police raid on homosexuals in June 1969 launched the modern gay rights movement. After that, lesbian feminists began to be far more vocal. A young NOW staffer named Rita Mae Brown called herself the "token lesbian," which set off Friedan who believed lesbians would undermine the movement. She began referring to female gay rights activists as "the lavender menace." "As four hundred women listened to the opening speeches at a purported Second Congress to Unite Women, the lights went out, then came up on seventeen women dressed in custom-made lavender T-shirts and carrying posters that said things like 'TAKE A LESBIAN TO LUNCH' or 'LESBIANISM *IS* A WOMEN'S LIBERATION PLOT.'"[16]

Laurel Thatcher-Ulrich explained that, "The rifts were predictable. The new feminism was not one thing but many. It was a *movement*—a tremor in the earth, a lift in the wind, a swelling tide. Although there were many groups, there was no unified platform, no single set of texts. Instead there was an exhilarating sense of discovery, a utopian hope that sometimes collapsed into factionalism. Self-appointed vanguards fought sexism, racism, capitalism, compulsory heterosexuality, and each other. The one common commitment was that women be heard."[17]

In the late 1960s, the U.S.-based women's movement significantly expanded its agenda. No longer focused on political rights alone, women made more demands for economic rights and for fairness in interpersonal relations. For instance, second wave feminists insisted that women should have independent credit so that married women were not reliant on their husbands for bank loans. The 1974 Credit Opportunity Act prohibited banks from refusing to grant women loans in their own name. This right to credit enables women to form businesses on their own. And women have done so since its passage, as will be detailed in subsequent chapters.[18]

Like the first wave, there was still a split between those who emphasized women's equality with men and those who stressed women's difference from men. "Feminist" came to be the term for the latter.[19]

1970s

One thing the second wave did was help get more media attention to gender inequalities. For instance, at the beginning of the 1970s, the *New York Times* printed a story about a woman attempting to rent an apartment who was forced to get her husband, a mental hospital patient, to cosign the lease. Women were appalled by such stories. In 1970, there were ten women in the House and one in the U.S. Senate. Three percent of the nation's lawyers were women, and seven percent of doctors were women. In North Carolina, only a virgin could charge a man with rape.[20] In 1973, Billy Jean King out-psyched Bobby Riggs in the "Battle of the Sexes," drawing great publicity to women's issues not just among feminists but among sports fans.

In the 1970s there were calls for unionization of prostitutes. In France, prostitutes staged a work stoppage to protest exploitation, while in the United States a group called COYOTE (Call off your tired old ethics) recommended unionization as well as a worker-owned collective to eliminate pimps and madams.[21]

Second wave feminists also helped usher in the first women's studies programs. In 1970, female faculty at San Diego State University (SDSU) taught five upper-division women's studies courses on a voluntary overload basis. That fall, the university approved a curriculum of 11 courses to make SDSU the first university with a women's studies program.[22]

In 1971, the Equal Rights Amendment (ERA) made it through Congress with little opposition. On March 22, 1972, it was sent to the states for ratification. Opposition mounted, as lawyer and political writer Phyllis Schlafly spun into action with her organization Stop ERA. Other groups also opposed ratification, including states-rights groups, who saw it as an unwanted expansion of federal power, some business leaders, who argued it would cost them money, and some fundamentalist religious groups at this time; the FBI was actually investigating the more radical end of the movement. "They simply didn't know what to make of groups that called themselves things like BITCH, Uppity Women, or Keep on Truckin', or how to deal with reports from the field that said things like 'This group has no leaders, dues, or organization.' A Washington, D.C., group ended up on the FBI's armed and dangerous list, even though its only identifiable weapon was a newspaper called *Off Our Backs*."[23]

Historian Gail Collins explained why the ERA was so controversial.

> Much of the fight over the ERA was due to the jockeying of conservative ideologues for a place in the shifting world of American politics. But it was easy for the amendment's backers to forget that for most American women throughout history, the goal had been getting into the house, not out of it. The vast majority never got a chance to reject the limitations of a career as a full-time housewife. Trapped in a world of endless work on the farm or in the factory, they yearned for a chance to exercise more control and creativity as wives and mothers. Susan B. Anthony had said that married women were only allowed to be dolls or drudges, but stay-at-home wives saw themselves as something else entirely—as domestic entrepreneurs whose accomplishments entitled them to some respect. When that status was threatened, both the women who had it and the ones who hoped someday to get it reacted with dismay.[24]

Women of color continued to emphasize the role that race played in their lives, and grappled with whether the movement was doing enough to address their needs. Yet black women were very sympathetic to the women's movement. A 1972 poll showed that two-thirds of black women but only one-third of white women felt this way. Rates were similar for Chicanas. A 1976 survey found general agreement with the goals of feminism among Chicana, although it also found that many viewed the movement as elitist and too focused on "men as the oppressors."[25]

1980s

By 1980, the term "feminist" was used to refer to anyone who challenged stereotypical gender relations.[26] This is when the stereotype of the unkempt white lesbian feminist was most powerfully disseminated by opponents. Feminists were called puritanical and anti-sex. Women who enjoyed sex or were sexually attractive were not considered to be feminists. Such images clearly competed with the "equally limited image of an elegantly suited, well-kempt, professional white woman with a briefcase that sometimes turned into a child or a vacuum cleaner."[27]

These labels and stereotypes further divided the movement. "In my experience, even wearing a short skirt was supposed to be odd, and elicited anti-feminist questions about this 'contradiction.' In fact, feminism has always stood for the right to bare, decorate, cover, enjoy, or do whatever we damn please with our bodies—and to do so in safety—yet the female body used to blame the rape victim ('Why was she dressed like that?') is also used to blame the feminist ."[28]

Men increasingly began to claim that they, too, were oppressed, even perhaps more so than were women. Susan Faludi has written extensively about this backlash, tracing it to white men's fear and feeling of reduced power.[29] Similarly, other scholars maintain that "Some men cite as evidence of their oppression their much-advertised inability to cry. It is tough, we are told, to be masculine . . . . But this is nonsense. Human beings can be miserable without being oppressed, and it is perfectly consistent to deny that a person or group is oppressed without denying that they have feelings or that they suffer . . . "[30] This perspective gelled well with the conservative politics of the Reagan era, which saw historically privileged groups expressing concern that minority groups had gained too many advantages through programs like affirmative action. For instance, U.S. President Ronald Reagan dismantled the Office on Domestic Violence as well as the National Center on Rape upon taking office, and his conservative agenda significantly cut support for other social programs.

In the 1980s, some feminists began to take a more global view. U.S. poet Adrienne Rich wrote about the "politics of location," calling up Virginia Woolf's statement that, "as a woman I have no country; as a woman my country is the whole world."[31] International organizations provided a forum for communication among diverse women's movements. The United Nations declared 1975–1985 as the Decade for Women, and regional and international conferences were held throughout that period, including the 1995 UN's Fourth World Congress on Women in Beijing. Women from around the world who were not official delegates held gatherings at the same time as the UN conferences. Many of the women were representatives of various nongovernmental organizations (NGOs). They found differences in the primary issues of focus—Western women were most concerned with equal rights to education, property, and political authority, while women from Asia, Africa, and Latin America cited poverty as the most critical human rights issue. "The NGO gatherings especially convinced many Western women that world poverty and national liberation were feminist issues because they affected women's lives around the globe. After attending the Copenhagen conference,

Charlotte Bunch, a radical lesbian feminist in the United States during the 1970s, came to the conclusion that *everything* is a woman's issue. That means racism is a woman's issue, just as is anti-Semitism, Palestinian homelessness, rural development, ecology, the persecution of lesbians, and the exploitative practices of global corporations'."[32]

In sum, second wavers were responsible for many critical achievements. At the same time, the divisions within the movement and the backlash it prompted threatened its very existence. It was not only conservatives who criticized the second wave. Many activists alleged that it was concerned only with the needs of middle- and upper-class white women, and failed to focus on the issues faced by women of color and lower-income women. Nor did second wavers do enough to elicit the involvement of women of color, according to critics.[33] Some second wave feminists, such as Susan Brownmiller, author of *Against Our Will: Men, Women and Rape*, have argued that women of color were not purposely excluded but that sometimes they were torn between advocating for women's rights and working with black men on civil rights.[34] Yet others feel the exclusion was far more intentional. Patricia Hill Collins, author of *Black Feminist Thought* and several other books, has argued that when white women say "we worked to include them," they are demonstrating the problem, which is their assumption that the movement was started by and pretty much belonged to white women.[35] Another issue with the second wave is that many who obtained leadership positions are today finding it difficult to let go and pass the torch to the newer generations.

Chapter Three

The Third Wave

Like Broadway, the novel, and God, feminism has been declared dead many times.[1]

—Katha Pollitt

IS FEMINISM DEAD?

The backlash against second wave feminists began in the 1980s and was exacerbated by the conservatism of the Reagan era. Common criticisms of feminism, mostly popularized in the 1980s, were that:

1. it is all about angry, whiny women who lack a sense of humor and who exaggerate discrimination against them;
2. all feminists hate men, want to be like men, or want to recreate society such that women now have power over men;
3. all feminists are lesbians;
4. feminists reject motherhood and all things feminine; and
5. feminism is exclusively a white, middle-class movement.[2]

By the 1980s, increasing numbers of people denounced feminism. As early as the 1970s, media proclaimed feminism as dead, or at least irrelevant. In 1976 *Harper's* announced a "requiem for the women's movement." In 1980, the *New York Times* told readers radical feminism was dead. In 1990, *Newsweek* denounced feminism as a failure, and in 1998 *Time* asked whether feminism was dead.[3] The articles all used a stereotypical depiction of feminists, setting up a "straw woman" to attack.[4]

There is statistical support that fewer women claim to be feminists. A *Time/CNN* poll on feminism in the 1990s, found 48 percent of women said feminism today is relevant to most women, and only 64 percent of self-identified feminists said so. Between 1989 and 1998, there was

a 12 percent reduction in the number of people who held favorable
impressions of feminists, from 44 percent to 32 percent. More recently, a
poll in 2000 asked women in the United States if they believed women
should have equal rights, and 85 percent said yes. When the same poll
asked if they identified themselves as feminists, only 29 percent said
yes.[5] Often simply called "the F word," discussions with young women
today "nearly always begin with the disclaimer 'I'm not a feminist
but . . . ' Young women assume that the feminist war has been waged—
and won. They think the struggles for the right to work, to control their
own bodies, to be safe in their homes, or on dates, or at parties, are rights
they can now take for granted, much as their mothers took for granted the
right to vote or drive a car."[6] One claim is that the women's movement is
dead because it was won, and thus nothing useful can be added by modern
activists.[7] Some have suggested that the women's movement in the United
States is less visible because we are in a time of "post-feminism." This is
clearly not true, as women still endure inequalities daily. "The glass ceiling
is only cracked, not broken; and there is a persistent wage gap between
mothers and non-mothers, with single mothers taking the largest wage hits
of them all. We are not in a time of post-feminism. We are in the third
wave."[8] Sexism is alive and well in the military, in corporations, in sports,
in politics, and in our own homes.

> Basically, we haven't come a long way, baby. Equal pay for equal
> work remains elusive. Barbie, with her distorted body image, is a
> perennial favorite. Female athletes are granted neither the respect
> nor the financial awards of males. It's still much more likely that
> your senator, doctor, lawyer, and boss are male. And odds are
> our preschool teacher, housekeeper, nurse, and receptionist are
> female. Feminist is not a dirty word. The opposition has simply
> coated it with an ugly patina, one that's effectively sticking at
> the moment. Even those who, 20 years ago, proudly wore the
> label that stands for equality, now back-step, side-step, and two-
> step, doing whatever it takes not to be caught in the flare of what
> is now considered the dirtiest F word of all.[9]

Women today tend to reject the stereotype, not the idea, of feminism.
For instance, Veronica Walker, supermodel, explained that she considered
herself a feminist, "but not in the fist-in-the-air kind of way."[10] Rowe-
Finkbeiner interviewed young women about their connection to feminism.
One woman, Traci, despite her belief in many of the traditional topics
central to feminism, rejected that term. She said, "When I think of feminists,
I think of those women who are totally against men. I wouldn't want to be
labeled a feminist. Actually, I don't like labels at all—I just want to be me
and have my own opinions."[11]

Advocates of gender equality today clearly struggle with the label of feminist and all that it supposedly entails. As Feminist Rebecca Walker explained,

> The ever-shifting but ever-present ideals of feminism can't help but leave young women and men struggling with the reality of who we are. Constantly measuring up to some cohesive fully down-for-the-feminist-cause identity without contradictions and messiness and lusts for power and luxury items is not a fun or easy task. As one women said to me at a small Midwestern college where I was giving a lecture, "I feel I can't be a feminist because I am not strong enough, not good enough, not disciplined enough."[12]

Commenting on interviews with young women who do not see how they fit into the mold of feminists, Walker explained that many young women have been exposed to specific ideologies or mythologies about what it means to be a feminist. A young woman might believe she has to be poor and unmarried and must constantly be devoted to gender issues. If she enjoys being "treated like a lady," loves misogynistic hip hop music, and can't wait to raise kids, she may feel she cannot be a feminist.[13]

Some second wavers say today's young women reject feminism because they are ignorant of their history. They claim today's women just do not understand how bad things used to be or could be without collective action. Others claim that young women have simply been convinced by the media deluge of stereotypes that feminism is undesirable. "The word is often hurled in insults on talk radio—think 'feminazi.' That's a lot of flack for a word that simply means the belief in the social, political, and economic equality of the sexes."[14]

Male feminist Jackson Katz has written at length about the term "feminazi." He discussed how ludicrous it is to compare feminists, the first people to publicly call violence against women a social problem, with Nazis, what he called "some of the world's worst hypermasculine murderers." It was second-wave feminists who founded the battered women's movement and started rape crisis centers. They were the first to draw attention to sexual harassment in the workplace, to openly discuss child abuse, and to demand freedom, dignity, and human rights for all. The Nazis, Katz argued, were obsessed with maintaining control. Although there were female Nazis, the most atrocious acts were perpetrated by males. "To link feminists with Nazis requires a breathtaking leap of intellectual bad faith. Not surprisingly, the person most responsible for popularizing that leap is the far-right talk radio icon Rush Limbaugh."[15]

Katz has also criticized the stereotype of feminists as "male bashers." Again, he points out the contradiction of calling women—the majority of victims of domestic violence and the ones who led the movement to end it—"bashers," which means to hit or strike.

The Orwellian quality of the term "male-basher" runs even deeper. It not only implies that women who speak out against violence are the violent ones; it also transforms men from the ones doing the violence into its victims. Unlike in the real world, where the vast majority of gender violence is perpetrated by men, in the strange world created by the term "male-basher," men— not women—are the ones being bashed.[16]

Of course, the effect of all this is very serious. Since most women do not want to be called these negative names or face other repercussions from an attempt to reduce gender inequalities, they either do not get involved or do so with less enthusiasm.

The repeated stereotype of feminism as one single and narrow thing serves to limit discussion in the mainstream press and, consequently, the information the average citizen likely has.[17] "If something or someone is appealing, fun or popular, it or she can't be feminist. Feminists are often assumed to be strident, man-hating unattractive—and lesbian. The idea that all feminists are lesbians is scary enough to keep some women, even those who are equality-minded, away."[18] The stereotype that all feminists are lesbians has been very detrimental. Homophobia is the irrational fear and hate of those who love and sexually desire those of the same sex. Suzanne Pharr explained that homophobia and sexism are major problems, but that feminists are also hurt by the more insidious heterosexism. It is the assumption that the world is and must be heterosexual. Systems and institutions, as well as socialization, are built on this so-called heterosexual normalcy. Almost anything a feminist might do to challenge the status quo can earn her the label of lesbian. Anything that suggests she is not being submissive or subordinated, like standing up for herself in the workplace, being financially independent, and speaking out when she hears sexist jokes. In order to keep from being called a lesbian, women may step back into the traditional roles that constrain them.[19]

Another interviewee, 22-year-old Matielyn, commented on why she does not like the term feminism. "Feminism bothers me because there are few, if any, positive 'isms. Racism, sexism, communism, hedonism, etc., all have negative connotations; therefore, many people subconsciously reject feminism without examining its foundations and theories."[20]

Walker, however, explained that it is not ignorance, naivety, or lack of concern that has kept young women from identifying as feminists. Instead, they shy away from the label because they want to live without conforming to any specific expectation. "We fear that the identity will dictate and regulate our lives, instantaneously pitting us against someone, forcing us to choose inflexible and unchanging sides, female against male, black against white, oppressed against oppressor, good against bad."[21]

Today's young women are critical of the compartmentalization and divisions they saw in the first and second waves. "For us the lines between Us and Them are often blurred, and as a result we find ourselves seeking to create identities that accommodate ambiguity and our multiple positionalities: including more than excluding, exploring more than defining, searching more than arriving."[22]

Rather than proclaiming that feminism is dead, we should, according to many, embrace the new voices, perspectives, and agendas. Feminism today has the potential to learn from earlier difficulties, including resisting the polarities of female/male, good/evil. Feminism "must continue to be responsive to new situations, needs, and especially desires, ever expanding to incorporate and entertain all those who wrestle with and swear by it, including those who may not explicitly call its name."[23] Some have suggested something as simple as a name change could help dramatically.[24]

The image problem has grown as feminists' work has progressed, and there has been continued backlash against these achievements and the threat they pose to existing power structures. Known as antifeminism, this perspective seeks to discredit and destroy the feminist movement. Interestingly, in addition to conservative groups and politicians, there are several successful female academics who have been the most vocal antifeminists. The list includes Christina Hoff Summers, Camille Paglia, Daphne Patai, Katie Roiphe, and Rene Denfeld.[25]

One way that the third wavers have challenged gender inequalities is by discarding traditional gendered language. They identify as "ze," "he," "hir," or "boi." This idea originated with second-wave feminists, who changed the spelling of "women" to "womyn." The respelling womyn was intended to show that women are different than men, not just a subpart. "Boyz," and the other new terms, however, represent a blurring of the lines between genders.[26] Some third wavers have referred to themselves as "femmenists." They define this as the intersection between feminism and lesbianism. "Femmenism is looking like a straight woman and flying like a dyke. Femmenism is being attracted to someone of the same sex who is very much your opposite. Femmenism is calling yourself a girl-girl and insisting that others call you a woman. Femmenism is playing up your femininity even when you know it can and will be used against you. Femmenism is using the master's tools to dismantle the master's house. Femmenism is political but not correct."[27] Some feminists have followed the lead of other minority groups and have attempted to take the power back from men by using terms like "bitch" (and others) to refer to one another. The idea is that derogatory terms begin to lose their impact when they are purposely used by the in group.

In regard to the lesbian stereotype, women who identify as feminists quickly learn how false is the notion that there is one sexual orientation for all their colleagues. Yet these women will indeed be subject to the accusation that they are "dykes" at some point. "However, simply denying that all feminists are lesbians is not the way to right this wrong.

We need to take the harder road of challenging the homophobia that gives this image its power."[28]

It is a new era, and just as new tactics were needed in the second wave, they are again needed in the third wave. Feminists have indeed advanced new ways of understanding. Standpoint theory explains that what we know is the result of our experiences, unique to each individual, and thus must be understood within a specific historical and cultural context. Authors like Carol Gilligan, Dorothy Smith, and Riane Eisler have utilized this idea to explain history and current issues. This is in contrast to the scientific method, which has long been proposed as the authoritative way of knowing. Yet standpoint theory is also rigorous and authoritative, as it is demanding of intellectual, emotional, and spiritual effort.[29]

Third wave feminists increasingly use standpoint theory to highlight the importance of lived experiences and reflexivity. Some don't know the concept academically, but do this instinctively. In doing so, they both honor the work of earlier feminists and at the same time carve a new path that incorporates the needs and desires of today's women.[30]

The third wave builds on the second wave's emphasis on women in professional careers and challenging of "traditional" gender roles, and adds to it an emphasis on the fact that there are many ways to be a woman. Young women today grew up with pop culture icons like Madonna and Jennifer Lopez (J Lo), who were confident in their bodies and in their sexuality. This confidence is viewed as a strength, not a weakness. This is in contrast to some second wavers, who saw sexuality as something that held women back from pursuing career opportunities. While the stereotypical second-wave feminists might have shunned makeup and short skirts (again, this is a stereotype), third wavers see femininity the way they want to, gleaned largely from popular culture, and still are able to run major corporations.[31] Yet others have critiqued this emphasis on popular culture, asserting that feminism has now "devolved into the silly."[32] Citing Ally McBeal as an example, these critics maintain that today's role models are not about women's rights but about personal or individual advancement. "Typically, a few unrepresentative but famous people are given as examples of feminist leaders, leaving many average and representative activists totally out of the picture."[33]

Further, feminism today has a strong base among specific groups. Many nurses, for instance, use feminist theory and ideas to redefine their work as advocates of patients and as holistic healers. Although older political groups like NOW still exist, young women (and men) use other means like social networking, the arts, and popular culture to spread the word. In essence, third wavers see social change as occurring through indirect action, rather than the more overt political or legislative tactics of the first and second waves.[34]

The third wave is, in general, less concerned with male oppression and more focused on female empowerment. It is more sexually and racially diverse than the first two waves. "It is not surprising, then, that there is no 'party line' feminism for this age group—you can be a corporate executive, a soccer mom, a transgendered person, and ultra-feminine woman, or even a full-time mother—and still be a feminist."[35] This is both positive and negative. Because of these ambiguities, according to some people, the third wave is not really a movement at all. It "is a large group of women in a certain age bracket who share many of the same daily struggles without a shared idea, or ideology, for solutions. The downside: Political leverage is lost without shared ideas and mobilized pressure for solutions, as with the first and second waves."[36] It is not just feminists but all types of social movements that have changed, however. According to Gloria Steinem, people working on equality issues today come together around issues or shared experiences, rather than as a larger movement. Huge movements against the war in Iraq, for instance, were organized largely through technology and less through direct action.[37]

Women today still face mixed messages, however. On one hand, women are encouraged to be wives, mothers, and caretakers, while on the other hand women are being told to be strong, career-focused women. Some women have learned from their mothers and from the earlier feminist role models that women are to forgo or postpone marriage and children in order to have careers. It is work and personal spiritual growth, not the family that they should look for to achieve personal satisfaction. The problem is that these ideas, too, limit and compartmentalize women.[38] Sometimes, women are at odds with one another over these issues, with those who work denouncing stay-at-home moms as unliberated, and stay-at-home moms denouncing working moms as uncaring. Similarly, women who pose nude or semi-nude for magazines butt heads with women who believe that this might be individually lucrative and liberating but for women as a whole, it does nothing.

Feminists today have focused more on privilege than oppression. Peggy McIntosh authored a seminal piece on unpacking what she called the "invisible knapsack" of privilege. She argued that men are often unwilling to recognize their unwarranted privileges—the daily benefits they receive simply by being born men in a male-dominated culture—even though they may recognize that women are disadvantaged.[39] The focus on privilege helps to make gender itself a topic of conversation. "Talking about gender for most people is the equivalent of fish talking about water. Gender is so much the routine ground of everyday activities that questioning its taken-for-granted assumptions and presuppositions is like thinking about whether the sun will come up. Gender is so pervasive that in our society we assume it is bred into our genes."[40] The idea that gender is socially created is difficult to understand in a culture dominated by an individualistic, instead of a collective, focus.

Since he served as U.S. president for eight years (2000–2008), George W. Bush and his administration had a tremendous impact on women and on the development of the third wave.

THE BUSH YEARS

President Bush campaigned for the presidency arguing "W is for women." Advocates were skeptical, although his first moves appeared good. He appointed a number of women to highly visible positions, and advanced some seemingly progressive policies, like the Family Time Flexibility Act and No Child Left Behind. His wife, first lady Laura Bush, declared that the fight against terrorism was also a fight for women's rights. But what happened under the Bush administration was not nearly so progressive—Richard Goldstein referred to it as "stealth misogyny"— in that Bush dressed up his cabinet and policies as women-friendly but his policies were anything but.[41]

Shortly after taking office, Bush cut funds to foreign organizations providing abortions and even information about abortion, called the Global Gag Rule. He appointed Kay Cole James as his director of the U.S. Office of Personnel Management. James is considered one of the nation's most vocal abortion critics. John Ashcroft, Bush's appointee as Attorney General, was equally if not more conservative.[42] Ashcroft appointed two women, Nancy Pfotenhauer and Margot Hill, to oversee the Department of Justice's National Advisory Committee on Violence against Women. Both had opposed legislation regarding violence against women in 1996 and 2000—the legislation they would now be overseeing.[43]

The war on terror was a more indirect yet no less damaging Bush policy harmful to women. For instance, the detention of Muslim men in the wake of 9/11 has had a heavy impact on women. Most of these men's wives were housewives who lost their breadwinner when their spouses were gone overnight. "Often what American feminists must do to help women elsewhere is not to focus on their governments but to work to change ours so that US policies and corporate forces based here stop harming women elsewhere."[44]

The Bush administration also pushed a marriage initiative, proposing $400 million in funding for projects designed to encourage single women to get hitched, in particular those with children. Further, they supported abstinence-only education in schools, requiring districts receiving state funds to teach only abstinence, not comprehensive sexual education.

One positive thing that occurred under the Bush administration was the reauthorization of the Violence Against Women Act. The reauthorization was cosponsored by U.S. Senator Barack Obama of Illinois, who went on to become the next president in 2009.

THE OBAMA ERA

Within days of taking office, President Barack Obama passed the Lilly Ledbetter Fair Pay Act, allowing women to more easily receive financial compensation when they have been the recipients of gender wage discrimination. Previously, he had cosponsored and signed the Illinois Equal Pay Act.[45] Obama has also retracted Bush's Global Gag Rule.

As a candidate, Obama was endorsed by NOW. He and Vice-President Joe Biden made women's issues a focus of their Web site, although it was not a primary focus of speeches or other campaign efforts. Obama pointed out the fact that more than 19 million women in this country are uninsured, and that women are more likely than men to delay or never receive medical care due to the high cost. His plan included encouraging insurers and providers to adopt electronic claim systems, electronic medical records, and patient safety reporting systems on order to cut administrative costs and reduce inefficiencies which drive up costs. Obama argued that these moves would cut health-care costs by 10 percent or more.[46] The federal stimulus package passed by the U.S. Congress in March 2009 included monies for these purposes.

Heart disease is the leading cause of death among women. Yet women's symptoms are often misdiagnosed, and after a first attack, research has shown women are less likely to receive diagnostic, therapeutic, and cardiac rehabilitation services. Consequently, women are more likely to die from a second attack. Obama cosponsored Johanna's Law, which was signed into law in January 2007. It was intended to provide education for women about the risks of ovarian cancer. Obama has also supported efforts to combat breast cancer, helping to pass legislation in Illinois to expand insurance coverage for mammograms. Obama has supported legislation that encourages research on health care disparities and to establish community outreach centers for women in high risk areas.[47]

Obama has been a leader in the fight against AIDs. Women account for more than one quarter of all new HIV/AIDS diagnoses today, with HIV infection being the leading cause of death for African American women ages 25–54 in 2004. Obama introduced the Microbicide Development Act, which will help increase the development of products that help prevent the transmission of HIV and other infections.[48]

In regard to abortion, Obama has generally championed reproductive choice. He has paid more attention to contraception and reproductive education and has pledged to reduce abortion rates. He has supported comprehensive sex education in schools, helped sponsor legislation that would increase insurance coverage of birth control, and promoted greater and more compassionate assistance for victims of rape. Obama cosponsored the reauthorization of the Violence Against Women Act which was signed into law in January 2006. It provides funds for community organizations, nonprofits, and police to expand services and to increase training and education programs related to domestic violence and sexual assault. Obama has been one of the leading Washington voices against the genocide in Darfur. A version of the Darfur Peace and Accountability Act, which Obama coauthored with U.S. Senator Sam Brownback (R-KS) was signed into law. He has visited refugee camps on the Chad-Sudan border.[49]

Obama and Biden know that a disproportionate number of Americans living in poverty are women and children. A contributing factor is that the federal minimum wage has not been raised in nine years. Obama said he would raise the minimum wage to $9.50 an hour by 2011 during his campaign, ensure that it was indexed to inflation, and increase the Earned Income Tax Credit.[50]

In regard to children, Obama has a record of supporting early childhood education. He helped establish the Illinois Early Learning Council, and has introduced the "Zero to Five" plan to increase support for families during their children's first years.[51]

In sum, columnist Katha Pollitt explained, "feminism has made the United States more equal, more just, more free, more diverse—more American. But it still has a long way to go."[52] The third wave is complex, but perhaps most important is its recognition that feminists can be many things, and activism can occur in a variety of ways. As Jones, Haenfler and Johnson explained in *The Better World Handbook*, "You can be yourself and fulfill your commitment to a better world. You don't have to follow some pre-designed path for making the world better."[53] It is this foundation on which this book is built.

Chapter Four

The Personal Is Political: Feminist Activism in Politics

Since the first wave helped earn women the right to vote, activists have worked for greater inclusion of women in political office. Research has demonstrated that having women in political office does indeed matter. One study by the Institute for Women's Policy Research found that when women held office, better policy for women was the result. Although far from equal, increasing numbers of women have been elected or appointed to major governmental positions, not just in the United States but across the globe. In the United States, the first woman was elected mayor in 1887—Susanna Madora Salter of Argonia, Kansas. Nellie Tayloe Ross became governor of Wyoming from 1925 to 1927. At the national level, Jeanette Rankin was the first female elected to the House of Representatives in 1917, in large part due to her active opposition to the war. In 1932, Hattie Wyatt Caraway was the first woman in a Senate seat, filling the spot vacated by her late husband. She was then elected to a full term later in that year. In 1981, U.S. President Ronald Reagan nominated Sandra Day O'Connor as the first female U.S. Supreme Court justice. Geraldine Ferraro was the first woman on a major party presidential ticket, running as Democrat Walter Mondale's vice presidential candidate. Outside of Washington, D.C., politics, Wilma Mankiller became the first female head of the Cherokee Nation in 1985. More recently, the 109th Congress (2005–2007) had a record number of female members—84, with 14 in the Senate and 70 in the House. In 2006, three states—California, Maine, and Washington—had women in both Senate seats. Democrat Nancy Pelosi is the first female Speaker of the House, and since 1997, the United States has had a female secretary of state (first Madeleine Albright, Condoleezza Rice, and then Hillary Clinton).

Globally, the twenty-first century has seen many women ushered into leadership positions, including as heads of state. For example, in fall 2005, Angela Merkel was sworn in as the first woman Chancellor of Germany. In January 2006, Ellen Johnson-Sirleaf was inaugurated as president of

Liberia, and Michelle Bachelet was elected Chile's president. In addition to Johnson-Sirleaf and Bachelet, Ireland, India, the Philippines, the Netherlands, Argentina, and Bosnia have current female presidents. England, Denmark, and the Netherlands are all led by female queens, and Iceland, Bangladesh, Haiti, Moldova, Ukraine, and Mozambique are led by female prime ministers.

Outside of holding office, feminist activists have been active politically, either advocating for or fighting against laws and policies of all sorts. Women have long been associated, especially in Western culture, with pacifism. Perhaps some of this emanated from the Greek drama *Lysistrata*, where women withheld sex from their husbands as a way to pressure them to end their warfare. In the twentieth century, reformers like Jane Addams and Emily Greene Balch created the Women's Peace Party and clearly linked pacifism to feminism. Both women later won Nobel Prizes. In 1915, feminist activists in the Hague, Netherlands, formed the Women's International League for Peace and Freedom. The group met with U.S. President Woodrow Wilson and shaped his ideas for later peace proposals.[1] In the 1920s, Virginia Woolf criticized war as the product of a masculine, patriarchal culture. From Cindy Sheehan, who got involved after she lost her son in Iraq, to women's organizations like Peace X Peace, women have taken the lead in advocating peace.

In was only in 1975 that women began to be called for jury duty. In 1961, a state assistant attorney general ruled in favor of women being exempted from jury duty because they had the more important "burden of providing palatable food for the members of their family."[2] This reasoning was not overturned until 1975.

Women have been central in calling for governmental change. For example, MoveOn is an online community of more than 2.3 million U.S. members co-founded by Joan Blades and Wes Boyd when they grew tired of the endless obsession with the Clinton impeachment scandal of 1998. Others have organized to draw attention to specific women's issues, as in the March for Women's Lives on April 25, 2004, in Washington, D.C. The march was cosponsored by over a thousand women's rights, civil rights, and health-care organizations, and approximately 1.15 million women turned out for the event. "It was, by some definitions, the largest (and possibly least reported) demonstration in history."[3]

The activists' entries in this chapter highlight the many ways feminists can advocate political change. From the Parent Teacher Assocation to chronicling history, from political analysis to fighting diabetes to mission trips, feminist activists are making a difference politically.

PTA ACTIVISM

Amy Barnickel

The world is full of opportunities to participate in armchair activism. One rather heartbreaking and not entirely successful example of my everyday activism happened at a Parent Teacher Assocation (PTA) meeting at my daughters' school. My girls were off to the side finishing their homework and the rest of the parents (i.e., mothers) met in the cafeteria. The subject came up of a two-year-old tradition the PTA had begun. The organization holds a father-daughter dance and a mother-son activity night (complete with miniature race car tracks and all sorts of other "boy" games). Because my husband and I had recently divorced and he had moved out of the country, my girls and I had been excluded from participating in these activities for the past two years: We are a mother/daughter combination. The PTA was not willing to let me attend the father-daughter dance with them, and the mother-son event was also off-limits.

So when the topic was raised at this year's first meeting, I calmly but assertively mentioned that the two events, while wonderful ideas, essentially excluded some types of families. I used my own example of not fitting either of their two eligible categories. I suggested that perhaps we could just label the events parent/child or caregiver/child rather than using the more exclusive titles and open them up so that families that don't fit those descriptions might attend.

I also mentioned that there were probably many other families at our school headed by completely different types of parents, such as grandparents, two moms or two dads, aunts and uncles, etc. The former PTA president quickly explained that, well, then a daughter could bring her uncle or her grandfather to the dance instead, but she dismissed accepting any other options.

Then, I made my fatal mistake: I said the word "discriminatory." That word set practically everyone off and everyone against me, though I really thought I had pointed it out in a most respectful way. The former PTA president went ballistic. I tried to explain that discrimination happens all the time and it's not a word we should shy away from but examine for what it is, try to change our behavior, and not perpetuate it. But the ears were deaf. The current PTA president finally chimed in only to demand that the discussion end and stated that both events would not be held this year. End of discussion. Meeting adjourned.

The next day, I wrote an e-mail to the PTA president and copied the principal. The principal never responded, and the PTA president's response included:

> Although I do not agree with some of your comments and claims, I would like to state that as PTA president I have made it a point to listen to all comments I receive from *all* the parents ... I aim to conduct all the PTA meetings in a calm, pleasant and fun atmosphere where all opinions can be heard and all those with concerns can express them in a *constructive* way ... I will not allow our meeting to become an arena to vent or abuse others. I will continue to explore your concerns and will contact you.

It's four months later, and she hasn't spoken to or e-mailed me yet. So much for listening to all parents and exploring my concerns.

But, although the PTA has not budged on opening these events to all families and it will not hold the events this year, the following e-mail exchange with the former PTA president (which she initiated, by the way) shows just how difficult diversity issues are to reconcile. This seemingly small matter that could have been repaired with a very easy solution resulted in depriving all of the students from a fun, family-building event.

Former PTA President: I apologize for engaging in an argument and debate with you tonight. I walked away upset over this, as I know you did and I definitely would not have let it escalate had I known your daughters were present.

Me: I do speak up about things that concern me, and I will continue to do so, and my daughters know that I will defend and speak up for them. There is no harm to them in seeing their mother stand up for what's right.

Former PTA President: I could say the same and say you are punishing the kids who do have a special male figure in their lives ... My husband has endured remarks numerous times and has always had to prove himself due to his small stature ... but I do not now or will not expect people to make special provisions just to accommodate him.

Me: These are not special provisions or accommodations ... [we're] simply opening [the events] up to significant adults and their kids ... [if they] remain the same, the fact is that some families will not be able to participate. There are many types of derogatory remarks and actions against individuals, as you note in your husband's case, but when entire groups are excluded, it does become discrimination . . . How are we to really succeed in our goals of gaining more members and more participant parents when we clearly exclude some families?

Former PTA President: I am willing to hear other ideas as I know the Board members are too. I think this could have been handled better on both sides.

Me: The same goes for me . . . I do not question your intentions because I know very well what they are.

Former PTA President: Agreed! I look forward to a great school year. Yes, we have to stick together, especially with the budget cuts this year and the lack of resources for our kids.

Honestly, I know that, at least on this former PTA president, I made an impression, and she has not stopped thinking about what I said, though she did not come completely around.

Armchair activism, contrary to what some may believe, is not easy. Doing it almost always requires our sticking our necks out to some degree. But the lesson in this PTA meeting drama is not that I failed to win everyone over, that the world is hopelessly closed-minded, or anything else—the message is that my daughters saw me acting on behalf of them and others who are silenced or excluded—and that's always a victory for progress.

HISTORIANS AS ACTIVISTS

Annie Warshaw

"Well, if you really want to help women, law is the perfect way to go about doing that!" My mother has uttered those words to me too many times to count. Her perception sadly is not an uncommon response to receive when I tell people I want to fight for women's rights as my career. It is thought that to help fight for women's rights and issues we must go through the judicial system. However, this is not the only way to help fight for equality; it is just a small part of the movement. By going through the court system one is just helping to change actions once they have already occurred, instead of preventing those actions from happening. Everyday feminism action to me is about preventing the inequality that exists from progressing, and to instead rewrite how we understand gender identity and norms. For equality between the sexes to exist, I think many different types of action must happen within the movement. Yes, the protesting is necessary and so is the law aspect but the actions that often go unnoticed are just as important. That is why I choose to write women into history as my everyday feminism.

I am currently receiving my masters degree in history. My work focuses on the triumphs and tragedies of everyday women throughout time. Not only does being a women's historian allow me to gain a better understanding of women's day-to-day lives throughout history, it allows me to understand how patriarchy manifested its way into society. I have learned about the great women who have resisted gender norms by cross-dressing in early modern England, the women of the English Revolution who fought alongside their radical husbands, the French women who marched to gain equal freedom during the French revolution, the early colonial woman settlers who shook men's confidence by defying gender roles, and the Russian women who helped to change familial structure during the Bolshevik Revolution. My study has also taught me about the forgotten heroes of the women's movement, including Sojourner Truth and her insistence that she was a human being just like men, Emma Goldman and Margaret Sanger who fought for birth control, Sophie Scholl who died for standing up to the Nazis, Ida B. Wells who fought for civil rights, Alice Paul the suffragist who constructed the ERA, Simone de Beauvoir who declared women were seen as a second sex and this could no longer be tolerated, Gloria Steinem who did not turn her back on African Americans and homosexuals during the second wave of feminism, and Angela Davis, the great African American heroine.

Learning about all of these women allows me to understand our current situation and system better. It gives me better insight to the workings of patriarchy and in turn makes me a better feminist. Giving women a voice in the history books gives women a voice within our current movement. By allowing the world to see that women were active throughout history, women are granted agency. Women having agency throughout history is radical and essential for the movement.

So although my activism is not flashy, nor in the news, it is an integral part of how we understand feminism and the feminist movement.

HOW DO WE BEAT THE BITCH?

Li-Hsiang Lisa Rosenlee

This infamous line uttered by one of then-presidential hopeful John McCain's supporters during the 2008 presidential primary, to me, is indicative of the problem of what I call "casual sexism"; that is, sexism is something to be brushed off, not to be dealt with, because most of time being sexist is just considered funny or at best mildly offensive. As captured on tape, this question elicited loud laughter from the audience of both men and women as well as from the presidential candidate McCain himself, despite the fact that John McCain and Hillary Clinton have a rather collegial relationship in the U.S. Congress. The "bitch" name calling then ignited *Saturday Night Live* comedian Tina Fey's rebuttal skit, where she equated "bitch-ness" with competent women and urged Texas and Ohio voters to get on board because, as Fey announced, "Bitch is the new black." This of course is not the end of the whole "bitch" saga during the primary. Roughly two weeks later, Tracy Morgan, another *SNL* comedian, offered his own rebut in favor of Barack Obama by calling out the racist nature of our nation and declared once and for all that "Bitch may be the new black, but black is the new President, bitch." Hillary Clinton, of course, is the "bitch" that everyone wants to knock down, not just by the Republican hopeful, McCain, but also her fellow Democrats, and even her own supporters embrace her "bitch-ness" as a sign of her competence. But what does this whole talk about "bitch-ness" have to do with feminist activism? As a professional philosopher and a feminist, I believe feminist activism must start with a clear thinking of the impact of ideas on our daily life. As simple as calling and embracing the "bitch-ness" of women, as shown in Fey's brief "empowerment" of Hillary as a "bitch," it has a far-reaching effect on our ability to transform our lot as women. After all, as comedian Morgan seemed to say in his rebuttal that a bitch is still a bitch no matter how chic she seems to be.

But one might say that Clinton *is* a "bitch," as the mother of Newt Gingrich, the Republican former speaker of the house, announced to news reporter Connie Chung back in 1995 when Hillary was still the first lady unable to accomplish anything on her own with the Congress. In 2008, 13 years later, things still haven't changed that much: Hillary, a second-term U.S. Senator and then a presidential contender, is still considered a "bitch" regardless of what she is able to accomplish now. This makes me wonder if a competent woman like Hillary Clinton—a Yale graduate, a high profile lawyer, an accomplished U.S. Senator, and a serious presidential contender with the mandate of 18 million votes—is unable to deal with the issue of sexism head on, what is the chance for the rest of us? Unfortunately, as shown in the 2008 presidential primary, critical feminist consciousness has always been relegated to the periphery, if it is acknowledged at all. People of any social group, whether it is religion, ethnic, or race based, don't take sexism seriously, since gender-based claims seem natural to them. And hence the fight against casual sexism is proven much harder than the fight against racism which has a different social structure.

For one thing, being overtly sexist is still considered funny, whereas being racist is not. Think of it this way: If Hillary or Hillary's supporters had called Obama the "n" word publicly, the world would not have tolerated it. Calling Hillary a "bitch," an equally derogatory term, has been a late night show hit and rap song top seller. There is, in a word, a casual sense of sexism in that we relegate sexist attitudes and claims into the periphery of our social consciousness, whereas we are generally more inclined to change overtly racist attitudes as an integral part of social justice. During the primary election, Hillary was mocked first and foremost for being a woman and criticized for her inability as a wife to control her unruly husband. In contrast, there is no equivalently forceful mockery that one can find aimed at Obama's self-defined African American racial identity. Of course, I am not saying that racism has disappeared in this country or in people's private consciousness. What I am saying is that being racist whenever it occurs is generally seen as a social problem, whereas being sexist makes one a comedian! Just like racism, sexism has not disappeared, but unlike racism, its existence is not acknowledged or taken seriously. The one who cries for being a victim of sexism is after all seen as a "bitch" who whines too much. For instance, unlike Obama, who was able to make a powerful speech on race to defuse the racial tension brought about by his former pastor, Rev. Wright. Hillary was not allowed to confront sexism head on, since that would have made her much more a "bitch" than she already appeared to be. The structural difference between racism and sexism is this: Accomplished women must shy away from addressing the problem of sexism, whereas accomplished men of color are free to address the issue of racism without apology.

But of course, it is not just men calling Hillary a "bitch," women do as well. After all, it was a woman supporter who asked McCain the question: "How can we beat the bitch?" Part of the problem of sexism, as I see it, is also women's own problem:

unlike race, gender doesn't foster solidarity among women. People see the skin color first and that is where they anchor their identity. But what women don't realize is when one "bitch" suffers, all of us do as well. For within any given race or ethnicity, women are still the second sex. Just look at the achievement gap between Michelle and Barack Obama: both are Harvard graduates and accomplished lawyers, but one is now the commander in chief of the most powerful nation on earth and the other plays the same supporting role that all mothers have done for thousands and thousands of years. I have no doubt that if Barack were a woman, he wouldn't have this kind of amazing ascendance that he has enjoyed now, just look at the kind of sacrifice that Michelle has to make in order for him to succeed and that sacrifice is still unnoticed and unarticulated. Paradoxically, Michelle, as our first African American first lady, is unbearably traditional and familiar, for she embodies the eternal virtue of motherhood: she is a wife and a mother first and foremost regardless of her prestigious Harvard pedigree, whereas Hillary is recklessly ambitious in spite of her motherly and wifely role. In other words, women of all stripes are seen as either a devoted mother or an ambitious "bitch" because of their gender. As a woman and as a mother, I dream of a better day for my daughter that she is not condemned to be the second regardless of her actual ability, that she is free to be ambitious and to be a mother if she so chooses, and that she is praised or blamed for what she has done, not what she is. In short, to borrow from Dr. Martin Luther King, I dream of one day when women are judged by the content of their character, not their gender. And that day will come only if women of all stripes stand together. If not, women will continue to be chained together by gender.

HELPING FIND A CURE FOR DIABETES

Ellen H. Ullman, MSW

"It was 20 years ago today" is not only the first line from the song "Sgt. Pepper's Lonely Hearts Club Band" by the Beatles.

That's when our son was diagnosed with type 1 diabetes, February 18, 1989. The shock was painful. I looked at the social worker in the hospital on the 21st after our son, our then nursing on demand toddler, was let out of ICU and said "please get me in touch with another parent who has been through this." Barbara Singer, one of the founders of the Diabetes Research Institute (DRI) called me while we were still in the hospital.

She was a beacon of hope then and continues to be now. One of the first diabetes support group meetings we attended (I was pregnant and our son had only been diagnosed a few months prior) was led by Dr. Wendy Satin Rapaport. We still attend groups she leads, and she continues to be a wonderful mentor.

It's been quite a journey. Our now 21-year-old son is empowered to take good care of himself. Over the years, we used a lot of positive language when we spoke about diabetes. We acknowledged what he did right. We acknowledged his efforts. We also validated his sadness, anger, and frustration surrounding the diabetes. We continue to do so. He does not stress over each high or low blood sugar, but he does take action and he does check and is beginning to embrace continuous glucose monitoring technology. One very important aspect of our job as parents was to raise our son to incorporate the diabetes tasks into his life and know he is a whole person, not just a person with diabetes. We are there for our son emotionally, as no one should deal with diabetes alone. We love him with all our hearts and souls.

Another important aspect of raising a child with diabetes was to reach out and make a difference in the lives of others. We never wanted any other parent to feel alone with this disease. We helped start a support group, we participated in groups and shared what we learned and learned from others simultaneously and continue to do so. We attended family diabetes camps, we sent him to diabetes camp, we attended numerous diabetes advocacy events so our son has always known others with diabetes. We've kept up with the research and technology. We have been available as contacts for many families over the years. Years ago, before insulin pumping was standard for children, our son had a wonderful goddess pediatric endocrinologist (then our fourth since he was diagnosed) who put him on a pump at age seven. For us, pumping was absolutely transformational (compared to life on two shots per day) and the relief we felt had to be afforded to others. I started a small pump Web site to share information so other parents could tell their uninformed physicians that their child was not too young for a pump and to provide the evidence in the literature that pumping was indeed effective for children. Fast forward 14 years—I am also a member of a two county outreach of professionals who work with patients with diabetes—and I continue to raise awareness among professionals to have their patients checked for celiac disease, let them know about newest resources available for their patients, etc. Our job of reaching out is ever important.

Our other most important mission as parents remains to raise awareness of the need to cure type 1 diabetes and to raise money for cure-focused research. We have been contacting the media for many years and even this past weekend we were interviewed for yet another article. My husband has been humble and tireless in his pursuit of raising money through his employer's charitable contribution program for the Diabetes Research Institute Foundation. We have toured the Diabetes Research Institute many times, are so grateful for the DRI's absolute dedication to a cure and approachability of each and every researcher there, the philosophy of collaboration with researchers worldwide, and we love being a family who continues to volunteer for this wonderful institute. I also cherish my position at the Children With Diabetes Foundation and am proud of our focus and goal to fund cutting edge research which will yield a cure that is safe, effective, and affordable for the masses. Our son can focus on his self-care, while we will focus and never rest until diabetes is cured as long as we live.

So my message to one and all is after the fog and depth of pain lifts post diagnosis, take baby steps to get involved. Find what works for you to pay it forward. Don't be afraid to step out of the box—you'll be amazed at how much you can accomplish.

Together we can all work to cure diabetes—hopefully at least within the next 20 years.

MY LIFE CHANGED IN AN INSTANT

Jennifer Nardozzi

Life is not measured by the number of breaths we take, but by the moments that take our breath away.

—Hillary Cooper

Your whole life can change in an instant. One experience can profoundly affect and shape who you are. My trip to Africa was like this, an experience that profoundly changed my soul.

I had always dreamed of Africa ever since I was a little girl. I first heard stories of Africa at church. My favorite Sundays at church would be when missionaries would visit and would share their stories. Our church was quite a majestic place for such a nondescript little town. The only other thing in the town of comparable stature and majesty were the mountains. My small American town was nestled in the Laurel Highland Mountains, part of the Appalachian Mountain range. The mountains encircled the town and had a lolling, rolling feel to them rather than the pointy, dramatic peaks you see in other parts of the world that say "notice me!" These mountains made me feel safe and secure as a little girl, like a big hug. No matter where you traveled in the town, you could see these mountains that simply said, "I'm here for you." As a kid, though, I barely noticed these mountains that were just the backdrop of my life growing-up. It was much later and after years of not living here, did I revere these mountains.

Church was like this too, another back drop of my life that informed me and formed me. A place that inspired awe and wonder, that made me feel safe and scared all at the same time. I imagine myself . . . this little girl with dark hair and almost black eyes, walking into the home of God—as I saw it then—with its marble pillars, large stained glass windows depicting bible stories, and a wooden choir loft high above the congregants where I would sing during my Catholic school years. Sister Eileen, the choir director would yell at us little Catholics-in-the-making, "Drop your jaw!" and would tell us that we were singing for Jesus. I took this seriously, knowing that if I missed a note God would not be happy with me. The confessional right below the choir loft provided safe haven for this and any other of my human errors.

The missionaries who came to share their stories from foreign lands held such excitement for me. Their stories were of hope, adventure, and excitement. They would tell of their travels to foreign lands and I would dream of similar adventures of my own, far away from our little mountain town of homogeny.

I would hold these dreams of travel for many years. I vicariously lived through my curry-eating, Hindu-praying friend Priya and her family to learn about new culture, food, language, and people until I could venture out on my own. It was not until my first trip abroad to Ecuador that I had the chance to experience living in a different culture for the first time, albeit a brief slice of newness. I remember being struck by the level of poverty there in a way that I had never witnessed scarcity and lack in my own life or the world around me. One experience in particular was going to a park in Quito in which droves of children from as young as three ran up to us begging for money. I felt overwhelmed and saddened by the great need, a need like I had never been witness to before in my mere 18 years. There would be a place that I would travel to where the need appeared even greater: Africa, though it would take me many years to get there. First came my education and choosing a path for my life.

While neither of my parents went to college nor many of my family members, it was never a question of whether I would further my studies after high school. My father had many quotes while growing-up and one of these: "Any job worth doing is worth doing right." This would become a mantra for my studies. I worked very hard throughout high school, which ultimately resulted in procuring an ivy league education and then graduate school. My mother who came from a different culture and who had life turns that did not allow for college at age 18, started college at the same time I did. I became the first person in my family and ancestry to receive a doctorate. Generations prior to this lived in Italy as farmers and laborers, I am told. The ones who immigrated two generations before me worked hard to live the American dream and to make a life for their families. My father worked hard which resulted in wealth and an ability to send me to the best of schools.

I decided after college that I wanted to further my studies and to go to graduate school for psychology to receive my doctorate. This decision came out of my first job after college in which I worked with troubled youth. The challenge and reward that came from serving those kids resulted in my decision to make a life of helping others. While I did not specifically know how I would use my psychology degree, I would spend the next 10 years of my life postgraduate school specializing in treating eating disorders. I have spent my time working at a residential treatment center called The Renfrew Center, which was the first residential treatment center in the country for eating disorders. I had various positions over the last 10 years whereby every 2–3 years, I moved on and up to a new position. Over the years, I have been a part of helping hundreds of women with their eating disorders both through this treatment center and through my private practice in Miami. The work has been extremely stimulating, a continual journey for me that is interesting and always new. Perhaps it is the complexity of the illness and the challenge of treatment that allows me to feel a sense of aliveness, even in the face of an illness that intends to destroy.

I have been more grateful for the opportunity to affect change both on an individual basis through the patients who come through Renfrew's doors but also on an organizational level, including developing new programming and generating new ideas to make an impact on others. I am most proud of my work through the spirituality committee and developing a spirituality track for our patients, which includes such things as a spiritual service and providing opportunities for residents to be of service in their community, such as through working with the Humane Society, Habitat for Humanity, or being of service to other residents who are struggling. Additionally, being given the responsibility to work with alumni who have transformed their lives through recovery has been a joy. The opportunity to be witness to their transformation and their incredible desire to give back has been remarkable. Providing opportunities for our alumni to give back to others who are struggling with an eating disorder has been a true privilege. I am reminded through the alumni of their struggles and their triumphs, and why I do the work that I do. This is why I have dedicated the last decade of my life to treating women with eating disorders. Being witness to a human being going through the darkest times in his or her life and evolving into a wise being of compassion and strength is a blessing and an honor.

I see that a cornerstone of my own life has been to be of service in the world and to be a catalyst for others to do the same. This mission of service work would manifest in the form of a trip to Uganda in the summer of 2008. While I dreamed of traveling to far away lands for many years to help others, this dream would not become an actuality until I was 38 years old. My original plan was to travel to a safe country in Africa with people I call friends, to possibly build a house or work in an orphanage. My trip to Africa could not have looked more different than my original conception. Instead, I was traveling to a relatively unsafe country doing work in psychology without knowing a single person. About 10 days before I was to leave, the enormity of what I was about to undertake struck me . . . . can I really do this? Who do I think I am to go half way around the world with strangers and to do what again? Help people who have survived civil wars and post-traumatic stress disorder? What did I know about any of this?

My conscious mind thought I was ridiculous, but my heart knew it was what I had to do. I knew it was right the moment that I spoke to Sharon Brown, the organizer of our trip and an immigration lawyer by trade. I began to cry when I first spoke to her on the phone and surprised myself. I did not know why I was crying, but a part of me knew. I knew that I had found my calling in that moment and that THIS was my trip, no matter how it looked or what it seemed like to my cognitive mind.

Sharon feels called to do this work in the world, to travel to distant lands, to create a team of "helpers" (which on this trip were comprised of mental health and medical professionals), and to make a difference to people less fortunate than her. She is a woman of quiet strength and enormous faith. A phrase she would say often on the trip: "It is well," in her Jamaican accent. She did not say this to reassure some of us who were fearful and anxious about the work in an unpredictable country with no formal peace treaty signed after years of war. She did not say "All is well" to smooth over an uncertain situation. No, she meant this as the truth, that everything is well, if you can put your faith in something greater than yourself. In her book, that was God.

We traveled to GULU town in the Northern part of Uganda to provide medical and psychological assistance to the people of this region who had few services and resources. We met with nearly 100 people from the local villages under a tent in Bungatira County for approximately seven hours per day. Uganda was coined the "pear of Africa" by Winston Churchill and Gulu means "heaven" in the local language. The name seemed fitting to me but not from the perspective of Churchill—a land of beauty and rich resources. Rather, the way this small pebble is formed through a process of constant irritation from which emerges a gem stone. Uganda has been like this small pebble in a continual state of stress, transforming with the hope to something lovely. It is in its transition, not still a pebble yet not a glimmering gem either but somehow trying to emerge into something it perhaps has never known itself to be. Similar to the women I treat with eating disorders, never knowing what is really on the other side of recovery if they take the leap to give up their disorder.

For many decades, this country and particularly the Northern area of Uganda have seen much strife and suffering. Many people have heard of the cruel dictator, Idi Amin, who ruled during the 1970s. Countless stories have arisen from the time of his rule, some fiction and some folklore perhaps, that tell of unspeakable acts of cruelty. Between 100,000 and 500,000 Ugandans are reported to have been murdered or tortured during Amin's seven years in power. This stream of violence and brutal atrocities had continued until the last two years when the country has united in peace. Over the last decade, Joseph Kony, leader of the Lord's Resistance Army, would terrorize people from his own region in Northern Uganda, many of them being children. While based in some twisted dogma of the 10 Commandments, this militia would abduct children and force them into their ranks. If the children did not comply, they were killed or made to kill others, sometimes even their own family members. Extremely high rates of depression, suicide, and post-traumatic stress disorder have resulted due to years of war and brutal violence.

One way the government tried to protect its people was through the creation of camps. The belief was that if people were united together in camps closer to access security and less vulnerable due to the increased numbers of people living together, the government could have a watchful eye over what was occurring in its lands. However, with these camps came other problems. Increased numbers of people living together resulted in problems regarding sanitation and food supply. Some of the camps were placed in areas where the land was not fertile. Thus, their livelihood was disrupted due to the poor conditions of the soil. The assistance from various organizations led to a dependency. The systems put in place to help created situations where the people relied on help from others and lost their ancient skill-base that allowed them to survive on their own for centuries.

Culture and customs were also impacted not only due to the warring militia and government but due to the haphazard social structures of the camps. To the unsuspecting eye, a camp may look like any other carefully designed compound with its specific blood lines and ties clearly defined. Prior to the camps, families would typically live on a compound together with their extended family members also included in the design of the living arrangement. Camps changed this structure, whereby changing the cultural customs and design of the villages. Upon further examination, it is clear to understand that the sources of "helping" created their own set of challenges. In addition to the war and violence that has impacted this small country, poverty, high rates of HIV, and other diseases are also of epidemic proportions.

Our team, lead by Sharon, was a group of medical and mental health professionals who went to Uganda to provide service and partner with local ministers and mental health professionals from Uganda. Our mental health team worked with 100 people for a week. We worked alongside a psychiatrist (one of three in the area) and the only psychologist in Northern Uganda. Due to the horrific atrocities that this area has suffered, there were high rates of depression, suicide, substance abuse, and post-traumatic stress disorder. Our work was to educate people about these mental health problems, to instill hope that healing can occur, and to unite a community to support each other for a better future.

About three-fourths of our participants were under age 25 years old. Some of these individuals had been abducted themselves and were rescued or had escaped from their captors. Some of the individuals were orphaned, having lost their parents in the war or to HIV. It was quite common to hear people talk about their families in terms of how many were their own children and then to discuss the orphans that were living with them. Sometimes these orphans were blood related or sometimes they were children in the neighborhood. The mentality however was, you take care of the people nearby you, no matter what. You help others, no matter how little you had. There was one man who was only 40 years old and discussed being responsible for 15 people in his house, but who no longer had a job to support everyone.

Coming to Africa as contrasting as it is from our western experience to say the least, in many ways it felt like a coming home.

I have heard others share a similar sentiment of the familiarity on a certain level. Perhaps it is more of an ancient understanding that on a cellular level or traces from previous lifetimes, that we were all born from this place and from this culture.

Many of the people that we met were trying as best as they could just simply to survive day to day. One young woman, Shilla, made a particular impression on me. Shilla was studying community psychology at her university in the capital city but had come to assist the American team with interpretation. Since Uganda was colonized by Britain in the 1800s, most people speak some level of English. The horrific and unspeakable tragedies in this area affected everyone and Shilla was no different. While Shilla's family was still intact, she too had been impacted in ways we can only imagine and her family had also taken in orphans. A major part of her desire to study psychology was so that she could help her people who have been traumatized from all that they have survived.

Shilla had this exuberant way of being and you always met her with a large grin of teeth on her face. She still had a sense of love and goodness of people. She had gratitude for the Americans, such as myself, who she met and came to help the people in her region. She had a deep faith in God and was elated when someone provided the money for her to purchase a bible. When we went to visit her home, her mother, Angelina, was sitting on a mat on the red earth preparing the meal for the day. Since there is no gas or electricity, they use charcoal to cook. Preparing dinner takes 2–3 hours. Thus, when Shilla was done assisting us in our day long workshop, she would then go home to assist her mother with the arduous task of cooking. Of course to us it was arduous, to them, it is just what you did to eat.

She did not live in a mud hut like many of the people we saw in Northern Uganda. Mud Hut. Do people really live in mud huts? I would see these humble abodes and could not wrap my westernized brain that they existed. Yes, people really do live in there. Another woman I met in Africa, named Avery, and her son Ferdinand allowed us to visit with them in their hut. Once again, this woman looked happy. Here was her two-year-old who was hungry with a runny nose, saying: "Daddy, I want a biscuit" and she was proud that she had built her home and had a family to call her own. She also had this huge grin and I told her: "You look happy." She said to my translator (even though we were both speaking English! She didn't understand my improper American English): "I am happy." Perhaps it is not until one has experienced deep sadness that there is understanding enough to be grateful for what one does have. A place to call home, even if it has dirt walls.

People to love—a community that unites and rebuilds their culture and lives together.

Shilla actually lived in a brick house with no running water or electricity, but she had four square walls rather than a circular home that was common in this area. She told her mother, who I think was embarrassed to have us in her home because the roof was not completed and there were holes to the sky, that she was grateful to have a home. How might our lives be different if we had few possessions and these few things we owned we cherished? While we have abundance of every sort in our Western world, there is a paucity of contentment and spirit. This is really what the women with eating disorders are suffering; it is a hunger of spirit.

What amazed me then and still amazes me as I recall the people there, despite the most brutal of experiences there is still love. There is something that I witnessed in Africa that is the pearl: a sense of connection, reliance on one another, and a mentality that was not about what life owed to them. Instead, it was about taking what little you had, planting it, and helping it to grow and helping others to grow what little they had. That is how they plant their garden: together.

In doing service work, we mostly get much more than we ever give and my trip to Africa was no different. I felt a sense of guilt when I returned to the shiny opulence of America and the city where I live. What also became heightened for me is that there are people in my own backyard suffering, not just the women I treat with eating disorders, but there are people who are living in a state of extreme poverty within the affluence of my own city and every city across America. What are we doing to help those in the backyards of our own gardens? There are so many ways that people suffer and we need each other to mend and heal our hearts and our lives. This is what I witnessed in Africa and the gift of seeing the resiliency of the human soul will always be a gift from them to me.

INTERNATIONAL ACTIVISM: REVEALING THE PLIGHT OF WOMEN AND CHILDREN IN DEVELOPING COUNTRIES

Lydia Bartram, MSW

As a young and aspiring social worker and activist, I have been blessed with many opportunities to bring a voice to impoverished, abused, and oppressed people around the world. My initial exposure to the plight of women and children throughout the world was during my first international trip to Romania. I was granted entry into a government operated orphanage for children with special needs and spent significant time with a group of orphaned girls ranging in age from 5 to 16 years old. I also had opportunities to interact with local community leaders and to build connections for future initiatives. This experience opened my eyes and led me to have a different perspective on world issues. It stirred within me a fire that would not be quenched.

In subsequent years, I joined short-term medical teams traveling to Mexico, Brazil, and Peru. In Mexico, the Tarascan Indians, one of the country's most impoverished groups, was our focus. Each day we traveled to a different village and set up a mobile medical clinic complete with general medicine, dental, and vision. The people were so poor they could not afford medical care and suffered from a host of health issues. The need was so great we were not able to help everyone and this impacted me greatly. During my trip to Brazil, I lived on a medical boat with doctors and nurses for several weeks. We traveled three days down the Amazon River into the jungle and provided medical care in the villages. People living along the Amazon River have no access to regular medical care and, as result, risk dying from injury and illness that Americans would consider easily treatable. Even if villagers could get to the nearest city in case of emergencies, they could not afford the cost of acquiring medical care. Our team rescued two people with serious medical emergencies during our trip. One was a young man who broke his collarbone in a fishing accident and the other was a woman in labor. My subsequent trip to Peru allowed me the opportunity to work with more orphaned children and interact with people within the local community.

My most recent trip was to Uganda where I worked with an HIV/AIDS intervention and prevention project. This trip heightened my awareness to the devastating impact of HIV/AIDS on whole communities. I participated in a program visiting the homes of women and children who had been traumatized by the ongoing civil war with Kony and his rebel fighters. Many women suffered unspeakable brutalities at the hands of the rebels and children were left traumatized from witnessing their fathers and mothers being killed in front of them. Many of those who survived the killing were suffering from AIDS and had passed it on to their wives and newborn children. As if civil war and HIV/AIDS was not enough, people also experienced chronic suffering due to lack of clean drinking water and overall poor nutrition. It was very common to see small children caring for younger siblings. Many children in Uganda are faced with uncertain futures because one or both parents have died from AIDS or are too sick to care for younger children. I witnessed many instances where children as young as five years old were taking care of infant brothers and sisters. I was fortunate to have my training in child-centered play therapy and reflective practice and used this knowledge when interacting with the young children. One of my favorite pictures from Uganda is of me holding an infant and watching how he responded to my voice and facial expressions.

Upon returning from Uganda, I became more interested in researching Africa and discovered a significantly troubling crisis . . . the trafficking of women and children. In reviewing the data, I discovered that there are more slaves in the world today than there has ever been in history, according to the U.S. Justice Department. Human trafficking is quickly becoming one of the most devastating global problems facing our generation and it needs to be brought to center stage. The more I research the issue of human trafficking the more I realize how widespread it is. The physical, mental, emotional, and spiritual trauma that results from the brutality of human trafficking cripples the human spirit and forever leaves an indelible mark on its victims. Through my advocacy work, I am consistently surprised at how little Americans know about the human rights issues facing women and children around the world. People have a hard time comprehending the fact that human trafficking and slavery even exist in today's society, let alone imagining that the number of slaves today far outweigh the numbers of the past. The many blessings we take for granted in America are the very things women can only dream of in many parts of the world. Millions of children, especially girls, never get to experience real freedom, the feeling of having a choice and getting an education.

My goal is to use my skills as a social worker and therapist and my passion as an advocate to highlight the need for international activism surrounding the human rights of women and children. Sometimes the problem seems so big that people think their efforts will not make any difference. This is a choice, a choice NOT to act. This cannot be further from the truth. All it takes is for one person to start the ripple, like the pebble that gets dropped in the water. One person can make a difference.

Are you ready to start the ripple?

Chapter Five

Class Matters: Feminist Activism in Economics, the Workplace, and to Eradicate Poverty

Without a doubt, feminist activists have made great strides in accessing opportunities for women in the workplace. For instance, three of every ten lawyers in the United States are women, ten times as many as in the 1960s, and women are almost half of all law school enrollments. Civil rights legislation in the 1960s required that employers advertise job vacancies, rather than rely on "old boy's networks" to fill positions. Help wanted ads were no longer allowed to state sex preferences unless they provided a specific reason for doing so. Employers also had to stop asking applicants about their marital status and inquiring if they were mothers or pregnant. Title VII of the 1964 Civil Rights act prohibited employers from discriminating on the grounds of sex and race. Complaints came immediately. By 1969, the Equal Employment Opportunity Commission (EEOC) had received over 50,000 accusations of workplace discrimination against women.[1] An executive order in 1967 changed the original affirmative action policy to include women. In 1978, the U.S. Supreme Court ruled in the *Bakke* case that while employers and schools were not to set strict numerical quotas, they could use general goals for hiring or including women and minorities.

Some professions are still very gender segregated, and some interesting changes have occurred in this regard over time. In the 1870s, there were fewer than 10 women working as secretaries in the United States. In order to use a typewriter, a physician had to verify that a woman was physically and mentally able to handle the job. Today, 95 percent of secretaries are women, generally because of its low pay.[2] Teaching provides another example of a female-dominated occupation. By 1900, female teachers outnumbered men by two to one. When compulsory schooling was established, laws to enforce attendance were added. Schools sought to control growing expenses, and thus began to hire women and pay them less. At the time, schoolteachers had to resign after marriage so as to concentrate on their duties at home.[3]

The majority of college students today are women, yet the National Center on Educational Statistics data showed women earned more professional degrees than did men in 2004–2005. There have been advancements, however. In 1970, less than 10 percent of students earning graduate degrees in law, medicine, and business administration were women—today women earn approximately 40 percent of those degrees. The Educational Testing Service has even altered part of the verbal portion of the SAT to better accommodate boys by adding questions on sports, business, and politics, although they have never altered the math questions to increase girls' scores.

Advanced degrees do not necessarily translate into greater opportunity or wages. Year 2005 research showed that while women earned 22.9 percent of PhD's in astronomy, they were only 9.8 percent of full/tenured professors. Worse, females earned 33.4 percent of chemistry PhD's, but only 7.6 percent of full/tenured professorships. According to the AAUW, women constitute less than one-third of tenured faculty at four-year institutions. Harvard University offers one example. From the time Lawrence Summers took the lead of Harvard University until January 2005, tenure appointments of women declined each year. There were no senior math professors, and only one in the 18 member department of chemistry.[4] Summers is well known for stating in January 2005 that biological differences are one reason why fewer women succeed in math and science. He went on to be one of U.S. President Barack Obama's top economic advisors.

Women still do not have equal opportunity in the military, although activists have tried to address the situation. Activists are working against powerful stereotypes, though, that suggest it is and should be a man's job to protect his woman, hence the following quote by Katie O'Beirne, "Good men protect and defend women in the face of a physical threat. If men in uniform are going to be expected to be sex blind when it comes to protecting their comrades, American mothers will have to get to work instructing their sons that it's okay to hit girls."[5]

There are still tremendous disparities in the workplace. Despite the Equal Pay Act of 1963, according to the Institute for Women's Policy Research, women in 2008 made roughly 78 cents to a male colleague's dollar. In 2005, the World Economic Forum (WEF) published a ranking of 58 nations based on their gender gap. The United States ranked 17th. The rankings include wage equality for similar work, economic opportunity, including the extent of government-provided child care, the percentage of parliamentary of congressional seats held by women, the male-female gap in average years of schooling, and health and well-being. The United States was eighth for educational attainment but 46th for economic opportunity and 42nd for health and well-being.[6] Sweden ranks number one, in part because of their lengthy maternity leaves—both parents receive 80 percent of their salary for 18 months, and child care is subsidized.

Pay differentials are greatest for women who are mothers. One study found that a working woman's earnings declined by $3,000 in the first year after the birth of a child and even more in subsequent years, which is only partly attributable to taking time off for childbirth. Women who reenter the labor force often find lower paying jobs, if any. Divorced mothers rarely receive alimony and often cannot enforce child support payments.[7] As of 2007, the United States was one of only five countries (out of 168) that does not mandate paid maternity leave, and working mothers get three and a half hours less sleep per week than nonworking mothers, a sacrifice they make to spend time with their children.[8] Even some longtime feminists have criticized the movement's failure to adequately address the work-family balance issue.

Some argue that the gender-pay gap is due to women's decision to work in lower-paying jobs. This might be because of the type of work or because they take time off for child care. That women are less productive than men is entirely erroneous, though. Women reentering the workforce have proven to be more productive than entry-level workers, as they are more motivated and skilled.[9] A 1981 study by the National Academy of Sciences attributed 50 percent of the gender wage gap to employer discrimination. A study by Rutgers University Law School in 1999 found that as many as two million American workers were affected by intentional discrimination in the workplace, with as many as one third of them women and minorities. In the fall of 1999, Ford Motor Company set aside $7.5 million to compensate female employees who were subjected to groping, pornography, insults, and other indignities at two Chicago plants.[10]

As a result of these disparities, women are far more likely than men to be in poverty. Over half of the Americans in poverty today are women. Nearly 40 percent of divorced mothers are officially impoverished. The gap in poverty rates between men and women is the highest in the Western world. Rates are particularly high for Blacks and Latinas. Eighty percent of custodial parents are women, and custodial mothers are twice as likely to be poor as custodial fathers.

As noted in Chapter Three, President Obama signed the Lilly Ledbetter Fair Pay Act. This decision overrode the Supreme Court's decision on *Ledbetter v. Goodyear*, in which they ruled that women must sue within 180 days of the start of payment discrimination. The effect of women's lower pay is of course felt far beyond the paycheck, as women earn less in social security and in pensions as well. Lilly Ledbetter, who worked for more than 20 years at Goodyear Tire, made $200,000 less over her career than did her male counterparts who did the same work, and she lost even more in additional income later in life.

Martha Burk has identified six ways the male corporate power structure keeps women out:

1. Power recreates itself in its own image—since we're most comfortable with people we're most alike, it is easy to see why male corporate leaders find others (males) who look and think like them;

2. Power-elites enforce norms and systems that guarantee continued power—those at the top set up structures to reinforce the status quo, like seniority systems;

3. Power creates a sense of entitlement—men at the highest levels believe it is their merit that got them there, and they are entitled to the privileges they experience;

4. Power creates a sense of invulnerability and flaunting of society's standards—more power means more people to control, and breaking rules (including those against discrimination) seems to be no big deal;

5. Loyalty to power overshadows all other loyalties, including gender and race;

6. Group loyalty combined with power can trump good judgment and override individual moral codes.

But without a doubt it is to a company's advantage to have females at the top of the ladder. Research has shown that the companies with the most female top executives outperform those with the fewest, although it is unclear whether this correlation is causal.[11]

Women's labor in the home has always been under-appreciated, yet it is of incredible economic value. In 1993, a family in the United States would have had to pay as much as $50,000 a year to buy all that a housewife contributed. In 1995, the UN Development Programme estimated the worldwide annual worth of women's unpaid or underpaid work at $11 trillion. In that same year, the World Bank found 59 percent of the wealth in developed countries is connected to human and social capital. Some have argued mother's work should be considered part of the Gross Domestic Product. In 1995, a UN study found that women in most developed countries contributed more than 30 hours each week in housework, compared to 10–15 hours for men.[12] Still, some claim that the work women do in the home is out of love and that it is only natural for women to be assigned these domestic tasks.[13]

Not all women agree that the workplace advances feminists have achieved are helpful. For instance, O'Beirne argued,

Feminists have made the workplace worse by waging an ideological campaign to portray working women as a victimized class, discriminated against in pay and persistently preyed on by male oppressors bent on enforcing the patriarchy. Not content with the equal opportunity women presently enjoy, these women demand a strict regime to dictate wages and regulate relationships between the sexes at work. Armed with distorted data and radical feminist theories, they reject other women's free choices and see potential rapists lurking behind every water cooler.[14]

In 2002, a controversy over access to the Augusta National Golf Club in Georgia, home to the Master's Tournament, erupted and drew national attention. William "Hootie" Johnson, the club's chairman, refused to change the club's policy that did not allow women to play there. Burk, head of the National Council of Women's Organizations, an umbrella group of about 100 feminist outfits, learned that the club had not had a woman member in its 70 years. Burk sent a letter to Johnson demanding that the club open its membership to women. Johnson refused to do so, arguing Augusta National was a private club and thus had the right to determine who could join.[15]

Women still face harassment in the workplace. In 1991, U.S. President George H. W. Bush nominated Clarence Thomas for a seat on the Supreme Court. The hearings turned contentious when Anita Hill, a law school professor who had formerly worked with Thomas, claimed he had sexually harassed her. Thomas was confirmed, but the publicity resulted in a 50 percent increase in sexual harassment complaints to the EEOC. Membership to NOW surged in the year following, and there were 117 female candidates for U.S. Congress in 1992. Still, sexual harassment in the workplace is very common. Up to 50 percent of all women workers in the United States and Europe report experiencing some kind of unwanted sexual advances. In 1997, *Essence* magazine published results of a survey conducted by the American Management Association and found that 72 percent of large corporations had recently processed at least one sexual harassment report. It is estimated that only 10 percent of sexual harassment incidents are reported.[16]

Globally, women have benefitted recently from microlending programs, which provide female entrepreneurs with small amounts of money to get their businesses started. Research has found that women tend to reinvest their income in food, shelter, and schooling for their children, thus the effects are felt both inside and outside the home.[17]

The following entries share insights about women as leaders in the workplace, one way or another. Through reflection, speaking out, and a general philosophy of authenticity, feminist activists have and continue to pave the way for greater opportunity and equality at work.

SEEING MORE WOMEN IN LEADERSHIP ROLES

Nancy Leve

Consider this riddle:

A father and son were driving in a car when they got into an accident. An ambulance arrives but can take only one passenger. So, the son went first while the dad stayed back. When the son got to the hospital, the doctor came to him and exclaimed. "Oh my God! It's my son!"

In recent years, women have made tremendous strides in the number of us represented in well paid and respected careers once dominated by men (e.g., doctors). Subsequently, it is not difficult to ascertain that the doctor in the riddle above is the boy's mother.

But in 1970, fewer than 8 percent of physicians (yes, eight out of every 100 doctors) were women. Since the word doctor did not translate into the visualization of a female doctor, someone's mom didn't come to mind when thinking of a doctor/patient family relationship. Something that seems so commonplace today wasn't commonplace 40 years ago.

Recently, I had the opportunity to take part in my city's Leadership Class. We were a diverse group of professionals (including bankers, lawyers, media professionals, etc.) who came together one day of each month for 10 months to learn more about the challenges facing the city in which we all worked. In the process, we also came to know one another better. At the end of our year, we were asked to vote for a group spokesperson. This class member would speak for the class at the upcoming graduation luncheon. Each of us took a slip of paper and wrote a name on it and handed in our ballot. As I looked around at my classmates, I couldn't identify a "natural" winner in the group. No one individual had consistently been smarter, more outgoing, more communicative, etc. Yet as I looked around, I thought that against the odds of females to males in the group, one of the "guys" would receive the most votes. My bet on us choosing a male spokesperson was based on my belief that when choosing a leader from within a mixed gender professional group, a male is much more likely to be chosen. I suspect that nearly all men will choose a fellow male as a group leader and furthermore, most women will choose a male from the group as a group leader. If women were as likely to choose from within their own gender as are males, the spokesperson chosen in this group would have been female. In an act of everyday activism, I decided to remove any of my male classmates from consideration and wrote the name of the female most likely to do well in this public speaking role. Not surprisingly, a male was voted in as class spokesperson.

Why is it that males are more likely to pick someone from their own gender but females are more likely to choose someone from the other gender? Why is it that women can continue to demean their own gender in management roles as in, I'd rather work for a man over a woman? I would suggest to my gender that we begin working in our own best interest, creating some group solidarity—because it is not going to come from males.

I understand that eliminating all the males from consideration for my vote was "not fair." And I do subscribe to fairness and "having the best PERSON chosen" regardless of gender, race, religion, etc. I hope the day will come when everyone will equally consider each individual as a potential for any leadership role. But in my experience, we are not there yet. Until that day arrives, I suggest that we would be better served by handicapping or counterbalancing for women.

I'm reminded of my experience with affirmative action hiring at a newspaper company where I worked 15 years ago. At that time, many white employees had difficulty with the concept of hiring African Americans with fewer credentials over supposedly more qualified white job candidates. The hiring philosophy from the top of this organization was that a newspaper cannot truly represent a diverse community without a diverse staff. As such, African American candidates were more likely to represent the voice of African Americans and it gave African American candidates an important credential that a white candidate could not meet. So only by living with a belief that the ends (a diverse staff appropriately representing a diverse population) justified the means (raising the importance of the race in the list of credentials) would we one day truly be able to hire the best person regardless of race.

So I'm suggesting that women make use of their own affirmative action when in a mixed gender group and are asked to choose a group leader. Make the most important characteristic be gender—must be a woman—and then vote for the most qualified. Is that unfair to qualified males in the group . . . yes, unfortunately, it is. But remember, in reality the criteria for the best choice is not a clear distinction but rather a perception about the best choice. Both sexes will someday be perceived to be equal in potential as far as leadership skills. That day will come when many more of us, in both sexes, have the ability to consciously and subconsciously really SEE candidates of both genders as potential leaders. That day can only come after everyone has had more experience with women being chosen and performing in leadership roles. It will be a result of more people SEEing women in leadership roles just as we now so easily SEE females as moms and doctors.

This is our responsibility. It will hopefully someday open the door for a woman to assume the ultimate leadership role in the world—president of the United States.

And as a footnote, let's please stop spreading the sexist message about preferring to work for a male boss. I've had many bosses. Most of them were pretty bad and most of them were also male.

MY FEMINIST PROPAGANDA

Iwona Lepka

"I'm not a feminist!" This was my initial reaction when my father accused me of sympathizing with feminist ideas. I was 11 years old and must have just voiced one of my controversial opinions that women are equal to men when my dad asked me that simple, yet symptomatic question. His vicious attack astonished me since I could not think of anything worse than being a feminist then. Despite my firm denial to the contrary, he just shook his head in disbelief and smiled. I was downright irritated by his remark.

Now, I am 24 and I consciously use expressions such as "accuse" or "vicious attack" because this is the language that is still employed in popular discourse in my country. In Poland, feminism is still misunderstood and unappreciated. Women's issues are ghettoized as it is widely believed that there are more serious problems that we have to tackle such as rising unemployment or drastically decreasing birth rate. Feminists are frequently ridiculed as humorless prudes. Our complaints are notoriously dismissed while, in fact, sexism is fairly acceptable and permeates our society through language, media representation, and stereotyping.

I had never considered myself much of a feminist activist before I started working as a teacher. I still find it difficult to call myself that way for I have always identified feminism with spearheading impressive campaigns against violence toward women or organizing workshops devoted to the issue of equality of women and men. Yet, I have finally found the area I want to work within, namely the field of education. Apart from trying to explain the intricacies of English grammar to my students, I also attempt to broaden their horizons.

My feminism is inextricably intertwined with my lesbianism and atheism. Hence, I am passionately devoted to ensuring the equal treatment of not only women, but also homosexuals, people from different religious denominations, as well as nonbelievers. I am lucky enough to teach English to high school students, which gives me an opportunity to design my lessons so that they provoke further debate and critical thinking on topics which are rarely discussed during other classes.

It is often said that school is the mirror of the society. For this reason, certain values and prejudices affect the life in school. Polish school is still misogynist and homophobic. Gender stereotyping is ubiquitous. This can be illustrated by the fact that the pictures in the textbooks often show a gender-specific division of labor where women usually take care of the household, whereas men are presented as successful businessmen or scientists. Furthermore, the presence of Catholic crucifixes in classrooms is no longer shocking. They are so commonplace that they have already become a part of the school panorama which is not so surprising if we take into account the crosses that hang in both the upper and lower houses of Polish Parliament. Homophobic remarks are another big problem in schools nowadays. This situation results from the generally unfavorable societal attitudes toward homosexuality, and in my opinion, is frequently aggravated by openly antigay rhetoric of some leading Polish politicians whose public statements about "promotion of homosexuality in schools" and "homosexual propaganda" may well be interpreted as a license to discriminate both students and teachers because of their orientation.

Despite all those obstacles, I think that change is not only possible but inevitable. The only way we can dispel ignorance is through education. To my mind, one of the most important things school has to do is to inspire a progressive change in students' mentality and that is what I have been trying to do. In order to encourage my pupils to clearly express their viewpoints, I often present them with some problematic questions to which they simply feel they must react. My students know that they are free to say anything as long as they justify their opinions. We have had many interesting discussions during which we were pondering whether women can find fulfillment through child rearing, if they are still considered second-class citizens, or who has the right to control women's reproductive rights. From my experience I can say that it is these highly emotional topics which inevitably polarize people, but which, nevertheless, provoke teenagers to think critically. I, myself, derive huge satisfaction from observing my pupils struggling to find some rational arguments so as to persuade one another. It is very gratifying to see them arguing about concepts to which they responded reluctantly at the beginning.

Of course, my successes are entwined with failures. Sometimes my students' prejudices are so deeply entrenched that they remain unwilling to even reconsider their peers' opinions. Quite often, their disinclination to open to new ideas is followed by laughter and derisive remarks. Their behavior, however, does not daunt me. On the contrary, it provides me with new energy and a strong conviction that what I do is right.

Although I and my students frequently have differing opinions on various matters, I am heartily glad to actually hear them express any views at all. This pleases me the most because it shows that these young people are not merely passive recipients of pop culture and are on a good way to become active participants in the life of our society. School is thus the ideal place where they can experiment with the practices of democracy and learn to confront other people in a peaceful way.

I am perfectly aware that most of my pupils will never have a chance to study gender or women's studies, nor will they participate in a feminist demonstration after having graduated from the high school. Moreover, I am afraid that some of them will never have an opportunity to become acquainted with different feminist theories such as essentialism or radical feminism. Hence, my classes may be the only occasion to deepen their familiarity with women's rights. I simply hope that when they see an activist advocating fair treatment on TV they will not switch the channel. They will stop and listen.

SUBVERSION, ACTIVISM, AND GENDER PLAY: THE UNDERGROUND FEMINISM OF EROTIC PERFORMANCE

Marianna Leishman

I always felt a kind of bemusement at the way my feminist literature and pink highlighters would look sprawled out next to my seven-inch black, thigh-high PVC boots. As a pole dancer, burlesque artist, and queer performer, I always had uncanny pleasure at the way my feminist academic background sat with my constant desire to take my clothes off in public.

At the same time as I was lacing up fancy corsets and applying body shimmer backstage at Sydney clubs, I was surrounded by law textbooks on sex discrimination and half-written essays on sexual assault. In my head were a thousand thoughts from hundreds of hours of volunteer work around gender-based violence at community legal centers, international nongovernment organizations, commercial law firms, academic institutions, nonprofit charities, and scholarly journals. In my past were countless occasions when I had feared or experienced violence, harm, and discrimination because of my gender. I was armed with feminist theory and experience that taught me to question and dispute the representation of ourselves and genders in popular culture, and a resentment for the way narrow stereotypes are echoed throughout legal judgements, policy, advertising, journalism, and societal expectations that govern how we should look, act, and behave. Even among my fake eyelashes, cheeky-cut hot pants, and diamante jewels, my wardrobe seemed replete with reminders of my feminist core, one singlet reading (a tongue in cheek reference to militant radical feminism), "Newtown Lesbian Militia"!

And yet there I would sit, backstage in my right leg split, negotiating my anger toward sexism and my love for sexual expression, trying to reconcile these thoughts with my emerging, insatiable, and exhibitionist desires to both dress up and undress. At buck's parties, I would see strippers embodying modes of feminist resistance in their control, domination, and making fun of their male subjects. From upside down, I saw pole dancers challenge expectations about female strength and passivity through defiant athletic and gymnastic skill. In interviews, I read showgirls deconstructing the way in which their depiction of "woman" is merely an artifice, caricature, and drag-like comedy; and sex worker friends told me that during sessions, they would educate their clients about safer sex, female pleasure, and employ kinky measures that subvert ideas about heteronormativity. In the BDSM community, I found levels of trust, communication, boundaries, and an emphasis on safe spaces that were far more complex than I had encountered in any other commercial workplace environment. Upon their podiums, exotic dancers experienced the celebration of their bodies as an extension of ancient goddess spirituality and commanding female archetypes. Classical burlesque performers would often pay homage to courageous iconic female figures, while neo-burlesque stars played with the bent, the grotesque, and the circus-like bizarre to create theatrical narratives that engaged and questioned audiences. With their politically active performance art, queer performers used the concepts of strip, nudity, and drag to play with ideas about the body, gender, trans, and dyke stereotypes to voice new aesthetics, create new iconography, and underscore larger social injustices.

Within this underground world of hidden treasures, I began to find a distinct pleasure in deviance. I was overwhelmed by a fervent sense of belonging to a subversive and historical collective of women who had long challenged heteropatriarchal restraints upon how they should behave, from the female midwives and healers burnt at the stake in the name of witchcraft for fear of their sexual power and knowledge, to the activism of feminist guerrilla theatre and sex workers manifesting their profession as educative, spiritual, and political. I saw the multifaceted, innovative, radical, and challenging performances around me as tools for social change, and heard myself defending erotic performance as a form of sexual expression, pedagogy, art, and activism. The words of my fridge magnet echoed in my head, "Well behaved women seldom make history," and that thought made me feel wildly disruptive.

While we remain highly stigmatized, hidden, and shunned, while we suffer discrimination, violence, and harassment, and while we move beyond "good-girl" categories of modest, monogamous, passive ideas of "appropriate" female appearance and behavior, erotic performers can use the act of undressing or themes of sexuality to navigate a path forward to confront and combat sexism, stereotype, and gender-based harm; to assert active strategies of resistance to patriarchy and restrictive social mores; to transgress narrow ideas of sex and gender; to promote wider gender equality, open-mindedness and sexual freedom; and as release from the wounds of social taboos and prejudice about sex, nudity, and gender nonconformity.

Indeed there remains a long path ahead for feminism in a society largely dominated by *female* sexual display for *male* audiences, and one which privileges certain *brands* of sexuality above others. In this context, it is vital to look toward the fostering of spaces that are respectful and safe for all women, which are gay friendly and include gender-diverse and open-minded audiences, which give creative license to their performers to interpret eroticism and striptease in individual, unique, self-deterministic manners, and which showcase female, male, trans, and genderqueer artists, as well as drag kings, drag queens, and folk of all genders, ethnicities, cultural backgrounds, classes, orientations, shapes, and sizes. This way the profound and significant activism flourishing in small pockets of queer and underground subcultures can be embraced as a crucial site of resistance within the larger feminist framework.

The hidden world of erotic performance in Sydney, with its carnivalesque illusion and bacchanalian excess, remains perhaps one of the most underestimated and underutilized manifestations of feminism. The stage of erotic performance can act both as a window through which to examine wider constructions of gender and sexuality, and as a kaleidoscope, reflecting fractured, twisted, and bent subversions of cultural symbols and norms which advocate for wider social transformation.

ON THE SEMINARY: THREE POEMS

Andrea Dickens

I.

Saturdays in my urban Italian, Catholic parish:
alabaster Mary statues, candle-wrapped,
the light dances across her painted eyes.
Old women, cross themselves,
kneel, with bowed heads, waiting for the Confessional
door to creak open again.

The old nun and her assistant, a young mum
teach Sunday school, a felt board displaying
Noah's ark, animals 2-by-2,
except the giraffe—the class lost one to
Thomas Kelly teething last year.

The examples of 'women's work' were few:
mothers, nuns, and the 'crazy woman'
who left her husband, who may
have been independently wealthy:
no one ever stood close enough to her to ask
how or if she got by.

II.

My seminary teachers offered less: no women's
texts to read, no proof that women served
the church in decades past, even references
to women in the Bible carefully interpreted into obscurity.
The two female professors, distrustful of their own ovaries,
owning a lot of hurt, knowing in their
battle-scarred bones that we needed mentoring,
but scared to heal themselves first.

1995: I arrive at seminary, naïve, enthusiastic
planning to drink deep the knowledge of a tradition.

My entering class is the first with
more women than men. 51 percent.
But this 'tradition' was only a partial one,
at least as taught by greying men with golden
retrievers lolling by their feet:
syllabi devoid of women,
only men wrote those books, only men
studied and taught them, men alone owned the history of their
interpretation. Between the names of Tertullian, Irenaeus,
Augustine, Jerome, Notker, Bede, Chrysostom,
and Theodore of Mopsuestia, history's women
stood silent, in some foyer unknown to us.

Around my co-op's dining room table, our group
would form: women, studying, sharing laughs and tea,
tears and notes, quizzing each other about our lives,
the texts, a commitment we shared: to support, to find, to
advocate, and work for our future by learning our past.

TEACHING

Students shuffle in to school: years of
preachers forming their sense of self:
limited lines of fathers who have led them—
Jesus, Paul, Augustine, Luther, Calvin—
and the man who founded this school chapel,
for his wife, who died in childbirth
some cold Ohio winter, in a farmhouse
miles from anywhere.
(They will forget her name ten minutes
after reading the memorial plaque.)

First semester, I make them read stories
nearly two millennia old,
extolling breastfeeding Perpetua,
gored by a mad cow, before cheering
Roman crowds. They are confused by
philosophical Macrina, her discourses
teaching all the theology her
would-be Bishop brothers
Gregory and Basil, will ever know,
their minds the pride of their
native Cappadocia.

And they plumb Catherine
of Siena, as she imagines Christ

as a covered bridge, protecting weary
Church travellers. They laugh with joy
at how she told Pope Gregory to
get his ass back to Rome.

They muse quietly at Dame Julian,
writing joyfully in her cell, staring at Christ,
blood dripping from his crown;
they gawk at her wonder over the sheer improbability
of earth's existence, little hazelnut
that it is; Julian probing the Trinity and God's love
is a mystical text which my students
report makes more sense than dialogic
Anselm's abstract theories of atonement.

They read the words of Jerena Lee,
'a coloured woman called
to preach the gospel' all the way
to the end of the earth: Cincinnati.
Each groans in solidarity with her as
she explains to each man she meets, why
a woman travelled as she did, why a woman
attempted to preach Christ.

I watch these students arrive,
September-skeptical, fearing their new textbooks
as if history has the power to turn readers into
asthmatic library dust. By December's grey skies,
they go forth feeling the sharp cool breeze of history
against their cheeks, wizening them.
They know they are the inheritors of a past, filled
not merely with the images of dusty academic men, but
filled with martyrs, mystics, and circuit-riding pioneer women.

MENTORING

Fall break: alone in my office, surrounded
by last week's papers to grade, next week's
readings, an overdue review, and my calendar
showing 3 committee meetings.
Karen returns Tuesday for her reunion,
asks for a half hour of my time,
entering my office, apologetic as always
for taking up my time: 'My teens,'
she explains, 'loved me teaching them about
women in the early church. They can see

themselves ministers, missionaries, martyrs,
teachers, writers, advisors, scholars, preachers—
something I never knew, until God, on the
way to my own private Damascus—knocked me
off my horse. I want to teach them more . . .'
A broken-off request, as she ducks her head back down,
(afraid of her desire to learn?)
and I print off 'the list' compiled for requests like hers.
Even her request is part of a women's family history:
and I am thankful to be a 'mother'
to Karen and her classmates now.
After she leaves, I stare across the atrium, overjoyed
my seed has fallen on good soil,
wondering about the lives of these young women—
whom I imagine to be all braces
and first crushes and boy bands and Blackberrys—
who do not yet know they are my granddaughters,
wondering if I will meet them on the street and know
they are Karen's heirs.

MY WORK WITH PREGNANT TEENS

Kathlyn Albert

I have had the opportunity to assist many young teens, the youngest being 13, into the role of motherhood through my career as a nurse midwife and family nurse practitioner in the inner city of Milwaukee. This has been challenging yet rewarding. Many of these young women have lived through horrible experiences, very often including abuse of all types. It is my job to help them persevere and become wonderful, engaging mothers with their children. I try to teach and empower these young moms to continue school, gain employment, and seek services to assist them as needed, as over 95 percent of my patients get state assistance. Rather than shaming a teen for becoming pregnant at such a young age, empowering her to take an active role in raising her child is more supportive. To see these young moms mature is the biggest reward, most of them doing it alone without help from the father.

The role I play in caring for these young moms is not always easy. Too often I lose touch with patients due to disconnected phones, changes of address, etc. The prenatal care is often late and sporadic, even when I make a connection with the teen.

Once born, infants are not brought in as scheduled, and I often find myself calling the mother to get the child to follow-up, as a mother might tell a child. More than once has a teen mom come to me soon after delivery, missing her postpartum visit, only to find out she is once again pregnant. At times like those, I often feel like I am the failure for allowing this to happen, although in my conscious mind I realize I have minimal control over this and many other things in the teen's life.

Milwaukee still has a huge problem with teen pregnancy and the burden of disease, but in my experience, it is improving. There is much more work to be done in this area, and I realize my small subset of patients only reflects the larger problem in our society all over the United States. To help make change, I would like to start a free prenatal class for these young teens to help educate them, not only on prenatal and infant care, but also self-worth and independence.

WOMEN LIKE SPORTS, TOO

Emily Yanez

Last fall, I was an intern at a television station in Miami, Florida. On my first day, which was an orientation, there were approximately 30 students. I noticed we were separated into boys and girls. The guys were led into the sports department and the girls were led into the entertainment news and fashion department. After a while, another intern and I noticed this bizarre division and began to discuss why they would do such a thing. Ironically enough, she was desperate to be placed into the sports department but was too shy to speak up. I was not. Thinking it would not be a big deal, I asked the guide why we were divided in such a way, and she said "Hah—we go where we belong." At first I thought she must be kidding, since I couldn't believe she'd actually say that, let alone believe it. After laughing hesitantly about that superficial remark, I then asked sarcastically, "So, who decides where we belong?" Unfortunately, she looked at me as if I needed to shut my mouth right away. That was the extent of the conversation.

Now, every time I reflect on what happened, I come up with so many great comments I could have made to the guard to help her change her thinking. I think of ways my friend could have helped her change her ways, like saying, "Thanks but no thanks —I should be able to choose where I belong, not you."

I would argue that this is one of those cases that demonstrated gender inequality, because who is to say that the guys are only drawn to sports and the girls are only interested in entertainment news and fashion. I found the whole situation absolutely ridiculous and after a couple of weeks of the internship, I spoke with my supervisor. He told me that is just something they do to make sure everyone is "comfortable." I just did not see it. I could not see how dividing us up based on stereotypes made us feel "comfortable."

Although I let it go perhaps too early, I felt good that it troubled me and that I at least said something.

$6,000 A YEAR LESS

Enbar Cohen

"We can pay her less because number one, she's a woman, and number two, she will end up needing a man to receive and process shipment." These are the words that my district manager spoke as we were debating about a new hire's wage. Without a doubt, there are many inequalities between men and women in the workplace. Wage is an especially sensitive subject when it comes to gender. When my district manager and I spoke about how much "X" was going to get paid, I felt cornered. My district manager used the "she is a woman" card to justify why we should pay this woman *$6,000 less per year*.

The first time we spoke about her wage, I offered no rebuttal. I just nodded my head. The papers had to be signed within a week, though, so I had a week to think about that conversation. The woman we were hiring was indeed qualified, if not over qualified, for the position. She had a bachelor's degree and was previously a manager at another location. But the fact that she was petite evidently meant she would be unable to lift heavy boxes, something we are occasionally required to do. My district manager assumed we'd need to hire a man to do that lifting, so we'd cut costs by offering her less. This was not only morally wrong, but it was unethical and perhaps illegal. It certainly promotes gender inequality.

The day the papers needed to be signed, I confronted my district manager. I sat with her and told her that not only was "X" more than qualified, but that we had made some huge assumptions about her ability to lift and that these were unfair. I explained that we were being biased, sexist, and were promoting gender inequality in the workplace. I told her that "X" should be paid the same, if not more based on her qualifications, than the other managers at different locations. I essentially had to plead the case for "X," but it was worth it because at the end of the discussion, my district manager agreed with me and we decided to offer "X" the full base salary she deserved.

Even better, my district manager pulled me aside later that day and told me that my justification for "X" showed true leadership skills and that she was very impressed with my argument and my courage to confront her. At the end of the day, I realized that confronting my superior was well worth any risk I took. I spoke up not so much because I needed "X" to get paid more, but rather to begin doing something about the root of gender inequalities. I felt that it was the right thing to do and that if I wanted to make a change in the world, this was something I had to speak up about. I walked with my head held high for the rest of the week.

ON PUTTING IT, AND YOURSELF, OUT THERE

Laura Finley

In fall 2007, I decided to leave my job coordinating violence prevention programs at a domestic violence agency. Although I loved the actual work, I did not love the environment. I did not feel particularly supported and repeatedly got the message from my supervisor that the way I coordinated my department wasn't how a "director" was supposed to do it. It was the classic square-peg-in-a-round-hole situation. I truly felt that if I stayed, I'd soon be burned up and burned out. The decision to leave was at the same time easy and difficult. Easy, because I am fortunate enough to have a supportive husband and be in the financial situation that I could handle the risk involved with my next plan. Hard because what that next thing entailed—I didn't have another job lined up, and that was something I had never done before. My plan, with my husband's full support and blessing, was to start my own business providing training, education, curricula, and consultation on violence prevention, peace, and social justice. Prior to making this move, I had always been under someone else's employ. Although there are some definite drawbacks to working for others, and certainly it depends on the field, there is a certain kind of security in knowing where and when you will go to work, who will be there, and how much money you'll make. Further, given that I have been fully socialized in the protestant work ethic, I felt tremendous guilt at the idea that perhaps

I was getting off too easy—perhaps I just needed to work harder at my job and all would have been well. I also felt guilt in that I fully believe it is important and possible to change problematic social structures and institutions, as we all have the human agency to dismantle and recreate what it is we all contribute to creating. Yet at the same time, I felt like there's a pivotal point in which a person has to assess whether they can change a particular culture—be it at work, at school, in the neighborhood, in a relationship, or other—or whether it is healthier for them to leave because the culture is not ready to change yet. So, despite these risks and difficulties, I went forward with my plan and created the Center for Living and Teaching Peace, my own entity. I put myself out there to potentially fail, but more importantly, to potentially succeed.

The next step was deciding what, precisely, I would take on, and how I would solicit opportunities. Not really knowing how to do this, I decided on a "put it out there" strategy. The essence of my strategy was this: if an idea kept coming to my brain repeatedly, then it was some type of sign that this was something I should pursue. That didn't mean I went willy nilly or hastily about it, but rather that I had to figure out a way to make that idea a reality. In the year that I have been operating, I have submitted many proposals to provide training and speaking to a variety of groups, have submitted (and been contracted to write) proposals for three books (this one included), have sponsored four conferences and am in the works of another, have sponsored a benefit concert, have created a local chapter of Amnesty International, and have served on the board of directors of a new nonprofit devoted to assisting victims of domestic violence. Although these things may strike an outsider as random and unconnected, the common thread is that they all relate to social justice, peace, and the betterment of human rights. And they are all things I am passionate about.

What have I learned in the process? Many things. One: that I can be successful forging my own path. I do not have to work for someone else in a toxic culture but can create my own structure and systems of support that nurture, not negate, my true self. Two: that I can make a difference in the world while I also make enough money for my family's needs. Three: that people appreciate my efforts and creativity. Many people have expressed that they admire the fact that I took the risk and that I made something for myself. Four: that sometimes we need to redefine success. Prior to my "putting it out there," I tended to define success as receiving good feedback from my employers and/or other external forms of praise. Since I did not have an employer for a year, I had to learn that success might mean different things in different situations, and that the feeling of taking an idea from just that—

a thought—to an actual plan provides a wonderful sense of accomplishment. Five: that putting myself, and putting "it"—my ideas, my writing, my words—out there *is* activism and it *is* essential for social change. So, if readers take anything from my story, I hope it is the notion that we need to keep putting ourselves out there and change will indeed come!

THE LIVES OF OTHERS: ACKNOWLEDGING WOMEN IMMIGRANT SERVICE WORKERS IN EVERYDAY LIFE

Dvera Saxton

The Lives of Others. There are tens of thousands of Salvadoran immigrants and refugees living in the United States at present. At a university where I collected life stories from Latina immigrants, the majority of the over 100 housekeeping employees are Salvadoran women, displaced from their homeland by over a decade of violent civil war and associated economic hardship. The distinctions between the lives of the women I interviewed, observed, and interacted with and the students and faculty they clean up after are striking and apparent. An added complexity of this workplace environment is that many of these immigrant women did not finish school themselves due to financial, logistic, or safety limitations during a gruesome civil war that plagued El Salvador from 1980 to 1992. The aftereffects of this long and violent conflict continue to haunt survivors and limit the country's inhabitants' means to survive and live in peace.

These women now find themselves working at a U.S. college campus where undergraduate and graduate students pay tens of thousands of dollars per year for the privilege (some might say right) of higher education and life in a comfortable and affluent metropolitan area. A university education should foster the development of more conscious citizens and policy makers that will work to address and improve the lives of those that make privileged lives possible. Yet all too often, too much is taken for granted in white collar, post 9/11, anti-immigrant North America, including the immigrant service workers whose lives enable U.S. students to study and later prosper. Too many lives don't matter, even though these lives of others—in this case, service workers of color and non-U.S. origin—make privilege, namely white privilege in North America, possible. This is particularly evident in the ironic contexts of higher education and policy making, where people are engaged in discussions and actions that impact not only their own lives but the lives of countless others: others, who are not even the primary focus of consideration. With this essay, I intend to highlight the everyday struggles of working immigrant women, often overshadowed in everyday interactions, but also within mainstream North American feminist advocacy and activism and to suggest how we might change ignorance and neglect into meaningful and informed relationships and immigrant and human rights policies that acknowledge that importance and value of all lives. We must make the lives of others, too often neglected in everyday life, matter through gestures and actions, small and large.

A day in the life of an immigrant service worker. I went to work for a day with Beatriz, a woman in her mid 40s who has worked for the university's housekeeping department for the past 18 years.[18] Many of the women who work in the housekeeping department at the university rise as early as 4 AM to help their families get ready for their days and to commute. Upon arrival, they walk to the offices of housekeeping services, housed in one of the dorms on campus. The "clock-in" routine consists of standing in line, swiping an identification card, and scanning one's hand in a high-tech security and time monitoring device. When I first learned that the women scanned their hands to clock-in and clock-out, I expressed much shock (and perhaps some horror). Indeed, the women confirmed my surprise, stating that the system is *muy controlado*, very strict. Students and faculty may scan identification cards to enter select academic buildings, but we are not subjected to biometric scans and other forms of worker surveillance in order to accomplish our every day tasks and activities.

After scanning in, and walking to a building in the gusty and frigid February air, and after downing a few gulps of watered down instant coffee, Beatriz explains to me that we must clean the classrooms first so that they are ready for the students and professors. So back and forth we walked between buildings (as Beatriz has the heaviest load of all the women, tending to two academic buildings, whereas most women attend to one or two floors within a larger building or dorm). We wiped down chalk and dry-erase boards and desktops with hot, ammonia-laced water; dusted chair backs and legs, shelves, computer screens, window sills; swept crumbs and collected trash both in the waste bin and littered on the floor and desktops; and swept, mopped, and vacuumed the corridors. *Muy rapido*, she said to me throughout the entire time. I felt like I wasn't doing a very thorough job, but my perception of clean isn't at stake here; it's about getting a job done quickly and efficiently in order to be out of the way of students and faculty.

This notion of being "out of the way" has much significance later on in our day. At about 9:30 AM, the halls start getting busier. People walk past us, with an uncomfortable look in their eyes or perhaps a smile and a meek "hi" or "[soft cough] excuse me." Some of them stopped and waited for us to get out of their way. Still, others walked past without acknowledgement, their gaze totally evading the two women in front of them who are working very hard. I notice that Beatriz reacts to those who ignore her as if she were an indentured servant, in sight of the master or mistress; though this may seem romantic, it is a lived reality, a conditioned gesture evoked by housekeepers of the past and present, paid and unpaid. Beatriz steps aside, folds her hands in front along her lower-abdomen, puts her head down, and waits for people to pass before continuing on with the tasks at hand. At first, I, not being used to this sort of reaction, simply expected the passersby to move around me; however, Beatriz eventually signaled to me to get out of the way: *Muevate* (Move!).

We break for one hour at 11 AM. Lunch includes an assortment of things: McDonald's or Subway (the cheapest and least healthy on-campus eateries), Salvadoran cuisine made at home or from friends, pastries, coffee, fruits, sunflower seeds, and nuts. Some women don't eat anything because they are too tired, or have health conditions, like type II diabetes and chronic stress and pain, that diminish their appetites. Still, the women lunch together, chatting in Spanish, discussing current events and neighborhood gossip or venting about aches and pains from the repetitive motions involved in housekeeping work, or about how little trash seems to end up in the waste baskets, instead, being carelessly tossed around classrooms and dormitory hall floors. The shift ends at 3 PM. The women clock out the same way they clocked in and head to their cars or to the bus or subway for the commute home: on to take care of their families or in some cases to their second or third jobs at other locations.

Shadowing Beatriz provided me with insights as to how she, and perhaps other service workers in other locations, experience and conceptualize respect (or a lack thereof). Although some students and faculty say "hi" or "*hola*" or engage with her in Spanish conversation, others blatantly ignore her (which she seems accustomed to, based on her submissive bodily response). She laments that on numerous occasions while she is mopping the bathroom floor, students and faculty and other university staff walk over the wet floor, forcing Beatriz to stop what she is doing, wait for the person to leave, and re-mop the entire area to erase the dirty footprints left behind by naïve passersby. This is very frustrating to Beatriz as such acts of disregard cost her time and energy. She would appreciate it if people waited until she was done so that she could work more efficiently and speedily—two qualities her supervisors expect of her.

Other lives matter, too. A month after accompanying her at work, I had the opportunity to visit Beatriz's home to see what her neighborhood was like as well as to chat more and spend some time with her outside of the work environment. I discovered that Beatriz does not feel that she gets respect at work but she does feel that she receives it from her family, both in El Salvador and from those residing with her in the United States, and always has despite times of financial hardship, state violence, and societal woes. When she still lived in El Salvador as a young woman, she, her mother and father and several of her siblings and extended family members worked full time. Still, her family could not afford to send her to school beyond the second level (i.e., to high school) as school supplies, tuition, and bus transportation cost a lot of money in El Salvador: money that is often spent on bare necessities such as food, water, and shelter. Given the opportunity, Beatriz would have completed her schooling to become a secretary for a doctor, or perhaps a nurse. Both of these professions are still within the service sector; however, they are careers that garner slightly more respect from both clientele and society at large.

While perhaps Beatriz could not achieve her goals as a result of the violent and economically unstable conditions in which she grew up, and increasingly because of the racist and classist attitudes that further limit immigrants in the United States, she is not without human agency. She works to live and to enable life for her family and close-knit network of friends: all this, despite the disregard that many at the university where she works demonstrate to her in everyday interactions, as well as the neglect shown by those involved in making national and international immigration laws and human rights policies. Both these micro and macro arenas shape her everyday existence and experiences as an immigrant and non-English speaking woman of color, and unfortunately, not always positively.

As a result of numerous conditions, attitudes, and structures —racial, economic, social, political, linguistic, sexed, and gendered—on both sides of the border that divides the global North from the global South, the lives of Beatriz and others like her continue not to matter. Beatriz and others continue to move or be moved to the side, while, oblivious to their presences or value, more important people pass them by in the bathroom, in the hallway, on the street, and in drafting immigrant and human rights policy at national and international levels. Changing this unjust trajectory can start, as I learned, with something as small as a greeting, *hola*, hello, an acknowledgment of the presence of these and other lives within our lives. Evolving from this small initial gesture, today's feminists and concerned and conscious citizens, on and off campus, must make greater more meaningful and sincere gestures. We must engage in the lives of others at the micro and macro levels to promote immigrant, labor, and human rights agendas at regional, national, and international levels that both acknowledge the presence of others and enable peace and social and economic justice for *all lives*.

Chapter Six

Feminist Activism and Human Bodies

Women's bodies have long been controlled by others, as was documented in the earlier chapters. Feminists have had competing views about how to deal with this. Many of the first wave feminists associated the condom with prostitution. They also feared that contraception could make things worse for women because their husbands might be more sexually demanding. They feared that women might actually lose the little control they had over their reproduction when they lost the fear of getting pregnant.[1]

Women were often left to their own devices when it came to controlling reproduction. In the 1800s, couples might have used traditional herbal contraceptives, variations of the "rhythm method," or limited intercourse to presumably safe periods of women's menstrual cycles. In the mid-nineteenth century, new contraceptives became available and quickly very popular. An early form of the diaphragm was patented in the United States in the 1840s. It was called "The Wife's Protector." Condoms had been used earlier, especially among prostitutes, but they were not terribly reliable until the vulcanization of rubber in 1880. When all these methods failed, women turned to folk remedies or some type of home abortion to end unwanted pregnancies.[2] In the middle of the nineteenth century, the American Medical Association worked to criminalize abortion, telling legislatures that women who sought to terminate a pregnancy were immoral.[3]

In some cases, women were sterilized so that they could never get pregnant. This was not voluntary but rather the result of coercive policies like the eugenics movement, which was given legal support through the U.S. Supreme Court's decision in *Buck v. Bell* (described in Chapter One). It was generally poor women, immigrants, the disabled, women of color, and those dubbed "feebleminded" who suffered from these state-supported violations. These sterilizations occurred not just in the United States but in Europe as well. More than 60,000 Swedish women were forcibly sterilized between 1936 and 1976.[4]

Women have, for centuries, been the ones to provide plant and herb remedies for various maladies. It was simply part of their domestic duties. Although not credentialed in the sense that physicians are today, these women accumulated a great deal of knowledge about health and wellness. Midwives in particular had great knowledge of reproductive functions, and many received honor and respect in their communities. Over time, though, male practitioners began to replace women healers. Men were allowed to access the new scientific knowledge that was offered at universities, but women could not. Essentially, "when medical schools and state licensing requirements created a professional elite, they excluded women."[5] At the same time that this medicalization of women's bodies was happening, commercialization of the female body was also exerting tremendous pressure. By the 1900s, marketing regularly linked images of women with products that seemingly had little to do with sex, like cars, mouthwash, and especially, cigarettes. "Playing on the female body as a desired sexual object, advertising and popular culture saturated the Western media with image and innuendo."[6]

Although the situation is better today in that women are able to attend medical school and earn degrees to lawfully practice medicine. Gender bias persists in the medical field. Women have made huge contributions to the field of medicine. They have offered specialized care for women, and have also demanded that research and funding consider women and their needs. In 1997, 33 percent of U.S. hospitals had specialized women's health centers, an increase of 14 percent from 1990. Treatment has improved as well. For instance, legislation has extended medical coverage for hospital stays after childbirth. In 1993, Congress responded to activists in the women's health movement by enacting legislation requiring that women be included in clinical drug trials. Female patients continue to pressure health insurers, governments, and hospitals to address their gender-specific needs, such as their unique symptoms of stroke and heart attack.[7] Activists have also followed the path of Rachel Carson, who exposed the links between pesticides and cancer. Carson died of cancer in 1964.

Today, access to reliable contraceptives is far greater than it was historically. This is largely due to the work of feminist activists. In 1969, young feminists disrupted the U.S. Senate hearings on oral contraceptives because no women had been called to testify about the safety of birth control pills. Interestingly, some feminists initially opposed the sale of the pill because the early versions completely stopped menstruation. Women were concerned that they would constantly endure the stress of wondering if they were pregnant if they did not menstruate to tell them otherwise. In 1972, the Supreme Court finally authorized the distribution of contraceptives to unmarried women and girls.[8] On September 2, 1998, the U.S. Food and Drug Administration (FDA) approved sale of Preven Emergency Contraceptive Kit, one of several emergency contraceptive kits that can be taken within 72 hours of having unprotected sex.

Nearly three million teenage girls in the United States use contraceptives. Yet access is still not perfect. A major problem is that contraceptives are not always covered by health insurance, that is, if a woman has any health insurance. Approximately three-quarters of women of childbearing age in the United States rely on private insurance to cover the cost of contraceptives. This stands in contrast to the fact that "private insurers have covered the cost of the male potency drug Viagra since it hit the market."[9] Insurance industry officials have made the claim that female contraceptives are a "lifestyle choice," while Viagra is a "medical treatment."[10]

This is even more true in other countries, where access is notoriously poor. More importantly, education about contraception is lacking. The U.S. Agency for International Development has rewarded countries that implement long-term contraceptive programs, many of which are irreversible like sterilization. In Sri Lanka, a woman can get the equivalent of a year's wages if she agrees to be sterilized.

Abortion is perhaps the ultimate issue of debate when it comes to control of women's bodies. Before abortion became legal in 1973, with the Supreme Court's decision in *Roe v. Wade*, scholars estimated that a million women in the United States had illegal abortions each year in the 1960s. About 10,000 women died each year from complications.[11] In the decade after *Roe*, the number of abortions averaged 1.6 million per year. Some people assume all feminists are pro-choice, which is not true. Even early feminists leaders like Alice Paul denounced abortion as "the ultimate exploitation of women."[12]

Although women still have the legal right to obtain an abortion, many times they do not have the access. Between 1996 and 2000, the number of providers decreased from 2,042 to 1,819. By 2000, more than 85 percent of the counties in the United States had no abortion provider, yet more than one-third of women of childbearing years lived in those counties. The decline was greatest among facilities in non-metropolitan areas, although even urban areas saw a decrease. There have been repeated attempts to ban what has been called partial birth abortion, despite the fact that nearly 90 percent of all abortions in the United States are performed during the first trimester of pregnancy. U.S President Bill Clinton vetoed a bill in 1997. In 2003, Congress enacted the ban into law. In May 2003, conservatives began using Laci Peterson, who with her unborn baby was killed by her husband Scott Peterson, to push the "Unborn Victims of Violence Act." Opponents are concerned that protections of an unborn baby will lead to the eventual elimination of the right to choose an abortion.[13]

Sex education is also a controversial issue. During his presidential campaign, U.S. President George Bush pledged to spend equal amounts of money on abstinence-only programs for teenagers as was spent on the provision of medical services and the dissemination of contraceptives and information on how to use them properly. He did just that, authorizing an increase of $33 million for abstinence-only programs. The problem was that Bush's policies virtually required school districts to teach abstinence-only, as doing so allowed them to receive federal funds that otherwise they were ineligible for. Research on the subject generally finds that the only reliable way to reduce pregnancy and the spread of sexually transmitted diseases among teenagers is abstinence programs in conjunction with education about and access to contraceptives, not in lieu of them.[14]

Other body-related issues also divide feminists. "As in every transnational organizing effort, the legacy of colonialism affects the women's health movement. According to UNICEF, 130 million women have had some form of female genital mutilation or female circumcision done. Each year, approximately two million girls undergo these often unsterile surgeries. The procedures range from extreme infibulations, in which the genitals are sewn closed, to removal of the labia and clitoris, to a ritual bloodletting.[15] Yet activists are not sure how to handle this without imposing their own cultural norms on foreign women.

As noted in Chapters One through Three, images of women in media have often been detrimental to our health. Activists in the 1960s realized that they attracted the most media attention when they utilized these images. In 1968, radical feminists in the United States scored a major publicity coup when they protested the Miss American pageant. Outside the pageant, young women created a symbolic funeral pyre in which they burned what they called "instruments of female torture," including high heels, nylons, garter belts, girdles, hair curlers, false eyelashes, makeup, and *Playboy* and *Good Housekeeping* magazines. The movement caught on, and women around the world demonstrated against beauty contests.[16]

The preoccupation with thin bodies is just as bad today, maybe even worse. When *Playboy* first introduced the full-breasted centerfold in 1950, the women who posed were about 9 percent under the normal female weight. By 1978, the models were 16 percent under the normal weight. This emphasis on weight pushes women to diet, to exercise, and even to endure surgical procedures. Ninety-five percent of the clientele of Weight Watchers is women. One large sample of U.S. women found three-quarters considered themselves to be overweight. One-quarter of them were not, and 30 percent were actually underweight.[17]

Most of these images of women are white, and when women of color are included, it tends to be those with more typically white features or hair. "These images set standards for appearance and beauty that are internalized—standards that affect how we feel about our own bodies. As a result, most of us grow up disliking our bodies or some parts of them. We are especially troubled by those parts of our bodies that we see as larger than societal ideals. It is distressing that women often experience their bodies as sources of despair rather than joy and celebration. This is especially true as we age and measure our bodies against notions of youthful 'beauty.' These images of perfect bodies are fabricated by a male-dominated culture and are reinforced by multi-billion dollar industries that serve to maintain both corporate profits and patriarchal social relations."[18] Yet feminists have mixed views on how to handle this. For instance, some feel that it empowers all women when female athletes pose seminude on the cover of *Sports Illustrated* by demonstrating their strength, ability, and confidence. Others maintain that this would be nice if it were true, but the reality is that the bulk of readers of *SI* are still men who will not use this as indication of women's strength but as mere titillation. Some applauded female soccer star Brandi Chastain when, upon helping the U.S. team win the World Cup in 1999, she removed her shirt and, in her sports bra and shorts, swung it over her head in a gesture of joy and celebration. Others argued Chastain was fueling the problem of hypersexualized images of women's bodies.

Prostitution, often called the world's oldest profession, is yet another area of division. Prostitutes provide sex for male workers, soldiers, and sailors and fuel a huge international sex industry. It is estimated in the United States that 250,000 prostitutes service 1.5 million customers each week, with gross revenues from prostitution ranging from $7 billion to $9 billion. That figure does not include the sale of pornographic depictions of sexual acts, itself another huge industry.[19] Some argue that involvement in prostitution or even in stripping at a club is a woman's choice, and that the best way to protect women is to allow them to do this work but make it entirely legal and thus offer some oversight and regulation. Others maintain that no woman truly wants to strip or sell her body for sex, and that the best response is to work to increase other viable work opportunities that pay well for women.

The entries in this chapter highlight the importance of controlling your own body. They illustrate that every decision we make, every moment we speak up (or elect not to do so), we are being activists. These entries also demonstrate the importance of confronting damaging social norms related to our bodies.

HANDHOLDING AS SOCIAL PROTEST
Victor Romano

In the summer of 2006, I was four years into my graduate education at a top-tier research university when I learned one of life's most valuable lessons. My teacher was a 17-year-old autistic boy. I'd taken a job that involved teaching and caring for Daniel, a severely autistic teenager who was kind, gentle, and very energetic. Daniel was a tall and good looking kid whose mother dressed him in fashionable skater-style clothes so it wasn't immediately apparent that he was autistic—he looked like a typical teenage boy. Daniel loved to swim, bounce balls, take walks, and he was fascinated by cars.

One of my responsibilities was to integrate Daniel into the community and to make him more comfortable in social settings. As part of this education, Daniel and I would make visits to the local grocery stores, shopping malls, and parks. It was during these visits that I became aware of my heterosexual privilege—the social benefits and advantages that are conferred on heterosexuals yet denied to homosexuals. From a young age, Daniel had been taught to hold the hand of his adult caretaker when he was in public. This practice was necessary because of Daniel's attraction to cars and his dangerous desire to run toward them when he saw them on the street. As young males holding hands in public, Daniel and I attracted attention and were often perceived by strangers to be romantically linked. At first, the stares, objectionable looks, and occasional snickers we received made me very uncomfortable. For Daniel's development I had to take him in public, and for his safety I had to hold his hand, but under the gaze of passersby, my heart would race, my palms would sweat, and I'd feel embarrassed by their assumptions. Daniel, meanwhile, was oblivious to any negative attention. So, that summer, while I was teaching Daniel how to behave in social settings, he ended up teaching me. Taking my cues from Daniel, I soon learned to not let the judgments of others bother me. After all, they—not us—were the ones who should be embarrassed by their behavior.

More importantly, however, I learned the practice of viewing situations from the perspective of others. As a heterosexual male, I had never before had to consider the act of holding hands. It was simply something one did to take comfort or show affection. Holding hands with Daniel made me take into account a multitude of considerations that due to heterosexual privilege,

I could previously ignore. I came to realize that considerations such as

- Is this a safe place to hold hands or might someone want to harm us?
- If I am seen by an acquaintance, friend, or family member will they change toward me?
- If I am seen by a coworker will they gossip?
- If I am seen by a supervisor will my career be negatively impacted?
- If I am seen by members of my church congregation will I be ostracized?
- Will someone discriminate against us?
- How should I respond to negative attention or comments?
- If someone is rude, should I attribute their rudeness to my holding hands with someone of the same sex?

These are concerns that openly gay couples must contend with on a daily basis and are psychologically taxing and unfair. After this realization, I came to view my public excursions with Daniel as expressions of solidarity with those who fight for equal rights and sexual freedom. Later, recognizing the value and educational opportunities of my hand-holding experience, I began incorporating a hand-holding exercise in the introductory sociology courses I now teach. Having students hold hands with a classmate of the same sex in a public setting is a great way for them to learn a little about the stigma, difficulties, and discrimination that gay people unfortunately still endure. Moreover, the exercise is a great opportunity for students to step out of their comfort zones and practice empathy, while challenging gender norms. At the individual level, the exercise is an eye-opening experience that can help people recognize the social forces and proscription that serve to maintain and perpetuate sexual inequality. After exploring the social world from someone else's perspective, you become better able to identify with them and the issues they face.

It is for this reason that I challenge readers to find a courageous friend and try this exercise on your own (in a safe place of course). Take note of your feelings and the reactions of others. Also, consider when and where hand-holding by people of the same sex is not stigmatized (i.e., children at the playground or holding the hand of a child). If approached by someone you know, use the encounter as an opportunity to educate them on gay rights. Afterward, see if there are any gay-straight alliance groups in your community that you can join. If there are not, consider starting one on your own. Remember, only through the efforts of socially conscious and committed individuals can we bring about the change we desire.

REFLECTIONS OF A SCHOOL "SEX LADY": MOVING TOWARD A FEMINIST, RIGHTS-BASED SEXUALITY EDUCATION

Jacque Daugherty

I know how you can tell a girl is burning [has a sexually transmitted infection]. You just put a copper penny on her thigh and wait to see if her skin around it turns green.
Condoms come with holes in them and diseases can get through those holes so condoms don't work.
If you jump up and down after sex, you won't get pregnant.

The last assertion stunned one of the classroom teachers with whom I work, because she said this is what she used to hear in high school back in the 1960s. I hear this kind of misinformation from middle and high school students all the time. Working as a comprehensive sexuality educator (as students affectionately call me the "sex lady") in Southwestern Ohio, much of the time I spend teaching is devoted to addressing myths that many students either believe or don't necessarily believe but don't have other information with which to replace the myth so the myth persists. As a result, people have been systematically denied a right to even the most basic information about their bodies.

This is a human rights violation that has been played out across the bodies of a generation of young people and we have yet to see the full effects of it. Millions of dollars in annual federal funding for abstinence-only programs and weak state sexuality education mandates are largely to blame for the state of sexuality education over the past 10+ years. However, my intention is not to argue against abstinence-only sexuality education, as that has been done effectively already via various studies by the U.S. Department of Health and Human Services and the House of Representatives Committee on Government Reform. But as we continue to struggle for implementation of the comprehensive model, I offer some feminist reflections on what I have learned while teaching sexuality education during this moment in history in the hope that they will be helpful to those of us working to shape the future of the discipline.

Sexuality education should be required in schools. The mantra of proponents of abstinence-only and, to some extent, of comprehensive curricula is that parents and caregivers are the best sexuality educators because only they have the right to impart values around sexuality. While I agree that parents and caregivers are the first sexuality educators, I challenge that they are always the best. As a feminist, I see this as just another discourse in which nuclear/patriarchal family is privileged. As a sexuality educator, I hear disclosures from many students about surviving emotional, physical, or sexual abuse at the hands of a parent or caregiver. One of my students told me that she was being forced to perform sexual acts on men in a local park in order to support her mother's drug addiction. Although this example is extreme, the national statistics reflect the experience of family-based violence as one that is pervasive and crosses race and class lines. Because I believe that sexuality education should be about empowerment and pleasure and choice, I cannot depend only on the family to impart this information to children as these are not values taught in all families. This said, it has also been my experience that many parents/caregivers would like to talk to their children about sex and don't feel that they have information or know where to start. So I would add that schools should engage in a partnership that offers parents/caregivers and children some input into curricula content and design and information on how to support sexuality education at home. Sexuality education as a human right takes this knowledge out of only the private realm of the family and also into the public realm of the school and other community organizations.

Sexuality education should be taught across the life span. As an educator, the sessions I teach are at most one hour/day for three days in a middle or high school; and in a best-case scenario students will have already had a unit on it typically isolated to their health classes. One or two units over the span of a person's life are not enough (even during a student's school years). Information changes as do people's sexual and relationship experiences. A colleague of mine received a grant that focused on HIV prevention in people of age 55 and over, as this group's rates of new infections have been increasing over the past few years. Her sexuality education classes were often based in nursing homes and were largely female. Many of her students still believed that HIV could be contracted through saliva and that it was gay men who were at the most risk—not them. It seemed as if the residents' knowledge of HIV was frozen in the 1980s and this contributed to their potential risk. Additionally, she found that residents wanted access to other types of education such as some basic information on self-pleasuring (masturbating) and on postmenopausal reproductive health care. Because their own adolescent educational experiences were most likely based on the hygiene model of the mid-twentieth century and this information wasn't readily relevant to them in mainstream popular culture, my colleague was able to fill an important need and to support the human right to lifelong learning.

Sexuality education should incorporate the struggle for social justice that defines so many issues of sexuality. Women and men have struggled for much of this country's history and continue to struggle for the right to use contraception, the right to love and/ or be sexual with whomever they choose, the right to choose whether a pregnancy will end in parenting, abortion, or adoption and many more. Historical and sociological perspectives should be integrated into the curriculum as a way to acknowledge that the choice, for example, to have an abortion doesn't happen in a vacuum. At even the slightest mention of the topic in the classroom, I often hear that abortion should be illegal because it is "wrong to kill a baby." This is a common perspective that stems from an abstract argument about when life begins. However, I have found that re-centering this discussion to include more concrete notions is really eye-opening to students and provides a forum that begins discussion instead of shuts it down. Some of these concrete notions are the actual number of women who get abortions every year, the material and emotional reasons one might consider abortion as well as a brief history that both clarifies that abortion wasn't illegal during much of this nation's history and that many women choose abortion regardless of its status as safe or legal. These historical realities are also some of the building blocks of the reproductive freedom movement. I have only had the freedom of such discussions in college classrooms, and I understand that the reason for this is because K-12 education allegedly shies away from controversial or political issues. I would put forward, as many others have, however, that choosing to not discuss or teach a subject does not make a school neutral on it, it makes a strong statement that the subject simply does not merit discussion and it normalizes the status quo. Schools themselves are products of social struggle to make certain types of knowledge accessible to everybody. This broad history of social justice struggle, including that around issues of sexuality, should also be accessible in schools and included in sexuality education.

Finally sexuality education in the United States, even during the most supportive political climates, has been marginalized within schools. Some of my feminist activism has centered on a rethinking of sexuality education and reproductive freedom and an implementation of it in the classroom. As a feminist, I believe that sexuality education has the potential to be a democratizing force if we push its boundaries by pushing the boundaries of the educational institutions. Such a sexuality education that explores personal choice within a social context, that is available to everybody, that is responsive to their changing needs throughout their lives, and that is grounded in movements for a more just and equitable world is a foundation of a truly democratic society.

BIRTH OF AN ACTIVIST

Jackie Disarro

I have always referred to myself as a feminist, but never an activist. I always saw activists as people who are radical and vocally expressive, and I'm not that. In fact, anyone who meets me might say I'm rather shy. However, after a medical emergency, I began to understand where the urge to become an activist can come from. I had learned in my women's studies classes that the personal is political, and after nearly losing my life in a "medical mishap," the truth of that statement was driven home in a way I hope other women never have to experience.

After my son was born, I decided to use an intrauterine device (IUD) named "Mirena" which is designed to prevent pregnancy for five years. It seemed like the best choice for a busy undergraduate mom with no insurance who had no immediate plans to get pregnant. Unfortunately, 18 months after it was inserted, I was suddenly doubled over with pain. After visiting four different doctors, my IUD was located in between my left ovary and fallopian tube. In order to remove the defective device I needed painful (and expensive) surgery that caused me to miss time with my family, work, and two weeks of university classes.

Not only was the experience terrifying but, as students, my husband and I were in no financial situation to pay for this medical nightmare. We didn't have any health insurance, but surgery was the only way the IUD could be removed. To say that I was upset about the financial situation we were being forced into through no fault of our own is an understatement. I was angry about the product failure, and more upset about being let down by the doctors I had trusted with my health care. I felt like everyone in the medical community had failed me at the same time and there wasn't anything I could do about it.

When I returned to class, I found out that my women's studies professor had assigned what she termed an "Activist Project." The project was to be something that "spread the word" about feminism and feminist issues to the campus community and beyond. I could not think of a better topic than women's experiences with birth control. I decided to create a blog entitled "The Mirena Mishap," and told my story to whoever happened to read it. I was angry about what had happened to me and felt it was necessary that I make other women aware of the severe risks involved with using this particular IUD. Not only did I think the blog would create community among women who may have had a similar experience, but it also made me feel good to tell my story. I was soon reading multiple responses regarding dysfunctional birth control and the horrible and life threatening experiences of other women. I had no idea that I would receive so much feedback.

I had mixed feelings about the response. There were too many stories that mirrored my own birth control disaster and I soon realized that while I was making other women aware, I had only created a connection and a place to vent these experiences. I was glad that I received so many responses and that I had created a space where we could all share our common frustrations with the medical establishment, but I became discouraged that we had all had these negative experiences and were doing nothing about it. I met with my women's studies professor and discussed the feedback and my concern over the type of responses I was receiving. She encouraged me to make the blog more radical and call to the attention of these women that something should be done about our experiences.

The personal *is* political, especially when birth control is failing women and putting their bodies at risk. I am hoping women not only feel a sense of connectedness because of these negative experiences with Mirena, but also get angry and begin a movement against failing birth control and the constraints it has on the human body. From negative experiences with the hormones in birth control pills to doctors who treat women like uneducated lab rats, the stories the women shared on this blog showed me that more needs to be done about this dysfunctional birth control epidemic. The more I think about it, the more I'm sure this is a movement in the making. Women can only tolerate victim-blaming for so long before they recognize that their personal stories can, and should, have political impact.

The struggle I currently face is attempting to redirect the common experiences, anger, and a sense of solidarity we have expressed into a movement that will lead to change rather than passive behavior. My personal experience has turned me into an activist. In addition, I have recently hired an attorney to address what I consider a medical injustice. The women who have found my blog have begun reaching out to each other, sharing their stories and encouraging one another. These small steps remind me of how the women's movement first began—with just a couple of women talking to a few more and taking their personal experiences into the light of public activism.

THE BREAST DIALOGUES

Corinne Becker

I have been obsessed with my breasts for most of my life. As a teen, I was eagerly watching and waiting for them to grow, expecting they would blossom into the size "C" cup that all of my female blood-relatives had (they never went past an "A"). As a young woman, I judged my breasts as not only too small, but criticized them for their changes in shape from the pregnancies and breastfeeding of three children. Then, as an older woman in my 40s, I spent many years fearing the possibility of getting breast cancer, as my mother did at age 43, dying just five years later.

It's no wonder I have surrounded myself with breasts! For more than 18 years, I have been sitting in circles of women, hundreds of thousands of women, where the main topic of discussion concerns breasts. I am a registered nurse and a mind-body fitness specialist. As a Transformational Women's Workshop Leader, I have developed numerous empowerment, healing, support, and fitness programs for women. Whether I'm working with pregnant women, breastfeeding moms, menopausal women, or women touched by breast cancer, I've been exposed to the pain, shame, pleasure, pride, fear, loss, and the grief women experience over their bodies and, in particular, over their breasts.

Collectively, as women, we complain about our breasts, criticize them, judge them, and compare ours to others, oftentimes against an unrealistic standard portrayed in magazines and other media. Many women feel their breasts are not enough. Not pretty enough, big enough, shapely enough, high enough, healthy enough, basically, *not enough just as they are*. We forget what we have breasts for.

In her book *Creative Menopause*, Farida Sharan writes, "Breast lumps, cysts, fibroids, and tumors are a result of physical, mental, and emotional toxicity. Feminine breasts have become the focus of diseases at an ever-increasing rate. They (breasts) are meant to be fountains of love, comfort, and nourishment, but they are now retaining the disease and despair of the planet, as well as reflecting difficulties in giving and receiving love."

Media brainwashes us into believing that breasts are what make us sexy, whole, feminine, and attractive. How can the average woman feel whole and complete, just as she is, when she is bombarded with Victoria's Secret ads, *Sports Illustrated* Swimsuit Covers, and enticing advertisements from plastic surgeons for implants with promises that our lives will change just by altering our breasts? In our obsessed culture, big breasts are emphasized more than a big heart.

Breasts aren't even called by their anatomical name anymore. This is a disrespect to our bodies that affects our breasts. They are given nicknames like tattas, jugs, boobs, tits, knockers, racks, "the girls." I Googled it and got over *300* euphemisms for breasts!

How do our breasts feel about all this? What would they say if they could speak? They carry the energy of the words, thoughts, and beliefs of ourselves and society at large. They have been covered, hidden, exposed, removed, "cut off" both physically and emotionally, radiated, rejected, injected, squeezed, sqwooshed, poked, and prodded. No wonder the incidence of breast cancer has been rapidly increasing. We have abused our breasts in the same way that we have allowed ourselves as women to be abused—by ourselves and by others.

If we gave ourselves a voice to speak our truth—to say "no" to the demands and expectations of others, and "yes" to ourselves; to say "no, I don't want to be touched there," or "yes, please touch me this way"; to ask for what we need and want—our bodies and our breasts would be happier and healthier.

I recently led a retreat for women with breast cancer diagnoses. The energy of 50 breasts that had been either removed or radiated spoke to me in that room. I **got** the loud and clear message that this is not just about breast cancer. This is about *women* ... what we have allowed, what we have denied ourselves, and to what we are finally ready to say "enough" to.

Most of my programs in the last five years have been for women diagnosed with breast cancer. Whether it's because of myself, my mom, my age, or because of the increasing number of my friends and students being diagnosed, *I* have reached my

"*Enough!*" My personal *enough* for judging my breasts and not accepting them just as they are. *Enough* years of fearing that I would get breast cancer like my mom (Dr. Christiane Northrup says many women view their breasts as "sacks on their chest awaiting a breast cancer diagnosis") and for not feeling *enough* gratitude that my breasts are healthy. *Enough* words and thoughts saying, "I have a history of breast cancer in my family." Or "My breasts would be prettier if I had implants." (Not to mention my breasts hearing those same words from others.) *Enough* obsessive reading about breast cancer prevention. I *now* focus on breast *health* (not disease or disease prevention) and body health, and encourage my students and clients to do the same.

To know we have a choice is very empowering. We have a choice in how we speak to and about our breasts, in how they are treated by us and others. Our bodies, including our breast and chest area, desperately need to know that we love and accept them; that they are safe . . . that we will protect them.

I wrote a *pledge*, modeled after our country's *Pledge of Allegiance*. How can I love and honor my country if I am not loving myself? How can I love others . . . my children, husband, friends, if I am not loving myself? This pledge is printed on the front of a shirt *right over the chest/breast area* to affirm my respect, love, and acceptance of my breasts . . . and of myself:

> I Pledge Allegiance to Myself ~
> and to the Magnificence of who
> I am.
> One Beautiful Woman ~
> Created by God
> Loving, Accepting, and Respecting Myself ~
> Once and for all!

THE BEST THING I NEVER DID

Rebecca Nicholson

I was pregnant once for five weeks and two days. Violent nausea woke me up around 7 AM. The headache and dizziness kicked in around 9. I could neither stand to smell anything nor move from my chair until it stopped at 3 PM. Every day. I endured crippling agony for eight hours, unable to read, talk, or think. Women who want babies may not mind this, but I do not want babies. Those pregnant hours were a prison sentence. I feel the same way about life with a child. Boring, mundane activities would hijack my life. Shopping at Baby Gap, changing diapers, and reading monosyllabic books doesn't do it for me. I am not having kids.

People seemed shocked by this because they consider me excellent breeding material. I am tall, fit, and intelligent. My features are symmetrical, and my appearance is pleasing by Western standards. Thus, most people I encounter believe it is my duty to reproduce, and they say so. When I tell them I have no intention of breeding, people have three standard responses. They tell me that I am selfish, that I have not met the right man, or that I will change my mind.

They ask about my life preference and then slight my answer. I could smile and agree, allowing them the comfort of interpreting my silence as consent. It would end the conversation and make things easy, but I have never been able to do that. Instead, I embrace these situations as opportunities to voice my opinion, which by these responses, they attempt to silence. I am polite and fierce at the same time.

"You're selfish."

The thoughtful soul telling me how selfish I am typically follows it up by telling me quite earnestly that motherhood is a woman's ultimate fulfillment. I do my best to keep from gagging. Perpetuating this cultural myth of how motherhood is bliss confuses every smart women. My best friend was 27 and starting graduate school when she got pregnant. Her life got forced in a completely new direction. Her plans of working in Africa were out of the question, because according to her, you can't take babies to Africa. For years she had no energy to exercise, she had no social life, and she had no boyfriends. She got mean looks when she took the baby into a place that serves alcohol (which happened all the time—she lived in New Orleans). She complained that she had no time to read, to write poetry, or just to sit and think. The baby took up all her time, and he just lay there doing nothing. She kept wondering when she would be overtaken by the magic that is motherhood. Words like "bliss" and "ultimate happiness" never came to mind.

The part that gets me is that she seemed genuinely shocked by this reality, like somebody tricked her. Like she ordered a chocolate martini and received toilet water instead—this is not what she'd been sold. Motherhood was supposed to be something more enchanting than mounds of dirty diapers and weeks of no sleep. She took pains to assure me that this was the happiest time of her life, and I assure you that this is not what happiness looks like to me.

Choosing my own life path is not being selfish. I study conflict resolution. My field develops strategies to stop war. Baby life is not conducive to the work I want to do. I elect to spend my time differently than a parent. Am I selfish for focusing my energy on a population of thousands, is a parent selfish for focusing his or her energy on a family of four, or is my friend selfish for focusing her energy on one? This is a matter of perception, and only non-breeders get judged negatively.

"You haven't met the right man."

Here we revisit cultural idealism about marriage and babies: I should marry a man, have him impregnate me, and care for the offspring. My career should be stunted, and my life should be about babies. Women attain ultimate happiness this way, according to the speaker. This deal might be okay if I get fulfillment from doing baby things. It works right up to the minute my husband leaves me because having a baby has wrecked my body, and baby talk has made me wildly uninteresting. Now I have to raise a child, and I have to fend for myself financially. Glad I found that man. Good thing I put my career on hold.

Relationships do not always last, but motherhood does. The two are very different. I want a relationship, but I don't want a baby. This person is saying that I need a man. I need a man for what? To make up my mind on this? To take care of me? I am perfectly capable of both. I have a relationship because I *want* it, not because I am missing anything without it. My life is enhanced with a good partner, but it is not deficient when I am single. Besides, people say the same thing to lesbians.

"You'll change your mind."

I really like this line. It gets used like a backhand in conversation. The speaker intends to signify superiority in his or her own life choice by suggesting that something like age or unplanned pregnancy will enlighten my view. To this speaker, I reveal my five weeks and two days of pregnancy. I took a test, made a phone call, and underwent a five-minute termination procedure. I didn't hesitate to make the phone call, and I don't live with regret. Pregnancy tortured me; it did not change my mind.

The fact is I just don't want kids. I don't want to be incapacitated for several months and suffer from weight gain, nausea, and no sex. I don't wish to spend my money on cribs and strollers when I want dresses and books. I don't want to learn baby talk. I don't want to change diapers. I have no desire to go to playgrounds and play on the slide. I prefer to be exhausted from jet lag than from running my offspring to soccer practice. I like the option of hitting happy hour more than the obligation of attending a parent-teacher conference, and I will not alter my life path based on where the good schools are located. I am not a fan of infringement on my free movement, and no man or woman will move me on these points. I don't want kids.

These myths assert that women without children need a man, that we don't know what we want, and that we lack compassion and judgment. Do those things describe you? They sure don't describe me. I refuse to have other people tell me what constitutes femininity, or what it means to be a woman. I have these conversations with strangers and relatives and coworkers because I believe in pushing folks out of their safe social constructs of assumption. I reject the double standard of people who reproduce never being questioned or told their choices are wrong. These conversations play like political debate. They are right, I am wrong, and I can only be right when I think like they do. I'm not buying what they're selling.

I encourage you to have these conversations when people attack your preferences. These canned pieces of pseudo-wisdom have been repeated invariably for years. They are a result of social conditioning, not insightful reasoning. Do not allow people to define you with clichés. Refuse to be told what it means to be a woman. Recognize your personal worth, and construct your identity based on qualities that you believe are valuable. Each time we have a conversation like this, we help to weaken social myths that tell us we are lacking as women.

INSIGHT FROM A BREAST CANCER, CELIAC, AND JUVENILE DIABETES ADVOCATE

Renee Bernett

I am a wife, mother, sister, daughter, and friend. I impact multiple lives. As a former teacher, I touched many lives, but as a breast cancer survivor and advocate for patient empowerment, I hope that I have been able to touch and inspire the most lives.

My own journey began with a mammogram on December 8, 1997, that led to a diagnosis of stage 2 infiltrating ductal carcinoma. Suddenly, I was inundated with unfamiliar words. A bewildering whirlwind of information and decision-making was made much more comprehensible, thanks to the input of other women who freely shared their courage, personal experiences, suggestions, and inspiration on an AOL message board.

Although my medical team was supportive, those women afforded me something intangible that my doctors could not. I eagerly embraced stories of women whose diagnosis and tumor pathology mirrored my own. Even at 3:00 AM, I could connect online with dozens of women in distant cities—empowered women whose words could allay my fears. Their support was so palpable, so priceless, despite the miles between us, that 40 of us convened in Las Vegas in October 1998 to "celebrate life."

Even before that momentous gathering, I knew I wanted to find local forums in which I could reciprocate. More than 11 years later, I am still connected to Living Beyond Breast Cancer. LBBC's focus on educating and empowering women to live beyond breast cancer echoes my own beliefs. Completing surgery, chemotherapy, and radiation shouldn't be a "finite" moment. In order not just to survive—but truly to thrive—I believe one must give back.

Initially, I attended every conference and posted my own summaries online so others could benefit. I spoke publicly about my breast cancer. I was honored to be asked to review research grants for the Avon Foundation and the U.S. Department of Defense. And nine years after I was trained, I am still answering calls on LBBC's Helpline and still reviewing those research grants.

Yes, I could have chosen to consider my cancer journey a "closed chapter" and gone on with my life, but until we can celebrate a cure, breast cancer is never a finite moment.

Through sharing what I've learned and reiterating an oncologist's quote that "patients can live with the word incurable, but they can't live without the word hope," I try to make a difference and add meaning and value to having survived when speaking to those who are still fearful that they will not survive!

That same passion and thirst for knowledge extends to my two other disease advocacy efforts on behalf of my child. Following my daughter's diagnosis of type 1 diabetes in 1992, I became increasingly involved with the Juvenile Diabetes Research Foundation. Not only have I participated in their national lay review program, helping to assess which research applications receive the coveted funding, but I have also served as my local chapter president and created an outreach "Moms' Bunch" encompassing hundreds of local families whose children also have type 1. The same kind of priceless camaraderie, information, and support that strengthened me during my cancer journey could now be accessible to families overwhelmed by the demands of caring for a child with a chronic illness. While speaking at local gatherings and support meetings or even in cyberspace chat rooms, I encouraged parents to become advocates for their child's best interest, even if it meant challenging the medical status quo that their physician endorsed.

Yet despite espousing that proactive approach, even I failed to advocate on behalf of my daughter when her endocrinologist scoffed at my request to test her for celiac disease. Despite learning of the increasing concordance between the two autoimmune conditions, by NOT challenging the physician, I prolonged my child's suffering needlessly. Within days of removing gluten from her diet eight months later, she experienced a dramatic and lasting improvement in her demeanor, her energy level and her health. The osteopenia that came from years of failure to absorb calcium and other minerals completely resolved five years later on her follow-up bone scan. Knowledge is unquestionably the greatest weapon in the patients' personal armamentarium. Every time I disseminate cyber "updates" to my celiac circle, or my diabetes friends, or my breast cancer survivor sisters, I am hopefully reminding them of their own power to impact their lives.

The invaluable lesson learned is that diseases like breast cancer, diabetes, and celiac may rob us and our loved ones of our breasts, our beta cells, our ability to consume any food, but they can never take away our most powerful asset: our voice. In honor of all patients who deserve to be treated with dignity and respect, who deserve to be "heard," I proudly and willingly do whatever I can to promote that philosophy.

Chapter Seven

Birthing New Activism: Feminist Mothering and Fathering

After the important decision whether to have children is made, many other challenges arise for parents. First and foremost is the decision regarding how the baby is to be brought into the world. As many scholars have pointed out, historically childbirth was the domain of women—that is, females assisted in the delivery of babies. This all changed with the development of specialized knowledge that was to be acquired through formal education only available to men.[1] Today, many women are working to reclaim the birthing process through home births with midwives and doulas. Television talk show star Ricki Lake chronicled this history wonderfully in her documentary, *The Business of Being Born*, demonstrating how women benefit from alternative birthing arrangements. As many of the contributors in this chapter point out, the birthing process is profoundly moving, even spiritual, when it is done as naturally as possible.

Once a child is born, the challenging work of parenting begins. Feminists have worked to encourage both men and women to parent in ways that challenge gender inequalities and allow for the free expression of all. Some have argued the best way to do this is to raise children androgynously, so that gender is not a significant factor of their identity. From resisting the urge to dress our babies in solid pink or blue depending on their sex to raising them to play with gender-neutral toys, parents can encourage children to be themselves, not just a stereotype.

Feminist activists have encouraged fathers to do more with their children, and for women to step outside of the role of "mom" to more deeply explore their own identities. Many fathers elect to reject what has been called the "tough guise"—the idea that men have to be aggressive, tough, non-emotional, and controlling to be masculine—and simply enjoy spending time with their kids. There is evidence of just such a shift. The average number of hours per weekday fathers spend with children increased in the last decade to 2.5, 6.3 per weekend. There is great payoff for this decision, not just in terms of male empowerment but for the children as well. Children of involved fathers are at lower risk for

delinquency, substance abuse, low self-esteem, academic underachieve-
ment, and other behavioral problems.[2] Despite this positive trend, however, in many families women still do a "second shift," as sociologist
Arlie Hochschild called it.[3] That is, they work full time and then put in
another full time shift in the home.

As noted in other chapters, mothers who work outside of the home in
addition to their domestic work still face significant hardships. In 2007,
the *New York Times* referred to this as "maternal profiling," and defined
it as "employment discrimination against a woman who has, or will have,
children." In fact, the term was coined by MomsRising, a group of activists that advocates for dramatic change to end workplace discrimination
against women, especially mothers.[4] The gap is true of virtually any field,
from higher education (where mothers struggle to obtain tenure and be
promoted) to law (where mothers are less likely to make partner), for
instance. Studies have shown that while women make .90 cents less than
men for comparable work, mothers make just .73 cents to the dollar.[5] Only
five countries in the world fail to offer some type of paid leave for new
mothers—Lesotho, Swaziland, Liberia, Papua New Guinea, and the
United States.[6] With a dire economic recession that has created huge job
losses for men in 2009, many mothers are doing extra jobs out of the home
as a way to make additional funds for the family.[7]

Critics contend that the feminist movement has blended the roles of
husband and wife to the point that neither has a clear understanding of
their place in the family today.[8] Feminists in the second wave were often
called "antifamily," and conservatives still denounce feminists in similar
ways. Barbara Ehrenreich and Deirdre English explained that, starting
in the 1940s and continuing today, the trend is to blame mothers for anything that goes wrong with the family. Many times, these people are holding on to nostalgic images of the "ideal" family. As historian Stephanie
Coontz pointed out, these images are not reality; they are what we wish
we were, not what families were ever really like.[9]

Instead of antifamily, feminists oppose the patriarchal family and
seek more egalitarian forms. Feminists have argued that when women
are limited to the roles of wife and mother, they become subordinates—
to their husbands, first, and in civil society next. This, feminist activists
assert, is good for neither women nor men.

At the same time that mothers are blamed, burdened, and under-
appreciated, they are also glorified and honored to the point that few
can live up to the expectations.[10] Witness the image of the "supermom,"
who works all day, spends quality time interacting with her children
and sharing learning experiences, has an immaculate house, and still

looks fit and beautiful. Politicians love to both revere and blame the mother, a paradox that makes it difficult to find out exactly what one is supposed to do to be considered "good."

Many groups of women (and some men) have organized to focus on parenting issues. Groups like MomsRising work to end discrimination against mothers and advocate for a nation in which all children, parents, and businesses thrive. They have organized national and state-level campaigns to eliminate the gender-wage gap, pass legislation to provide paid sick days for all people, update unemployment insurance, support breastfeeding mothers, keep children safe from toxins, and much more. Because mothers cannot always be available to attend meetings or organize marches, the group utilizes creative ways for "naptime activists" to get involved.[11] One of their primary vehicles for raising awareness is their documentary, *The Motherhood Manifesto*. The National Association of Mothers' Centers offers support for caregivers, emphasizing the economic impact of "mothering" (whether it be done by a male or female).

Mothers Acting Up (MAU—see their Web site at www.mothers actingup.org) is another organization that "works to inspire and mobilize mothers (and others who exercise protective care over someone smaller) to advocate on behalf of the world's children." It was launched on Mother's Day, 2002, the day Julia Ward Howe envisioned in 1870. Howe saw the day as a way for women to rise against the horrors of warfare and to, above all, protect the children. One of MAU's activists, Amie Brooke Nelson, who is also author of *Celebrating Mothers: Global Portraits to Inform and Inspire*, explained, "I believe that mothers are the world's hope for social change: the leaders who will honor the needs of women and children. For years I've watched in awe when moms, for the love of children and community, pull off five-star school fundraisers with little to no budget! What would happen if mothers used this same commitment to speak up for children who don't have access to education at all? What would happen if mothers spoke out for the diminished rights of mothers in other nations? What would happen if the collective strength of mothers was unleashed around the world?"[12]

This section opens with the editors' own letters to their daughters, highlighting their wishes for the future of feminist activism. The other contributors in this chapter show how we can unleash that potential—how we can create a better world for our children. Not just the domain of mothers, the chapter makes it clear that fathers are powerful feminist activists as well.

A LETTER TO ANYA

Laura Finley

My dear, sweet Anya;

I know that you will make the world a better place. How can I be so confident, when you are only five? Because you are already doing it! You already get that any little thing you do has consequences—it makes some type of change. This is true whether your actions were intentional or whether you acted spontaneously. And you know good things not only lead to good results, but that they come back to you. I think I learned about karma at probably age 19, but you already know the term and, better yet, you understand how to live it.

I don't know if you'll remember this when you get older, so I want to remind you of it now. When you were four—in Pre-Kindergarten—you came home one day with your lunch box and asked me, "Mama, why do they make us use paper plates to eat our lunch on every day? That's wasteful and bad for the earth." I responded that I had no idea that the school did that, assuming that you just pulled each item out of your lunch box and ate it from there. So I said I agreed that this was wasteful. But you didn't stop there. You asked if we could get a plastic, reusable plate you could take each day, then wash each night. Of course, I said. Then you went farther, asking if we could buy your whole class, even your whole school, plastic plates so no one had to waste. We stopped short of doing this, but agreed to let other parents know what we were doing and offer to purchase plates for those who might be interested. A few kids did start using reusable plates, but more important was your curiosity about what you saw as a problem, your willingness to do something about it, and your thought to include more than just yourself.

I think that story highlights the five things I love most about you. And these five things are, not coincidentally, the same qualities I believe are essential to activism of any sort, and particular toward reducing any kind of social inequality.

First, you have to be observant. You are definitely that! I recall the first time I wore eye makeup that you could remember—you were perhaps four—and you said, "Mom, you don't look earthy like you normally do." You have to notice things, and keep on noticing things, in order to see what is in need of change and what is already right on.

Second, you need to ask questions. Like most kids, you did a lot of this! Always "why" with little ones. Adults often lose that inquisitiveness. Please always ask questions about why things are the way they are. Too many people just accept.

Third, never be afraid to say what you think and ask for what you want. When I was your age (even much older—pretty much until I went to graduate school), I never spoke up. I was mortified if a teacher called on me in class, and I never went out of my way to offer anything. You are a strong girl who has a lot to offer, and I love that you say what you think. Once when we were on a busy corner holding signs to call attention to torture and abusive treatment at the detention camp at Guantanamo Bay, Cuba, a lady pulled over to harass us. Not knowing her intentions and seeing her big smile, I assumed she was in solidarity with our cause and walked closer to her car. Her smile was not friendly but creepy, though, as she called us "terrorist lovers." I was flabbergasted, and I think you recovered faster than I did, as you said to her "We just want people to teach peace." Never let that gumption go! As Laurel Thatcher-Ulrich has said, "Well behaved women seldom make history." You can be polite and respectful—which you are—and still assertive.

Fourth, you have a big-heart and know that doing something—even if it is small—indeed makes a difference. Please keep on doing something! Your little something done by lots of people eventually becomes a big something.

Finally, I love that you understand how it truly feels good to do good. Once when we were stopped at an intersection and saw a man with a sign declaring that he was hungry, we decided to give him the $3 dollars we had with us. He was incredibly thankful, and as we drove away you said, "Mom, that made my tummy feel good to do something nice for that man." I don't think anyone has ever said it better. Always remember how good it feels to do something to help.

My wish for you, my love, is that you continue to create a better world. My hope for myself and your dad is that we did everything we could to help you do that.

With peace and love,
Your mom

A LETTER TO LILAH

Emily Reynolds Stringer

My Little Bundle of Love, Lilah Jean,

You my dear are a being full of wonder. Although you are a growing seven-month-old baby girl, I see how you already make a difference in the world. Your joyful smile and radiant pureness offers hope and peace wherever you are. Whether it is in the grocery store line or in the arms of your grandparents, you bring people together with your toothless grin. You have a warm charm about you and a curiosity that seems endless. We can all learn from such newness and purity.

The future for you is ripe for the picking. As a young girl I imagine endless opportunities to make the world a better place, and my hope is that you continue to act upon them as you grow to be a woman. You may begin with sharing your toys and continue on to sharing your dreams but any way you slice it the possibilities for you are abundant.

My job, as well as your father's, is to allow you to grow and become the woman you choose to be. A woman with courage, strength, and curiosity as your roots; inner beauty, unity, and love as your branches; and bountiful peace as your leaves that you spread to the world. As your mother I wish to be a nurturing source for you to grow. I will be another sturdy tree to lean on and to trust along your own journey.

As I look into your eyes I see that you already have all the tools within you to create an amazing life and contribute to the lives of others. I see that although you are small physically your spirit is gloriously large. When I am having a tough day and I look within those beautiful eyes you tell me (without words) not to sweat the small stuff. You allow me to love you unconditionally, and show me what love really is, a love so pure I have never known until I met you. I see that within your seven months outside of the womb, you have already brought people together. You have offered hope to our family after a year of loss and grieving, you have given your father and me a new found sense of purpose, you have brought new friends into our life, and I know for sure you have made many people's day brighter just by looking into their eyes with your pure heart. You, my dearest, are already an activist and someone we can all learn from. You teach me that combining hope, purpose, and unity, you can make a difference no matter what age, gender, size, or color you are. I see that what the Buddhists call a "beginner's mind" is what you live daily and what we adults strive to grasp a moment of. No moment for you is left behind or wasted. You have an ability to capture each second of life and learn from it no matter what the task. Whether it be riding in your car seat, learning how to crawl, or tasting carrots for the first time you embrace these new experiences with a curious delight.

It is you my sweet dearest girl that has brought me to become the greatest title I could ever ask for in all my journeys within life, Mom. I thank you my bundle of love for being my muse and my own personal slice of heaven. I can only wish for your journey to continue onward and upward wherever your dreams find you, and I can promise I will be there by your side wherever you decide to land.

Much Love and an Endless Sea of Admiration,
Your Momma

BORN AT THE RIGHT TIME

Emily Reynolds Stringer

This is a story about the most incredible day of my life. The day my daughter was born. Like some women, I chose to have Lilah in a birthing center, without pharmaceutical assistance. This experience was the greatest act of activism I have made in my life. My husband and I created our own path and chose a mid-wife, Alice Palloy, to deliver Lilah. It was a beyond wonderful experience that I wish to share within this book, to enthuse others to choose a more natural path as a birth choice. Many women overlook this option, as there is a lot of fear in the world around giving birth naturally. We are trained to think that giving birth is a medical condition and not the miraculous gift from Mother Nature. I encourage you to look beyond the lines and explore midwifery as an option even if you choose to deliver in a hospital.
"Born at the Right Time..." Paul Simon
Lilah Jean Stringer Born August 26, 2008, at 8:48 PM

Dear Lilah Jean, My Queen,

This is the story of your amazing birth. The story began early on an early August morning. As your Daddy and I were anxiously awaiting your arrival at 2 AM Mommy woke up to your little kicks. Your tiny feet were awakening mommy to let me know it was time for your grand entrance. Then at 5:30 AM on the dot mommy's water broke and we called Alice Palloy our midwife. Alice told us to head to the birthing cottage as soon as we could.

Daddy packed the car and the three of us drove to the place you were to be born, the birthing cottage of Winter Park, Florida. We arrived at the cottage to find out that Mommy was dilated only 2–3 centimeters, and so our jobs began. Mommy and Daddy power walked for one hour as fast as mommy's legs would let her go, and with each surge that both you and I were feeling Daddy helped Mommy squat to let you know it was OK to come out. In between walks, Mommy sat on the birthing ball while daddy massaged her back and we listened to spiritual flutes playing in the background and your lavender birth candle burning its sweet smell. All we could think of was how excited we were to finally meet you, our beautiful daughter. After a lot of hard walking from both Mommy and Daddy, and a lot of hard moving from you, things were still moving slowly at 3–4 centimeters.

Knowing how much we both loved the water, Mommy asked for a bath to help both you and she relax. As soon as I heard the bath water it was like we both knew things were going to move along smoothly and a bit quicker. Meg, our birthing assistant, dropped some lavender in the bath water and off we went, relaxing and feeling your little bottom move up and down with each surge. Meg was so helpful in supporting mommy's breathing so you could get lots of air. Mommy and Daddy knew you were coming soon. Mommy moved from 4 to 7 centimeters in a matter of a couple of hours and Daddy got a little rest in while we were enjoying the bath. Then with the support of Meg and Priscilla, another birthing assistant, we did lots of stretching, bouncing on the birthing ball, deep breaths, and one more bath, which did the trick! After much movement and excitement you were telling us you were ready to come into the world at around 6 PM on August 26. After two and a half short hours of pushing your beautiful round head and body came out into the world to great us. Daddy caught you and cut the umbilical cord that connected us for nine months. Your cord was strong! It took two hard snips and daddy was so fascinated with the feel of it he couldn't help but to hold it up to the light and admire the magnificent plumbing you designed! It was a miracle to finally meet you; both Daddy and Mommy had tears of joy as you greeted us with a songbird scream and puckering your lips for your first taste on Mommy's milk. Your grandparents were on the phone with Daddy and your Grammy and Auntie Mimi were waiting for you at "Uncle Jay's" home in Florida. After we all washed up and rested for a bit we went home at 3:00 AM Wednesday morning, and you slept through the night, peacefully and soundly, you knew you were home.

The world will never be the same now that you are in it, Lilah Jean My Queen. Mommy and Daddy and all of your friends and relatives are so in love with you. All you have to do now is grow and explore, the world is at your finger tips, which you love dearly to eat!

THE FEMINISM OF BIRTH: ONE WOMAN'S STORY OF BIRTHING NEW LIFE AND DISCOVERING NEW STRENGTH

Jeff Nall

At 7:46 PM, Sunday, November 16, 2008, April Lee Nall birthed our daughter, Mimi Lucille Nall—we call her Lucy. She was 21 inches and 8 pounds, 7 ounces.

Lucy is our amazing "special," as April likes to call her, but she is not a miracle. Nothing miraculous or "medical" brought Lucy into the world. She wasn't rushed to the hospital. Her birth didn't involve forceps or IVs. No one threatened to conduct a c-section less her body quickly deliver Lucy. There were no nurses or doctors darting between a dozen "patients." The birth attendants did not need a file to know April's name. There was no beeping technological gadgetry; no multimillion dollar machinery; no white-coated obstetricians. No one forced her labor process according to an arbitrary deadline. No one broke her water and she was not induced. There were no drugs coursing through her blood stream. And so there were no drugs in her newly born daughter's body.

April and the creative power instilled in her by nature brought Lucy into the world. April birthed Lucy at home. In doing so she became part of the 1 to 2 percent of the U.S. population who choose to have a home birth.

Home birth wasn't even in consideration until a birth class doula named Ruth showed us Elena Tonetti-Vladimirova's 2006 film *Birth as We Know It*. The film presented childbirth as we both had never seen it. Instead of an agonizing disease which men were lucky not to go through, the film presented birth as an opportunity for women to experience a sacred and empowering communion with nature, showing 11 natural births taking place in various environments. Up until then neither of us knew much of anything about the furtive debate raging beneath the surface in American society about how best to birth. We began reading numerous books and scholarly articles. The more we read and questioned doctors, the more we began to question the sensibility of conventional birth. We also watched another incredible film that put everything into perspective: *The Business of Being Born* (2007 by Abby Epstein and Ricki Lake). In addition to demystifying home birth, the film shows that medicalized child-birth's "innovations" have often been responsible for harming women and the natural or normal birth process.

We discovered the c-section rate in the United States was 31 percent and 40 percent in Palm Beach where we were living. In 1970, the c-section rate was just 5.5 percent. The leading causes of maternal death in the United States are complications from cesarean surgery along with those from anesthesia. We also learned that the United States had a deplorable infant mortality rate, one of the lowest among industrialized nations. In much of the rest of the world, midwives take care of the majority of births.

Throughout the majority of the pregnancy and before our eventual break with the hospital, April went to a traditional obstetrician. But things changed dramatically when we began to experience first hand what we were learning about, particularly the hospital's love of the serious and often unnecessary cesarean section surgery. April sought to ensure her favorite doctor could deliver Lucy, since three had been assigned to her. When she asked how she could make sure he was the delivering doctor he told her, you could always schedule a c-section or an induction on a day I'm in. On April's last visit to the hospital the ultrasound tech noted the estimated size of the baby. The doctor's probably going to schedule you for a c-section, she commented. Fiercely, April shot back: "No she's not." And when April's blood pressure was minutely elevated her doctor joined in, warning that if such numbers persisted she might need to consider a c-section. Suffice to say, that was the last day April went to the hospital and the last time she heard the "c" word.

Our birth class instructor, Ruth, suggested we contact a midwife named Lori. Over the course of 18 years of midwifery, Lori learned to listen to women's bodies. She developed a keen ear for the sacred, rational knowledge stored in women, aiding them in birthing more than 1,100 babies. Only once had a child not made it through the birth. Compare that ratio to the United States's infant mortality rate which is above 6 per 1,000.

About a week shy of her due date, Lori stopped in for her first official checkup of April. What I witnessed in the next several hours changed everything I thought I knew about pregnancy, birth, and the beautiful power of woman. By the small trace of bloody show and the way April's cervix felt, Lori determined that Lucy was on her way in the next 24 hours. April and I exchanged cynical, excited glances. April was looking for good news but neither of us thought she'd be having a baby that day. Lori's prediction went from probable to definite as April described her Braxton Hicks contractions and the location of the tightening she was experiencing. "She's definitely coming today," said Lori. "I'm going to bring in some of my stuff and stay at my sister's house." Her sister's house was nearer to our home than Lori's.

Lori later returned around 5 PM. April was 1.5 cm dilated. About 90 minutes later, April's water broke as I loaded our two children into my mother's car. I walked into our bedroom to find Lori stepping back before a soaked floor. April was 5 cm dilated. Laughter over the splash her broken water made turned to serious breathing. The contractions grew stronger.

April climbed into a warm shower where she labored privately for several minutes. It was here she faced her first great struggle. April let out deep, primal intonations as I had never heard her make. She was speaking to her body, stored with thousands of years of nature's evolutionary knowledge, trying to find her way through the agonizing but creative wilderness of birth. "She's so in-tune to her body," Lori commented as we stood outside the bathroom door.

When April called me in I sat beside the tub where we held hands. She experienced tremendous pain. She pulled me into our tiny shower. Fully clothed, I sat on a ledge at the back of the tub where I helped support her weight. When she turned around to sit down in the tub she asked me to sit behind her. April groaned and cried out. I couldn't empathize with her. I could only encourage and love her. I revered her. Despite the way in which medicalized birth had distorted reality, birth and the creation of life was the realm of woman.

Between contractions, April managed to move from the bathtub to the bedroom. It was all she could do to make it to the foot of the bed. Head on the bed, knees on the ground, April labored intensely. Lori suggested that she lay on her side on the bed. We helped her stand and push forward. April's legs trembled with exhaustion. I held her left leg behind the knee, still holding her hand with my other. Lori said, "You're almost there." April cried out. She felt burning. Positioned with a view I watched as Lori worked olive oil into April's skin. "Can you see her," Lori asked me. Lucy's head began to crown. A full head of jet-black hair. Lori grabbed April's hand to touch. "She's coming," Lori smiled. April cried out for Lori to get her out. "She's coming out, but you're the one doing it, not me." This was April's birth, no one else's.

Lori massaged April's perineum, preparing the passage. April writhed and squealed with pain. "Push it down to your bottom, don't let it out through your mouth," Lori advised. Half aware of anything being said, April collected the pain and pushed it into a low growl. Lori watched in absolute confidence in April's birth. April's face turned to me, no anger and no cry for help. She was silently asking if Lori and I believed in her. Her expression seemed to say, seriously, am I going to have this baby? With absolute confidence I beamed back, "She's really coming honey, you're doing it."

April pushed, giving a deep lasting moan. Lucy's closed eyes appeared over the horizon of her mother's birth canal. April cried out. Lori expertly oiled and massaged the edges of the passageway. No urgency, just confidence and anticipation, Lori replied: "Keep going, she's almost here." April looked to me once more, searching my eyes for honest confirmation. I replied with a careful, earnest smile. April groaned. The head emerged. I moved closer.

Lori placed her hands around Lucy's head, tugging with April's determined push. Soft, milky shoulders. April pushed, Lori pulled. Small drops of water touched my face. A deep, earthy groan. Lucy's soft, watery body poured forth with her legs and arms compressed around her torso. Then Lucy's body unfolded before my eyes like a flower bud bursting into bloom.

Lori quickly checked Lucy and placed her on her mother's stomach. April looked upon her with shocked satisfaction. Her pain was so great and the struggle so intense, her mind had left her skeptical. But April's body knew; it was stronger than she could have imagined; she was capable of more than she was taught to believe. No book, no film could convey the truth evident in Lucy's cries beneath her mother's chin. Exhaustion. Pinches of pain. Joy. This was the way new, innocent life should be brought into the world.

Soon after, April delivered the placenta, and Lori brought April's bleeding to a stop. When the first feeding was done, I joined April and Lucy in bed. The three of us laid there together in the serenity one could only find at home. I began to realize that I had just witnessed April bring new life into this world.

Early on April had doubted herself. She struggled to overcome the years of conditioning women in our society experience, taught that they are powerless and that their ability to birth new life is akin to a sickness needing treatment. Before she birthed Lucy, April hadn't realized her own creative power. But now Lucy lay on her naked breast, proof of the potency, and the agency of her body; proof that she could do anything because she birthed a new life.

The word "spiritual," though loosely bantered about, was created to describe what I witnessed that night. I witnessed April and nature in sacred communion; and a midwife who trusted women and the natural process, working with it rather than seeking to control it.

A PRAYER FOR MY SON

Doreen Maller

It is early Sunday morning; I wave at the front door as our eldest leaves with his father to look at colleges up north. He is 17. It feels like yesterday I took the same trip with my own father. I can remember driving down the eastern seaboard, groggy in the morning mist, roiling with the mixed adolescent emotions of resentment and gratitude, all directed at my poor father who was, I imagine, filled with love and confusion as he clutched the steering wheel and tolerated my venom. At 17, I wore my equal rights amendment tee shirt to telegraph my political views and as a fuck you to anyone stupid enough to notice my breasts underneath (even though I can admit now that I wanted them noticed). At 17, I was looking for my tribe. I was anxious to begin living. At 17, I was running from my father and his generation. At 17, I wanted to change the world.

At 17, my son is searching too. As his mother I can barely stand to let him go. As a woman looking back, I know he will leave no matter what I want. I know he must. I have to believe, as my father must have, that I have done well by him. I know that he is a wonderful person, that he is kind, that he is fair, that the world will treat him kindly, or if not, that he will survive its unkind moments, and like his mother, grow from them.

I remember being 17 and the dreams I had for myself and for all women. I can remember how hard I was planning to fight to be afforded my rightful share of the American Dream. My parents, children of immigrants, parents of girls in a time of change, encouraged me to explore my possibilities. Not without trepidation, mind you, not without fear. Maybe they knew that there was nothing they could do to stop me, that the best thing they could do was let me go and hope that I would be safe. Ours was a clash of paradigms. Theirs: be good, be pure. Mine: be everything, do everything. Watching the car pull away I remember being 27: my move across the country. My possessions plus two beloved cats packed into the back of a VW Rabbit. A stick shift I could barely master. Landing in a new state, starting over. Twenty-seven was a year of sorrow, realizing that the marriage I had hoped for was not the one I had. California and its cabbage-sized roses would be my home, but not this house and not this man and not this job. At 27, I told my parents I could not be who they wanted me to be. At 27, they told me my failures were my own. At 27, I was cast adrift. For years I floated, undoing and redoing, finding new love, starting a new life. At 27, I was no longer daughter. I was only self.

By 37, I was torn: climbing the corporate ladder, yearning for more, more money, more status, more validation. At 37, I had a new husband, a new house, and children—two beloved cherub children whom I left with a nanny during endless corporate days. I was the woman I had hoped to be at 17; busy, vital, an equal in a man's world and the best woman/mother/wife I could manage. I was up at dawn baking cookies, racing home at night to sit at the dinner table. I used terms like quality time and meant it and tried to ignore the moments I missed: first steps, first words, school plays. At 37, I was exhausted. Having it all was beginning to feel like way too much. Unnecessary. Overblown. Overrated. When I discovered a lump in my breast, I knew I had to make changes for those two boys who needed their mother home and well, and for my husband too, equally exhausted, wondering if I would ever hit a point where enough was enough. I wondered too . . . had I done enough, if this kills me, had I lived enough?

By 47, I had retired, was back at school, cancer free, earning a Master's degree and beginning my Ph.D. At 47, I was a mom and student, an intern, a wife, a daughter again, a friend, a sister. At 47, I shifted from getting to giving: I ran a mentoring program for girls. Oh those girls! Hard girls. Angry girls. Broken girls. The women I trained to mentor them walked willingly through prison doors, scared, open hearted, reaching out, while I provided guidance and support. Success was measured in moments and hope. Maybe these girls will remember this or that. Maybe we will ignite one tiny spark of possibility. At 47, success was measured in stamina and attitude.

This morning, waving goodbye to my son I think about calling my father. At my 50 and his 81, we talk on the phone three times a week. I worry about his eyes, his heart. I will tell him that his grandson, now almost a man, approaches the world with kindness. I will thank my father for his love. I will share my worries about letting my son go, and my pride that as his mother, I have prepared him as well as I could for the vast possibilities of a life richly lived. The rest, I will tell my father, will be up to him.

At 50, my husband and I work together to run the household, drive the carpool, cook meals, put away the laundry, walk the dog. My husband and I are a team. We know that we can launch this boy into his life as we have done everything else, as partners.

I sent them off with a prayer.

That my son's life will be rich. That he will find his way. That he will know kindness. That he will know love.

RAISING CHANGE: FATHERING, FEMINISM, AND HOPE

Craig Elliott, PhD

As a feminist, I am inspired by the potential for long-term significant change. As a parent, I am pulled by the immediacy of child rearing. For all my grand intentions and desires for social change, some days the work of being with, listening to, guiding, assisting, and playing with my sons is all I can manage. This tension is intriguing and as much as this lack of grounding both inspires and frustrates me, within it, I find hope. I believe that a model of feminist parenting allows me to navigate the space between.

Feminist living requires me to address my dominant socialization and develop other models of engagement that are not rooted in force, fear, anger, and strength. I am very much a product of the society in which I live and as much as I work to transcend this model, I occasionally slip back into the role of a traditional, dominant patriarchal father, sometimes in uncomfortable ways. Anger and force are tools of dominance and, as a man, I have been socialized to use these first. Although I consciously choose other tools, I find that I resort to these when I am stressed, tired, or frustrated despite my intentions. I struggle with these choices, and I am deeply uncomfortable with them, because these reactions feel so natural and so counter to my being at the same time. Ultimately, I feel sad when I use them because, while efficient in the moment, I see the fear they bring up in my children's eyes and worry about the longer term impact on them. Choosing to be a feminist means that I work to be mindful of these dynamics that are not normally part of my consciousness and choose other models that are based in empathy, compassion, and love.

Existing as a feminist and a father also requires me to continually examine the structure of our family, the foundation of our gender roles, how they specifically show up on a day-to-day basis within our family, and the impact that these roles may have on my sons. In acts of the mundane and the extraordinary, I engage our family in exploring why it is important to place a toilet seat in a particular position, what it means to be "nice," who can be superheroes, and subtlety expanding the socially defined limits of gendered behaviors like celebrating my son's choice to paint his nails and wear them proudly at his school. Even larger sociopolitical decisions take on new layers as my partner and I involve our children in these considerations: where to live, how to live (and what values are implied in that answer), and how to engage within a community.

On an individual level, I practice honoring my partner as a strong, intelligent, and autonomous woman, also celebrating that she feels respected when I open doors for her. This nuanced, feminist living requires a more comprehensive understanding of social justice mechanisms as well as connected knowledge of those whom such choices might impact. Intention coupled with a consciousness brings new lenses, and new possibilities for engagement in this disconnected and gender-defined world.

But these transformations come with pain as well; in many ways becoming a feminist parent requires me to redefine my masculinity, and that counter-cultural effort can layer on painful criticisms from those entrenched in the traditional gender roles (it also layers on the oppressions of homophobia and sexism as masculinity is re-expressed in new ways). Every day I attempt to give up my gender privilege. This is sometimes painful and brings about loneliness, even in a supportive, loving family. Research is showing that men who act outside the patriarchal norm are not treated well, and bell hooks notes this as well by adding that men who honestly and authentically confront sexism in their lives find that they become isolated. Shunned by conventional men and distrusted by women for not conforming (even from some feminist women), I feel "kicked out" of one home and unwelcome in another. On one hand, becoming a feminist man should be less painful, and less "different" from the "normal" man; on the other hand, this is also the nature of transformation—and the painful experiences often provide the most meaningful transformations.

Perhaps a fear of the pain is what prevents more men from imagining a change; yet avoiding this pain will not cease it to be —the only way to be free of this pain is to relinquish the privileges, including power, that come with being a patriarchal man. The hopes of our future, and our children's futures, rest in our ability and determination to do so. Figuring out new ways of being "male" requires a vision of what is possible, the courage to step outside "the box" and a dedication to prevail despite resistance. Being engaged in this process is exactly what makes the presence and engagement as feminist men and fathers all the more powerful and important. Reflecting back on my experiences, I have been able to turn my pain and sadness into hope and inspiration for change. The journey is indeed worth that pain.

How parenting is done influences in great measure the heart, soul, and consciousness of the next generation. Any hope of creating a more just world based on another paradigm for the children rests in part on how parents actually perform this very act. Fathers can, and must, play a key part in developing this new parenting paradigm; anything less continues to root society in the patriarchal, dominator model. I dream of a world that allows children and adults to express their whole selves free from gendered limits, one that is free from wars and aggression, one that is based on love and compassion. This world is possible and within our abilities. It begins with me. It begins at home.

THE FAMILY MATRIARCH: *HER*-STORY IN THE MAKING

Dianne McDonald

Honor thy father were words to live by. Historically, American family units have been patriarchies as praise and honor were reserved mainly for the breadwinner, which was typically the male head of house. Women remained the unsung heroines who cooked, cleaned, and cared for the children. Domesticity was the arena where women were expected to flourish and revel, satiated with their blessed lot in life.

When you investigate the life stories of these matriarchs, you can find new appreciations for an older way of life.

In generations past, women did not have access to the inundation of global information that we are currently accustomed to. Because their world was theoretically much smaller, women were able to focus on their immediate surroundings and were provided the opportunity to fine tune micromanagement skills. The matriarchs of the past ruled the family with great pride. They did it all, and did it well.

Without use of cell phone or GPS, your mother knew where you were and who you were with. The neighborhood mother-network had many eyes. Verbal reports were given amongst a network of moms way back when people spoke to each other in person.

Home cooked meals were the status quo, not the exception. Preservatives and chemicals were less likely found on your dinner plate because some of the food was from a garden, and everything else was fresh from the butcher and grocer. Time and attention was given to meal preparation ensuring a balance from the basic four food groups, not a pyramid.

Post–World War II mothers did in fact have the opportunity to work outside of the home, and often became the first women in their families to obtain a paid wage income which supplemented the family's income. Baby boom moms embraced newfound freedom when they furthered their educations becoming the first females in many families to obtain higher degrees of education, therefore expanding opportunities.

Matriarchs have integrated into our patriarchal society with a subtle strength that enabled them to become the core of the family unit, ensuring domestic stability. Our mothers and grandmothers held onto familial traditions while integrating newer modern day expectations such as learning to use computers, which were a new invention during their lives.

The elder women were likely to outlive their husbands and still continue to thrive and pursue admirable ventures such as volunteering within their respective communities.

Family traditions continue to be practiced by the matriarchs. Favorite recipes and traditional ethnic meal preparations are shared with current generations ensuring continuation of foods that have been an integral part of one's heritage. Family gatherings may seem like seamlessly flowing events, but usually the party preparations are done by the elder women in the family.

The matriarch is also likely the family storage unit for information regarding your family's ancestry. Your family trees have often been watered and groomed by the female relatives who took the time to contribute and ensure the accuracy of ancestral documentation.

Appreciation of the matriarch's beauty is crucial to altering the subordinate position wherein lies the status of women within the familial infrastructure. Lines on one's face represent the wrinkles in time where stories of the past can be found. Appreciating the inner and outer beauty of a senior aged female member of your family allows a person to use an explorative lens which proactively dismantles the slanted media infiltration of what "beauty" is.

Listening to the oral *her*story of the family matriarch is like listening to a beautiful recording from the past. These historical accounts are sacred information and can only be researched first hand by listening intently. Documentation of her stories is a way to honor her and to preserve a written account of your family lineage.

Through time, family units have transitioned away from the standard patriarchal structure into a more egalitarian environment. Both men and women within the household more equally contribute toward child care, domesticity, and supplying a monetary income. This shift has created a less subordinate position for women, but it also neglects to exalt the position of older women in the family, who never got the attention and societal admiration they each deserved.

Modern day matriarchs are ideally positioned as the people who have experienced the times that we consider "old-fashioned" and also exist in our modern world. They have experienced wars and presidents that we can only learn about in history books and PBS specials. They have experienced multiple fashion trends, musical genres, and iconic fads. They have forged paths in civil rights movements and paved the way for modern day feminists.

I asked a dying matriarch once if she had any advice to share. She said she wouldn't have worried about cleaning her house so much. I am not saying we should live in squalor, but I do think we should learn from our beloved matriarchs. Matriarchs value their families. We should too.

We should return the care and attention they have dedicated to us. Their sacrifices should never be forgotten and their respective *her*stories should be treasured.

Honor thy mother: words to live by.

For further reflection . . .

- In what ways does your family and community honor the matriarch?
- How have women's roles shifted within the familial infrastructures throughout the past several decades?
- Is there clear division between the matriarch and patriarch in the family? If so, how are the differences perceived by family members?

Chapter Eight

Until the Violence Stops: Feminist Activism to End Violence against Women

An estimated one in six women in the United States will endure a sexual assault in her lifetime. College-age women are four times more likely to be sexually assaulted than women in other age groups. This all adds up to a sexual assault on a woman every two minutes in the United States.[1] Every year, an estimated 1,300 women die at the hands of their abusive husbands and boyfriends. Domestic violence is a tremendous problem on military bases. Yet it wasn't until four women were killed by their spouses at Fort Bragg in North Carolina in a five-week time period that much attention was devoted to this specific issue. Estimates are that up to one-third of women in the United States will be victims of domestic violence, while globally estimates are as much as one-half of all women suffer from abuse. According to the World Health Organization, women ages 15–44 are more likely to die from domestic violence than cancer, malaria, traffic accidents, and war.[2]

It was feminist activists who helped devote much needed attention and resources to violence against women in the 1970s. These women started grassroots networks in which they provided shelter in their homes for victims, petitioned for legislation against domestic violence, and ushered in an era in which these problems were no longer considered "family issues." In 1977, Oregon became the first state to pass legislation outlawing marital rape, but it was not until 1993 that all 50 states had such prohibitions. By 1980, every state had some form of rape shield law to protect victims of sexual assault from being re-victimized when attorneys grilled them on their sexual history. It wasn't that earlier feminists were unaware that rape and sexual assault were problems, though. For instance, in the 1870s *Woman's Journal* editor Lucy Stone and her husband Henry Blackwell publicized "crimes against women." They wrote about rape and urged reforms such as temperance, which they thought would prevent men from abusing or assaulting their wives.[3] But it wasn't until the second wave that activists really focused on this issue.

The 1994 Violence Against Women Act was perhaps the largest move to date to address the problem of domestic violence and to devote resources to services and prevention. Today, activists, nonprofits, and nongovernmental organizations have pushed the United States to ratify the Convention on the Elimination of All Forms of Discrimination Against Women and to enact the International Violence Against Women Act. In 1997, 200 organizations from around the world formed the Women's Caucus for Gender Justice that prompted the International Criminal Court to include wartime rape under its jurisdiction and to condemn this violence during conflict.[4]

According to the U.S. Department of State, as many as two million women and girls are bought and sold each year. Approximately 80 percent are women and girls. In 2000, activists helped get the Victims of Trafficking and Violence Protection Act passed. It is intended to protect victims, punish traffickers, and prevent trafficking.

Many men have spoken out against domestic violence. Jackson Katz is known for his work creating Mentors in Violence Prevention, as well as his documentaries and books that address men's violence against women. Paul Kivel has written extensively about men's activism to end sexism, racism, and other "isms." One of the most famous men to speak about the domestic violence he experienced as a child is New York Yankees manager Joe Torre who has started a foundation in his mother's memory to raise money for domestic violence programs. Katz explained,

> Men who work in gender-violence prevention—especially those men who are recognized and self-rewarded for our work—have an obligation to acknowledge women's leadership in this area whenever we get the chance. Some of the biggest fears women have about men's entry into this movement are that they will replicate traditional patterns of egocentric male behavior, women's leadership will be supplanted by men's, and women's voices will be drowned out. These fears mirror one of the most frequent complaints that women have about men: that they do not listen to them.[5]

The entries in this chapter come from a diversity of sources, but all involve individuals who have been impacted by or suffered from violence. They emphasize the need to break the silence about these problems and for all people to take action to prevent violence.

SHATTERING MY SILENCE

Lauren Pilnick

It is time to forever shatter my silence. It is time to destroy the shroud of secrecy so often enveloping domestic and sexual abuse **survivors** like me. It's time to make my voice heard. It is in listening to others, those that have triumphed over similar experiences, that I have found this **courage**. It has been through this **courage** that I have realized how much I have to say, and how many want to listen. I know now, after years of difficult **healing**, that I have survived some horrific things and that that just might be so **powerful** in itself that others need to hear about it. Especially for other survivors. This chapter is not only for me, it is for *you*. I've learned that I needed to stop protecting other people and start watching out for myself. In doing so, I call on others to do the same. These acts of **speaking out** are one of the greatest forms of activism in and of itself.

This is for those people who *have* found their **strength** again —those who speak up and speak out at candlelit vigils, marches, and events like "Take Back the Night"; for those who write letters, make phone calls, initiate campaigns, and pester the hell out of the people who have more power than we do; for the ones who encourage their friends to seek help and shatter *their* silence; for the people who raise their children to be nonviolent, pro-woman, gentle, and caring human beings—these are all huge gestures of activism.

I have attended countless candlelit vigils, seven Take Back the Night rallies and marches, been a producer of *The Vagina Monologues*, voted in elections, taught women's studies courses, worked for social change in several jobs as well as my current position, and made my **voice** heard in many other ways.

The most **symbolic** and **meaningful** activism I have pioneered, though, is shattering the silence in my own life and surrounding my personal experiences with rape and relationship abuse.

When I was 16, I met Mitch. We dated for three years and there wasn't one day that was abuse-free. In fact, it was abuse-riddled. He was emotionally and verbally abusive every minute of every day; telling me I was fat, unwanted, stupid, ugly. He was financially abusive; making me pay for things I didn't even want. He was physically abusive less frequently but would often put his hand around my neck, with his thumb pressing on my throat sending a clear message of how much power he could exert over me at any given moment. He would grab my arms and shake me leaving bruises. He was sexually abusive; taking my virginity and raping me nearly every day.

Mitch's coercion, lies, manipulation, power, and control have long since been battled and triumphed over. The damage he perpetuated in my life will never be forgotten but I have healed and will continue to **heal**. He still visits me through vivid nightmares which shake me but I remind myself that I escaped his hands of destruction and will not only survive this, but thrive because of it.

While I was still with Mitch, I went away to college. Once there, I was raped by another man, Brett. My act of making a police report and letting Brett know that what he did was wrong—getting me drunk to make me pass out so he could have sex with me—was yet another form of my activism.

Good *can* stem from evil. I am unsure whether I would have answered my true calling of working to prevent and educate about violence on a day-to-day basis had I not experienced these acts of violence. For me, it is in helping and educating others that I find and experience the greatest satisfaction and affirmation of being able to **survive** violence. What Mitch and Brett did to me was an attempt at control . . . **take this you evil men!**

The most **satisfying** activism that I just cannot wait to carry out is sending Mitch a copy of this book. He has been called out for the pain he inflicted upon me and I look forward to confronting him through my typed, black and white, nonnegotiable words.

I encourage you to break your own **silence**, make your loud voice heard and make it impossible to ignore. Use your own judgment and trust your comfort level on how you want to accomplish this.

I serve as the sexual violence education coordinator at Minnesota State University, Mankato in their women's center and educate people on a daily basis about issues of violence. Most of my position involves advocacy and crisis intervention for survivors and secondary survivors. It is, of course, their decision what they want to do after working with me, but what many of them don't realize until I **affirm** them is that they've already taken the first and largest step to break their silence by talking to me. My greatest goal is to **empower** survivors with knowledge, resources, and information to make them more equipped and powerful. Abusers and rapists work quite hard to take that away from us. Take it back!

This **courage** to speak out is exactly what I'm talking about. I urge you to reach out to whoever you feel most comfortable: your partner, your family, your friends, your local sexual violence or domestic violence agency's advocates, and if you're a student at a university, your women's center. I also urge you to contact me to learn about your many options and avenues to shatter that silence that your abuser(s) desperately count on you to *not* shatter. Please contact me at laurenpilnick@yahoo.com or pilnick @mnsu.edu and know that I truly and most sincerely commend you for reading this chapter and seeking the tools you need to stock up that emotional ammunition and strength to start filling and overflowing that toolbox of survival.

Activism can be "big" or "small." What I want you to know is that it is all **significant** and **meaningful**. Make your voice, ideas, and experiences be known and heard . . . **LOUDLY!**

RAGE AGAINST THE SILENCE

Rebecca Ajo

A few days out of every year it takes a hold of me. But I will never let it beat me.
Anonymous

Ayn Rand once wrote, "She fought it. She recovered. Years helped her reach the day when she could face her memories indifferently, then the day when she felt no necessity to face them. It was finished and of no concern to her any longer." This was her process.

It starts with a nightmare . . . a recurring nightmare that instills a crippling sense of fear and despair . . . a relentless reminder of pain . . . an ever long anathema. . . . It was not my nightmare, but the description of a loved one's nightmare . . .

She ran as fast as she could in the dark, gloomy night. Her heart raced almost as fast as the tears which rolled down her face. She called for help, but, except for the man chasing her, she was alone, and no one came . . . just he whom she hated. He who stole her innocence. He who laughed in her face when she begged and pleaded . . .

"Stop!"

"Please Stop!"

She continued to run. She was running back to a place where there was no fear and no nightmares. She was running to a time when she could sit in her room in peace without wondering whether or not he would come for her.

She felt him nearing. Suddenly, he reached from behind her and grabbed her arm. Both of them fell to the wet ground together. She fought to get free but failed as he overpowered her.

She looked at his blue eyes. Eyes that showed no mercy, no compassion, and no kindness. Eyes that were filled with perverted-
ness. Eyes that were dirty, lewd, and lascivious. She looked at
him, a look dripped in agony, pain, and disgust . . . one more time
she pleaded in her soft voice . . .

"Please stop."

He did not stop . . . he continued and then took out a gun and
shot her.
She woke up in a sweat and in tears. Her heart was racing.
She shook as she thought of her vivid dream and prayed to
God. She asked for strength even though she's stronger than
she knows. She got up and got ready for work, determined to
not allow her past or her dreams to affect a beautiful day. She
refuses to let him win.
I was 18 years old the first time my best friend told me she
had been molested as a young girl and raped at the tender age
of 12. I had never seen devastation or paralyzing pain until that
night. I did not know it then, but that conversation would impact
my life forever. The topic would arise several times proceeding
that night, usually because a few days out of the year would bring
the experience back to her in the form of a dream. No matter how
many times she described these dreams, no matter how many
times I saw her cry, it never got easier. I never knew what to say
or how to help . . . and then it came to me . . . Rage Against the
Silence.
The last time this dream was described to me was a few
months ago. I remember it was a Saturday night and I remember
being frustrated because I still did not know what to say or how to
help. Three years had passed and her past still controlled her.
I could not sleep that night. Every single conversation about her
being molested or raped raced through my mind incessantly that
night. I saw every single tear drop fall all over again.
The next day, I decided I wanted to coordinate a fund-raiser
for rape victims in collaboration with the high school I graduated
from in 2005. I decided to call it Rage Against the Silence.
I thought the title was appropriate as sexual violence is grossly
underreported. Because of the nature of such crimes, thousands
of women are silenced each year. Shame, guilt, fear of retaliation,
or a lack of faith in the criminal justice system means that justice
is very seldom served. The silence must be broken.
My idea for the fund-raiser is as follows: I would like to have
two alumni basketball games. One in which the current Varsity
Girls team plays the women alumni and another game for the

Varsity Boys team against the men's alumni. The entry fee would be $5 per person and the monies raised would be donated to an organization in South Florida which aids victims of sexual violence.

Additionally, I would like to get a local radio station involved as well as an alumni Miami Dolphins player to come out and sign autographs so as to boost attendance. Moreover, I would like the event to be set up like a human rights fair with booths from different agencies and pamphlets with information for the guests to visit. For example, I would like to have a booth from the criminal justice department as well as a No More Tears booth. No More Tears is a nonprofit organization which aids immigrant women that are victims of domestic violence.

My goal is to bring awareness and help an organization without ample resources to help those who have been victims of sexual or domestic violence.

The biggest challenge thus far has been choosing the right organization. I graduated from a Catholic high school which means the organization I choose to donate the monies to must be a Catholic-based organization. There are not many to choose from.

I told my best friend about the project the day I came up with it and she loved it. In fact, I think that is the day she decided she was never going to let her past beat her again.

My philosophy is this: one voice can make a difference. Martin Luther King Jr., demonstrated this. So, if one solitary voice, standing steadfast with nothing but a sense of bravery can make a difference, imagine thousands of voices relentlessly and indefatigably thrashing ... blaring ... RAGING AGAINST THE SILENCE TOGETHER.

MY JOURNEY

Roslyn Parker

I am a survivor of domestic violence. No longer treading water to keep from drowning in a sea of abuse, I am on the shore, completely aware of my past, yet fully engaged in the present. As a mother of a two adult children, an entrepreneur, survivor, and advocate for women's causes and empowerment, I bring all that I am into all that I do. I understand now that every experience in my life, both good and bad have presented me with opportunities for growth, understanding, and sometimes forgiveness. Today I look at that time in my life as an opportunity to take what was a bad situation, and lift it up for a greater good.

Starting on this journey of advocacy work was not an easy one. As a survivor, for many years, I was angry and bitter. I didn't realize it at the time, but looking back on it I guess I was. One day I finally came to the realization that my anger and bitterness was really serving no one, and that in fact it was impeding my own healing. I was also very ashamed. The shame weighed me down even more than the anger and bitterness did. I internalized a lot of the shame and hurt that came from being a victim, or should I say survivor. Little did I realize that internalizing this shame would also keep me treading water, and that even though I was keeping my head above water, any minute I could go under.

As a result of my own shame and fear, for many years I did not feel comfortable sharing my story. Twenty some odd years later and it is still sometimes difficult. The fear of being judged kept me in the shadows of my former life and my former self. Yet the opportunities to share kept finding their way into my life. It is amazing the number of people, from all walks of life, that I have encountered who have been impacted by domestic violence in some way.

In time, I realized that what I had to offer in sharing my story, my own abuse, my own pain, my own hurt, and my own shame, was much bigger than me. Perhaps something I will say will resonate in some woman's soul and prompt her to make a new choice, in fact a better choice, one that might even save her life. Perhaps something I say will give her the courage to say "no" more. In recognizing how powerful this work could be, I finally began to more readily share my own experiences and to let people know that they were not alone and that they did not have to isolate themselves because of the abuse. I have walked in those shoes and know what it looks and feels like to not think rationally, while putting your own life and your children's lives at risk. I know what it feels like to not be able to look at yourself in the mirror because your self-esteem is in the toilet. Been there, done that, even bought a t-shirt. I understand the importance of sometimes just offering a listening and empathetic ear and allowing people to talk, cry, or do whatever. I don't judge because I don't want to be judged. Last but certainly not least, I also understand the strength it takes to walk away and the courage, support, and tools needed to stay away. I understand that because that was my story too.

About seven years ago, a friend and colleague was killed by her estranged husband. People, including myself, were in shock after her death because we did not know that she had been abused. She was a dedicated mother and a beautiful person overall. As a community advocate, she worked for a non-profit organization that helped people secure housing. I don't believe that even her family knew the pain that she was going through. Her friends did not know. Her colleagues did not know. It was only after her estranged husband broke into her apartment and killed her while their five-year-old daughter lay sleeping that we knew. He unsuccessfully tried to commit suicide. Today, he sits in jail for the horrific crime he committed that fateful day in August. After her death, it became clear to me that I had to step out of my own shadows of pain and do more. I had to recognize that what I had gone through had more meaning and purpose in my life than I was giving it credit for, and that by lifting those experiences up to a higher cause, I could serve others.

They say when you are ready the teacher will appear. I was now ready. It was during my tenure as a manager with Verizon Information Services, and my work through the Verizon Foundation, that I became connected with the Safespace Foundation, a Miami Dade nonprofit organization that had been dedicated to serving victims of domestic violence for over 30 years. They are the advisory board to the Miami Dade County Victims Advocates Programs which has under its umbrella a variety of services and programs for victims and survivors of domestic violence, including a 24-hour crisis hotline, the Safespace Shelters and Inn Transition housing. It is through this collaboration with the county that the Safespace Foundation is able to provide financial support for programs for housing, emergency services, relocation assistance, counseling services as well as a variety of education and empowerment programs for victims and their families. The Safespace Foundation has enabled me to grow as a leader, as an advocate, and as a person.

As president, I am now able to make a real difference as an advocate of women's causes. I take my role very seriously. I have taken core competency training and am always in the mode for development and growth. Very recently I traveled to Tallahassee to lobby state legislators regarding two priority bills on behalf of the Florida Coalition against Domestic Violence. My goal is to lead by example by creating a legacy of education, awareness, and empowerment. As the cocreator of the shelter's women's empowerment program, I am now able to infuse some of the life skills and tools for healing that I learned while on my personal journey of healing. It's rewarding to know that I am part of a process that embodies the foundation's core beliefs of empowerment, education, and advocacy. In addition to our work at the shelter, it is also the board's goal to further expand our efforts through additional outreach programming and counseling services.

The beauty of this work is that you can step into that space at anytime or anyplace. During a recent trip to the Dominican Republic, because of my role at Safespace, I was asked to speak on domestic violence to some of the women in the tiny village of Cienfuego. I was on a travel to do good through a "voluntourism" project with Airline Ambassadors and Kids for Kids to deliver aid to the impoverished community that is ravaged by a variety of social problems including abuse.

Even though I was speaking through a translator, I found the women to be eager for information. They patiently waited as the program manager translated. I listened as they shared their stories. I had to remember that this was the first step in a long process and that I could not solve every issue in one trip. At least the process had begun. That evening the ladies in attendance met me more than half way and I was grateful for that.

After that trip I was inspired further to develop my travel to do good programming concept. By incorporating my life's purpose and passion to help others into my professional life, I have now created a business model that allows travelers to integrate a volunteer or service project into their travel destination experience.

To sum it all up, my work as an advocate against domestic violence is part of a personal journey of being in service and giving back to others. Every life experience, both good and bad, has brought me to where I am today. It is a gift and honor to be on this journey. Thank you for allowing me to share a part of this journey with you.

TRYING NOT TO CRY

Khadija Charles

My journey to being a feminist activist started six and a half years ago, the very first time I had ever had my power taken from me. While attending a night school program in the tenth grade, I was pulled into a classroom and sexually assaulted. As surprising as it may seem that was not, for me, the most severe silencing of my power. Three days after the assault I told my mom. After calming down and calling our family doctor she drove me down to the rape treatment center. Once I arrived a basic physical exam was done along with the answering of a few standard questions. Then as a part of procedure the police were called and asked to come in. When the police officer heard my story he asked to speak with me and I retold him what happened over the phone as he instructed me to do. And then he told me he didn't believe me. I remember feeling like my heart sank to the bottom of my feet as I passed the phone to my mother. The police officer was forced to come in after my mother complained and he brought along his other male partner. They took me to a room and told me that my mother couldn't be in the room when they questioned me. At this point I remember still feeling hopeful that I would be able to stop the man that hurt me, it must have just been a misunderstanding between the police officer and I. They took turns asking me questions beginning with asking me to again restate my story. After finishing the same way as before he replied to me that he didn't think that was quite what happened but that we wouldn't leave there until we had "resolved" everything. For the next two hours or so, they asked me questions and then talked amongst themselves in a language I couldn't understand. They asked what I was wearing, if I knew his friends, how I was wearing my clothes, how I said no, how many times, how loud. Then he asked me to get up and pushed me up against the desk to show him how I was forced up against a similar desk, standing close enough to me for me to feel his breath. I couldn't take it anymore, I just wanted to go home so when he asked me yet again if this wasn't just all a misunderstanding I nodded my head yes and left the room. A police report was never written. While he explained everything to my mother I went somewhere else in my mind, I remember her looking at me and believing me but not knowing what to do. It was the middle of the night and we were two women who were being told something by two male law enforcement officers. I always knew I couldn't change what happened but from the day it happened I hoped I could help prevent it from happening to someone else. It would be five years before I would even come close to doing that.

At my university's Take Back The Night, I spoke out about my experience. It was hard, I had never done anything like it, and I cried through the entire thing but I knew it was important to do. I remember looking out into the crowd and seeing a few faces I hadn't known crying with me, sharing my hurt and my survival. I knew it was important to take a stand against violence, and to put a face to the person many college students didn't think they knew. I as an individual went up and gave a voice to the women that had lost theirs and to some who just weren't ready to use it. After that night I got numerous thanks from my fellow students and professors, but there was one that changed me. It was a young woman about my age who came up to me and told me her story. It had happened years ago for her and she never shared it with anyone, and she wasn't even at the event but she knew someone who was and she confided in me. I was able to refer her to our on campus services as well as serve as a support system for her. I was able to help her find her voice. It was after that that I realized that I could make a difference.

I wanted to learn more about making a difference and so I took my first women's studies course and that showed me through learning the history of the feminist movement that my voice is one of my very best assets. I was able to grow more confident in using it to promote change through awareness. There is no way anything will ever change if I don't stand up and say that the way I was treated is wrong, that as a society, not just the police, we need to change the way we perceive rape. I recently landed my dream job in a domestic violence agency in their social change department through an AmeriCorps term. I have been able to work with a group of amazing people to help change the way the world sees not only rape but also domestic violence. I have been able to share my story with my coworkers and at another Take Back The Night, and this time I didn't cry!

NO MORE TEARS: THE LIFE OF SOMY ALI—FILMMAKER, HUMANITARIAN, AND FRIEND

Laura Finley

At the age of 24, Somy Ali returned to the United States after an eight year, very successful career as an actress and model in India's Bollywood. Tired of what she now calls a superficial life, Somy wanted to do something that made a difference. Having dropped out of her Florida public school at age 16, a school she admits she rarely attended (preferring instead to hang out at the bowling alley across the street), she worked hard to pass the GED exam. She flew to Tampa from South Florida to take the TOEFL test to prove she was proficient in English, and then enrolled as a student at Nova Southeastern University. She earned incredible marks and accolades from her professors, but not without a lot of work. Somy explains that she monopolized her professor's time during office hours, as she was so inexperienced and so needy that she required one-on-one attention in addition to attending classes. In 2002 she earned her bachelor's degree of arts in psychology, despite being told by her father that she would never achieve anything and that women had no business doing anything but marrying, having kids, and taking care of the home. After graduating from NSU she earned a degree from New York Film Academy, focusing on documentary filmmaking, and then took additional courses through the Connecticut School of Broadcasting. She has created several documentaries about social justice issues. Her 2005 film *I Can Survive*, about Mukhtar Mai, a Pakistani woman who was gang raped because her brother dared to communicate with a girl from another caste, helped prompt Somy to find her precise calling: helping women who suffer as victims of violence. Mai went on to be a vocal advocate for women's rights and has founded schools and shelters in her community. She even insisted that the children of her rapists attend her school—she sees them every day—so that she can help prevent them ever becoming like their fathers. Somy says if Mai can do it, she can too.

It was more than this, really, that has made Somy commit her life to helping victims of abuse. As a young child growing up in Pakistan, she saw abuse in her home, among the servants who worked for her parents, everywhere she looked. Rather than an oddity, domestic violence seemed to be the norm. Somy recalls wondering at about age nine who would help these women. Everyone told her that was just the way things were. She knew better, even then.

When the family moved to the United States, Somy continued to witness abuse. In 2006, she was again confronted with the issue of domestic violence when one of her South Florida neighbors knocked on her door asking for help. She was being beaten by not just her husband, but by her in-laws as well. Somy helped her obtain a restraining order, supported her emotionally through a divorce and child custody hearings, and helped her get a job. In December 2006, Somy formalized her ability to help these women by founding No More Tears (NMT), a nonprofit devoted to providing individualized assistance to victims of domestic violence and their children. Insistent that NMT never be "cold or corporate," she runs the nonprofit from the heart. She takes no salary from this full-time organization, and plans to grow it with a staff of volunteers. Bucking the norm among social service providers, she provides very personal help to the survivors. As I write this, she is providing one survivor transportation to work, and is making plans to babysit the woman's daughter for the bulk of the weekend while she earns a living. NMT provides long-term mentoring, pro bono legal services, child care, assistance with financial needs, and much more.

I am in the fortunate position of being able to assist NMT and my good friend Somy. I agree with her when she says there is nothing more gratifying than listening to a little girl who has been isolated in an apartment by her abusive father giggle hysterically because she loves the way sand—a foreign object to her, even though she has lived all her life in Miami—feels on the bottom of her feet. Somy is remarkable for her resilience, having been exposed to abuse as a child but being determined she will be part of the solution, not the problem. She is amazing for her heart and her generosity, opening her door (literally and figuratively) to anyone who might need help. And her commitment to social justice and human rights is tremendous. In addition to NMT, Somy founded a socially conscious clothing line called So-Me Designs in 2006. Appalled at the stupid comments people would advertise on their clothing ("Who needs a brain when you have these" written across the breasts), she decided that fashion can be sexy and smart. Ten percent of the net proceeds from So-Me Designs go to NMT. And, beyond the fact that the messages emphasize human rights and the money supports victims of abuse, she has recently moved the line to be almost exclusively organic and eco-friendly. She takes great pains to ensure the t-shirts are not produced by sweatshop labor. She did all this with no background in business or fashion, just a dream to rectify something she saw as a problem. As her friend and colleague with NMT, I think Somy truly represents the best of humanity.

ON SURVIVING: SARA'S STORY

Laura Finley

Sara (name changed to protect her identity) was born in Jordan and is one of nine children. Two of her brothers were afflicted with Duchenne muscular dystrophy, and she has already lost one of them. At age 19, she was wed through an arranged marriage to a horribly abusive man. She soon became pregnant, but lost the baby when her husband kicked her in the stomach. Although she wanted to tell the doctor the real story of why she miscarried, she could not because no one at the hospital except her husband spoke Arabic and thus the doctor asked him to translate for her.

Sara endured horrific control, isolation, and physical abuse at the hands of her husband. He prohibited her from learning English, something she desperately wanted. Over time, Sara would sneak around and ended up teaching herself English from books. When she wanted to go to school to earn a GED, he became enraged. Sara pleaded with him and endured more physical abuse, but eventually prevailed. But each time she would ask for something else—to go on to community college after earning her GED, then to enroll in the pharmacy program at a university—he would retaliate with more abuse. Again, she endured so that she could gain the education she so wanted.

It wasn't just getting his approval to enroll that was difficult. At times, her husband would take her books and study materials, just to mess with her. He once locked her in the home for months on end, not allowing her to go anywhere. When she was finally allowed to leave, her eyes burned since she had not seen the sun in so long. But Sara pressed on.

Her husband grew more and more confident that Sara would do nothing about the abuse over time. He manipulated her cultural beliefs, exploiting the fact that he knew her culture frowned on asking for help and dissolving marriages. He controlled all the finances, so she did not believe she could take care of herself and the children alone. He knew she was generally unaware of U.S. systems of support, including the simple fact that what he was doing was illegal and that she could call the police during an incident but also up to one year later.

In November 2009, Sara's husband attacked her and threatened to kill her and her children. He hit her so hard she passed out. She tried to call the police twice, but he took the phone. She called her mother, who relied on cultural beliefs and advised against calling the police. The next day, she went to her university to ask for an extension on her exams, and they told her she had to tell them why. She did, and they encouraged her to call the authorities. Sara did, and ended up filing for a restraining order, which she obtained. Criminal charges of domestic violence battery are pending, and a divorce is in the works.

So, how is this awful story an example of feminist activism? As a board member of NMT, a nonprofit organization devoted to assisting victims of domestic violence and their children, I have been able to not only help Sara, but to get to know what a remarkable woman she is. Her LIFE is an example of activism for women! Despite the odds, Sara has never lost her goal of becoming a pharmacist. She has maintained her position on the chancellor's list of students (the top five percent in her class) throughout all of this. She appeared in court—a very unfamiliar system—and not only represented her position, but did so with great conviction and strength. Her command of the English language is truly impressive—for anyone, let alone for someone who learned it alone from a book.

Sara wants nothing more than to be free, and for her kids to be free. Sara authorized me to tell her story so that other women may benefit. She is a strong, intelligent woman who will go on to make that life for herself and her family.

Chapter Nine

Love Your Mother: Feminist Activism for the Environment and Animal Welfare

The theory of intersectionality best explains how environment and animal rights issues connect to feminism. Intersectionality posits that injustice of any sort is the product of multiple layered and intertwined hierarchies.[1] The argument is that the commodification of people, animals, and land are intricately connected. Ecofeminists maintain that the subordination of women and male superiority are related to the degradation of the environment and speciesism, or the privileging of humans over animals. Even the language used to describe domination of land is rife with reference to women, such as "rape of the land," whereas the land itself is genuinely described in feminine terms, as in "Mother Earth." Some point to the disconnect between humans and nature that occurred some 20,000 years ago as the source of all inequalities, asserting that this was the root of domination over other things.

Women have often taken the lead in identifying environmental dangers. In 1910, Alice Hamilton, the first woman professor at Harvard Medical School, saw the connection between improper sewage disposal and the flies that spread typhoid. She also noted the health condition of Chicago immigrants was tied closely to their exposure to unsafe conditions and chemicals. She later became the director of the Occupational Disease Commission created by the governor of Illinois, the first commission of this sort in the world. It was Michiko Ishimure who helped expose the high levels of mercury near the Chisso chemical plant in Minimata, Japan. Her work also helped gain support for those who suffered from what came to be called Minimata Disease. Rachel Carson is one of the most well-known environmentalists in the United States. Carson, a marine biologist and author, shocked the nation with her 1962 book *Silent Spring*. In it, she chronicled the damages caused by pesticides, in particular DDT. U.S. President John F. Kennedy requested that the Science Advisory Committee investigate her claims, which they verified in 1963. Many women were involved in getting Earth Day recognized officially in 1970. In 1978, Lois Marie Gibbs found herself an accidental activist when she and her family suffered from the chemicals that had been dumped all over their home and neighborhood of Love Canal, New York. In the 1980s, Winona LaDuke, an Anishanaabe, worked with Women of All Red Nations to call attention to extensively forced sterilization of native women as well as environmental issues impacting natives. She is executive director of Honor the Earth, an organization she founded with the Indigo Girls. LaDuke was named *Ms.* magazine's Woman of the Year in 1997 and received the Reebok Human Rights Award in 1998. In 1996 and 2000, she ran as vice president on the Green Party ticket with Ralph Nader. One of the most widely known ecofeminist activists today is Vandana Shiva. Shiva has written about a variety of environmental issues and how they both create and result in poverty. In 2004, Dr. Wangari Maathai was awarded the Nobel Peace Prize for helping combat deforestation in Kenya.

Ecofeminists have taken all sorts of actions to make their points. Julia Butterfly Hill began sitting in a 1,000-year-old Sequoia tree named Luna on December 10, 1997. Her act of civil disobedience was intended to call attention to the damage wrought by the timber industry in Northern California, where only 3 percent of the old growth redwoods remain. She agreed to vacate the tree in 1999 when the Pacific Lumber Company agreed to save Luna and all trees in a three acre area. In 1999, Hill and other activists founded the Circle of Life Foundation. She found out in 2001 that Luna had been cut down with a chain saw. Women have also led the charge in fighting environmental racism, which refers to the disproportionate placement of toxic chemicals and pollutants in areas populated by poor people and people of color. In many cases, they have used their status as mothers to advocate for environmental justice. Activists organize "girlcotts" in which they refuse to purchase certain products or services that they learn are dangerous to themselves, their families, or the environment.

Activists have pointed out the damage we do to our bodies when we consume toxic foods and products. For instance, activists have noted that Premarin, a drug widely prescribed for menopausal women, is derived from the urine of pregnant mares and is thus not only potentially harmful to women, but to animals and the environment as well. Mothers have started blogs to call attention to environmental issues and to exchange tips and information on how to help—one example is http://organicmania.com/green-moms-carnival/. Women have started businesses devoted to a healthier environment, offering organic foods, fair trade and environmentally friendly clothing, baby products, and more.

Like the feminist movement, the animal advocacy movement is divided as well. Some argue for an animal welfare perspective, which generally pushes for more humane treatment of animals. Rights-oriented approaches go beyond this, maintaining that the quality of lives of animals is most important. Tom Regan summed it up by saying that animal rights advocates seek not bigger cages but no cages for animals at all. People for the Ethical Treatment of Animals (PETA) has been the most visible animal advocacy agency and has generally taken an animal welfare approach. This is likely due to their celebrity endorsements, provocative campaigns, and sexualized imagery. Women's sexualized bodies have been used in many PETA campaigns, including their "I'd Rather Go Naked than Wear Fur" effort that began in 1990. The campaign featured partially or fully nude celebrities and models, often posed in Lolita-like or schoolgirl-like settings. Feminists have repeatedly criticized PETA for this, and have been wary of the use of Pamela Anderson, best known for being scantily clad in various television shows and magazines, as a spokesperson. The broader question is whether groups advancing any type of social justice should ever utilize degrading images to publicize their cause. Feminists maintain that PETA's work should be informed by feminist principles and thus should not further sexist portrayals of women that have been called soft-core pornography.[2]

The essays in this chapter help readers understand what ecofeminism is all about. They also show that feminist activists of all ages can help the environment and animals through their ideas, words, and actions.

ECOFEMINISM 101

Dianne McDonald

Historically, most societies have been categorized as patriarchies. Men have reigned as the dominant gender within most families and governments as nations became industrialized. Industrial progressions have resulted in our earth's natural resources being used, therefore altering the world's ecological landscape. We now see the effects and try to fix what has been broken and dirtied.

The environment is a feminist issue. Environmentalism + Feminism = Ecofeminism. Ecofeminism is when women recognize the environment as an entity deserving of attention and activism. What's a poor little feminist to do? Anything and everything, that's what. It all starts with a conscious decision to make a difference.

Women are empowered to make a lasting environmental impact because we are situated prominently within many households. Within the role of mother, we are given the opportunity to teach our children positive ecohabits such as coloring both sides of paper used, gardening, and choosing natural and earth-friendly products. As we ourselves attempt to engage in daily acts of environmentalism, such as recycling, we have become living breathing ecofeminists now serving as mentors and role models. By infusing environmental activism with child rearing, we ensure a generation of people who are proactive in sustaining the health of Mother Earth.

Women are becoming more prevalent within government positions, allowing feminist issues to be highlighted as public policy. Women elected to and serving within societal positions of power is imperative because ecofeminist theory also recognizes the disparities between women from different regions of our planet. For example, women geographically located closer to the equator are more likely to live in poverty and less likely to have access to education and reproductive information and options. Some feminists address this gendered inequality by infusing information and opportunity to the women. Political policies can potentially bridge these gaps of inequality.

Women in the paid work force are also very important in ensuring programs that reduce, reuse, and recycle. Female leaders of industry are now in position to alter the available goods and services to better suit the needs of women and the environment simultaneously. Marketing strategies can include ecoawareness. Business women are quite aware of the desires of their consumers and can offer ecofriendly alternative products such as laundry detergents, feminine hygiene products, and make-up.

As technology advances, our world, theoretically, becomes smaller. This has allowed women to learn about environmental issues worldwide on a daily basis, not just on random nature programs that were shown too few and too far between. Ecofeminist issues can now be researched and addressed with great ease.

There are many ways to raise your ecofeminist consciousness. It is possible for people to include and embrace environmental activism throughout each day:

- Minimize water use in the morning by shortening your shower and shutting off the faucet while you brush your teeth.
- Recycle anything and everything as much as possible.
- Bring your own shopping bags to the market.
- Refill a water container rather than using plastic water bottles all of the time.
- Plant a sapling for every tree or wood based product you consume.
- Adjust your thermostat to save some energy.

These little changes go a long way.

Old habits die hard. It is challenging to pry one's own hands from a steering wheel at times. Idealistic and overexuberant intentions often fizzle. Embracing a realistic approach to ecofeminism will likely yield the greatest results over the longest amount of time. Similar to a successful diet plan, this activism gets the planet healthy.

Utilizing public transportation and avoiding use of a gas-guzzling vehicle like the popular sports utility vehicle (SUV) is a challenge for many Americans. SUV's are everywhere it seems. The bigger vehicles were almost seen as a status symbol. That's no longer the case. As people became more aware of the deteriorating health of our planet, the popularity of the SUV has declined. Hybrid vehicles have become the new car rage. Bravo to the masses!

Many rural areas do not have public transportation offered. In reality, personal car use is a necessity for many people. Ecofeminism encourages less driving for those folks. Multiple errands per excursion reduce multiple trips which results in reduced personal emissions. Every decrease in fossil fuel consumption minimizes one's carbon footprint. A "carbon footprint" describes the amount of greenhouse gasses one produces.

Ecofeminist groups and individuals are likely to have a more encompassing perspective as they recognize and address the term "ecological footprint," which includes the multiple ways we negatively affect the environment.

Ecofeminism is a very complex feminist theory, also considered people-friendly because it has a very accessible piece to it. Ecofeminism recognizes the simplest acts of environmental awareness as important contributions. There are many environmental issues that need your attention. Please investigate an environmental issue interesting to you and become involved in some way. This is OUR world. It may not have been perfect when we got it, but we can leave it in better condition for future generations.

Go green to preserve and save our Mother Earth! Go blue and become an ocean and waterway activist! Enjoy your newfound ecofeminism. Activism has never been easier.

For Further Reflection:

What do you consider to be the most prominent environmental problems which could have long-term effects?

In what ways could you personally become involved with ecofeminist activism?

Do you have any ideas for an event for a community to partake in to improve your city or town's ecohealth? If so, how would you go about implementing it?

CREATING THE WORLD IN WHICH I WANT TO LIVE: FEMINISM, VEGETARIANISM, AND GLOBAL TRANSFORMATION

Ariana E. Vigil

"Being vegan is like saying 'Fuck You' to everything I hate!" I shouted to my best friend Cristina. We were standing in the crowd-filled streets of Quebec City, Quebec, one day into a weekend of massive protests against the Free Trade Act of the Americas and just five months into my newly adopted vegan lifestyle. Looking back, I think, my excitedly screamed epiphany was more a reaction to the spontaneous community I discovered that weekend than a hazy response to the toxic tear gas clouding my eyes and throat. But I also have to ask myself: what does being a feminist of color have to do with being a vegetarian, and what do both of these things have to do with the things I want to reject and those I want to embrace?

I've always been convinced that there is a connection between my feminism and my vegetarianism but I've long had trouble articulating that link. While excellent research has been conducted into the theoretical ties between vegetarianism and feminism, I think my young teenage mind understood something less complicated, though just as important, as the connection between the fetishization of the female body and the commodification of animals for human consumption. Thinking back to the development of my feminist consciousness I realize what was so striking was the undeniable structural basis of sexism. It was the understanding that sexism wasn't something that happened only on an individual scale, but something that was enacted and supported at an institutional level that led me to realize that a similarly structured response was needed. What is most terrifying about acts of violence, dominance, and discrimination is their pervasiveness and the justifications used to support them. The understanding of, and opposition to, structural inequality has provided the bridge between so many movements with which I engage: feminism, antiracism, worker's rights, queer liberation; and it is structural inequality that is my link between vegetarianism and feminism. My commitment to feminism is what leads me to object when I hear a sexist or racist joke—not because such jokes are painful and offensive in and of themselves (though they are)—but because such rhetoric contributes to a larger structure that I want to dismantle. Similarly, my commitment to vegetarianism stems not from the concern over the contents of one meal (though indeed that is important), but rather my recognition that the contents of EVERY meal are part of larger oppressive structures. I refuse to laugh at sexist jokes because I refuse to contribute to discriminatory societal beliefs; I refuse to eat meat because I refuse to contribute to a system that is built on the exploitation of land, animals, resources, and workers.

The connections continue in the reactions that both my feminism and vegetarianism elicits in others. I am often accused of a strikingly similar set of trespasses against man and nature: I want what is "unnatural," I have "no sense of humor," I am "against everything" and "for nothing." A common joke amongst my family and friends is some version of—"what do you eat, anyway?" or, more accusingly, "[sigh], you don't eat anything!" Because we are so often caught up in pointing out racism, sexism, homo-phobia, and classism in our cultures, classrooms, and political systems it may seem to some people that feminists deserve a similar indictment—"you don't like anything!" or "you don't sup-port anything!" And indeed, sometimes I feel that I am hard-pressed to find political or cultural work that doesn't degrade or deny my ideals; or I grumble as I begrudgingly vow to "check my politics" as I enter the movie theatre or open the pages of a novel.

As a woman of color, both my feminism and my vegetarian-ism threaten to place me outside the community with which I identify. Both feminism and vegetarianism are still considered "white" identities and while feminist communities have become much more responsive to the ideas and concerns of women of color in the past decades, the vegetarian/vegan community remains difficult to navigate for people of color.

While I'm happy to let my feminism, my vegetarianism, and my ethnic identity place me outside of normative lifestyles and activities, refusing to participate in established structures has its limits—if we really want change we need to begin creating the kinds of societies, institutions, and meals that reflect our values. Thinking back to that moment in Quebec City, that moment when I really thought that I was part of something *positive*, I am reminded of the words of Carol J. Adams. In the preface to the tenth anniversary edition of her important work *The Sexual Politics of Meat*, Adams acknowledges the danger of always say-ing "no": "Feminism should not embrace vegetarianism simply because it is a negation of the dominant world. It should embrace it because of what it is and represents. Vegetarianism is in fact deeply proactive and transformative" (Adams 1999, p. 22). My vegan lifestyle allows me to participate in this transformation. As a vegan I enact countless "yes's" every day—yes to sustain-ably grown food, yes to community economies, yes to respecting the living beings that make my own existence possible.

As I stood in the streets of Quebec City watching so much of what I consider to be wrong with the world take place behind closed doors, I was forced to ask myself: What would a world without exploitation and oppression look like? I'm not 100 per-cent sure, but I do know that when I take the time to ensure that the tools I use to sustain my life—my clothing, my transportation, my food—are grown, manufactured, and shipped in a manner as free of exploitation as possible, I am beginning to catch a glimpse of this world.

RESCUING CATS, RESCUING ONE ANOTHER
Kimiko Akita

It's 5:50 AM. The alarm clock awakens me. I get up, wash my face, skip breakfast, go outside into the dark, open my garage, load cages of cats into my car trunk and back seat, and start my car.

By 6:30, I arrive at Animal Control Services, unload the cages, take my place in line—usually first—and wait for the clinic to open at 7:30. I'm never alone for long, and I pass the time talking with other cat rescuers.

These are my Monday mornings.

I have been rescuing cats for three years. Upon moving to Florida in the summer of 2005, I noticed that many pets were being abandoned. I was startled by how many hungry and miserable cats were trolling trash bins. When kittens of the ferals began showing up the next spring, feeding on garbage and growing up in the shadows of the dumpsters, I felt compelled to do something.

I met Linda, another resident of my apartment complex who lived near the dumpster. Through research, we learned about the local feline rescue agency's trap-neuter-return (TNR) program, an inexpensive, effective, and humane way to limit animal reproduction. We became cat rescuers.

Our modus operandi: Linda and I would trap the cats over a weekend. I would care for the cats in cages inside my garage. I would transport the cats to Animal Control on Monday. Linda would pick them up seven hours later, after their surgery. I would minister to the cats (males are woozy but recuperate the same day; females require a longer recovery) until they were ready for release.

When Linda moved away, I was left alone to carry out the TNR. I managed to tame several ferals and was able to find them loving homes. Since 2006, I have "rescued" 111 cats; some diseased cats must be euthanized, and all fetuses are aborted. I adopted two ferals, Chame and Chibi, whom I have domesticated. They are my de facto infant children.

Cat rescue is a maternal and feminist act. Most of the volunteers I see weekly are women; all volunteers possess and display nurturing qualities. They not only take care of ferals before and after surgery but also keep feeding colonies for as long as they exist.

Trapping cats, which must be done late at night, is not easy. TNR must be carried out no matter the weather or the fire anthills in the tall weeds or the mosquitoes that swarm on summer nights.

Often, opportunistic possums and raccoons wind up inside the cages instead of the cats. A trapped wild animal may attack upon its release.

Human animals pose a larger threat. Near where I live, a jogger disappeared recently and was found murdered; her killer has not been found. Another fellow rescuer who tended a cat colony at the apartment building she managed spent several scary and desperate nights with me inside the grounds of her complex after it was evacuated and fenced off to be razed and replaced by a high-rise. Our plan to rescue two dozen resident ferals there proved largely unsuccessful. We can only imagine their fate.

I have discovered that some people who oppose human abortion will break or destroy traps once they learn the possible fate of the fetuses of cats targeted for TNR. Then there are thieves who find my expensive cat traps alluring.

The support of the network of volunteers encourages us to maintain our mission. Mondays, while we wait for the clinic to open, we tell one another our stories and exchange information, knowledge, and advice. Many wind up adopting a cat we've rescued. Otherwise strangers, we bond on common ground: the heartless environment into which cats get thrown away. We're better for the experience.

A woman in her 60s says: "My children complain that I care for my cats too much. I tell them, 'You come home only for Thanksgiving and Christmas, but my cats wait for me every day and show me affection all the time!'"

A grandmother in her 80s: "My cats saved my life several times. When I get asthma attacks while I'm asleep, my cat comes to me and scratches my face to help me wake up."

Another woman, same age: "Two years ago, when I was diagnosed with cancer and was told that I didn't have long to live, I told my doctor that I was going to give away my dog and cats. My doctor told me, 'Oh, no, animals are great companions and extremely therapeutic. Don't give them away.' He was right. My cats and dog were so comforting. Look at me. I survived cancer. I am well now."

Our shared stories empower and energize us; like Powder-milk Biscuits, they give us the courage to do what needs to be done.

At first I was intimidated by Jane, a volunteer who handles appointment phone calls for TNR. I had no idea what the acronym meant. Jane scrutinized me. I learned that she wanted to make sure I was reliable, responsible, and worthy. Once she decided I was committed, she became extremely supportive and encouraging.

I still have never met her in person, but her encouraging talk by phone and her trust in me kept me going.

Once, I was stuck with three abandoned but friendly cats. I could find only kill-shelters, where cats are kept for a few weeks, then put down if no one adopts them in time. Cat-loving friends in Chicago agreed to take the three and promised to find them good homes. We shared the cost of shipping two by cargo flight. The third I carried with me aboard a plane to Chicago. We found great homes for all three and felt great about it. Nurturing these cats, we nurtured one another.

Cat rescue is tough work and invisible to many as they go about their lives. I like knowing there are women working hard, while the city sleeps, for the betterment of the community and for the cats.

FEMINIST TRASH TALK: WHY I PICK UP YOUR LITTER

Kimiko Akita

When I moved to Florida a few years ago, I was heartened to find wild birds, fish, and other creatures living in my neighborhood. I was also saddened to find trash dumped along roads and into canals, lakes, and streams. It pained me to see the polluting of these creatures' habitat—the human habitat, too. Trash and litter that clog creeks and pollute ponds may eventually get swept out to sea. I started to pick up trash: beer bottles, dirty diapers, paper and plastic cups, aluminum cans, the occasional soiled mattress, food-encrusted Tupperware, the broken iPod, the used condom. It is as if trashy people believe that, once discarded, all garbage instantly biodegrades, or at least that someone else will pick up after them. They do not seem to think of consequences of littering, of tossing garbage, of trashing their planet.

When picking up trash, I have plenty of time to think while trying to ignore horn blasts from passing drivers, some of whom evidently think they're supposed to toss their empty bottles, cups, and cans directly at me. As I wonder why humans wantonly pollute their habitat, my mind wanders. I think, for example, about cultural differences between the United States and my native Japan. Generally, Americans and Japanese think differently about nature, dirtiness, public spaces, and the environment.

I have observed that Americans tend to alienate themselves from nature, rarely choose to encounter it, and prefer instead to attempt to control it. Most Japanese, by contrast, integrate nature into everyday life. A central example of this contrast is in the way we treat litter. Picking up trash or cleaning up public space voluntarily is a typical sociocultural practice in Japan; in the United States, however, to clean up someone else's mess is a dirty job most eschew because it connotes social inferiority and is publicly embarrassing and demeaning to self-conscious citizens. When I ask my college students about litter on campus —discarded newspapers, plastic cups, and other detritus of our throwaway culture—they tell me that they think little about littering because other people are paid to clean up after them and that it is uncool to be seen picking up trash.

In Japan, cleanliness is an extremely important cultural value, partly out of necessity because of crowded conditions and limited space on the island. Tokyo, for all its problems, could be worse, even unlivable. Most Japanese, however, devote time each day to cleaning. From kindergarten through high school, students clean their classrooms, rest rooms, and schoolyards after the last class each day. This instills in them the value of cleanliness, makes students feel more connected to and respectful of their school, and helps them appreciate that cleaning can be difficult and dirty work. Community residents get together usually once a week to clean their neighborhood and public parks. In Japan, December 31 is spent cleaning before welcoming the new year.

The cultural differences may derive in part from ideology, religious beliefs, history—and gender. In Japan, physical cleanliness signifies inner cleanliness such as one's mind, mental purity, sincerity, and honesty. According to the ancient Shinto beliefs, the indigenous animistic religion (the feminized and matriarchal shrine Shintō, not the militarized and masculinized state Shintō of the twentieth century) that lingers in most minds and lifestyles in Japan, anything that blocks the flow of air, water, or energy is considered dirty and must be removed. Shintoism worships spirits believed to be present in nature and treats nature with utmost care since we are creatures of nature and because, eventually, we return to it.

And, ancient Shintō treats women as sacred. All Japanese once believed women to possess divine and purifying power, and women often conducted religious rituals. Coincidentally, the Shintō virtue of ablution, cleanliness, and purity was reinforced through Buddhist rituals such as the washing of a corpse and symbolically eliminating from it all defilement. For me, picking up trash is a personal act that grants me private moments during which to cleanse my mind; but it is also an other-directed act in which I clean for others and clean up nature. It connects me closely with the rest of the world.

Cleaning may be perceived as domestic work that radical feminists would eschew. Mass-mediated images present cleaning as the purview of the socioeconomically lower classes, for undereducated people such as the housewife, the cleaning lady, or even prisoners in day-glow orange vests. When a man, alone, picks up trash along a road, people might look at him suspiciously. When I do pick up trash, people regard me without too much suspicion. Still, they do not know quite what to make of me; I think they would not suspect I have a Ph.D. Occasionally, passersby ask me, "I see you picking trash around here often. Why do you do it?" I always reply: "I am from Japan, so I am used to picking up trash. I do it because I care about the environment and I care about the fish, the birds, and children of future generations."

Perhaps I am fortunate that because of my gender I can pick up trash publicly without arousing suspicion. Most modern patriarchal societies (and even those that are nearing gender equality) expect adult women to take care of children (and even parents), keep a house, and create a safe environment for family. Women take pride in these activities. I do. A woman who willfully chooses to engage in such daily chores is a feminist. I pick up trash daily along a stretch of road and in parking lots where I live, work, and shop because I care for Mother Nature, Mother Earth: for all living things now and yet to come. Not because I consider myself inferior, but rather because for me as a feminist, it is how I nurture, protect, and sacrifice myself to help sustain the world in which I live and thrive as a global citizen. It is a courageous act, a maternal act—a reproductive act. A purely feminist act.

COMMUNITY GARDENING WITH REFUGEES

Jenney Stringer

In the spring of 2007, as a student at a small liberal arts college minutes from downtown Utica, New York, I was told by a professor who knew of my recently discovered passion for community gardening that a woman I will call Stephanie (her name has been changed to protect her privacy) and I could be of some help to one another. I took heed of the advice and soon thereafter met with Stephanie in the public housing complex which she and many other refugees from European and African descent call home. Within minutes of our meeting, Stephanie explained the ins and outs of a problem her neighborhood was struggling with for quite some time. For the past several years, many refugees living in the housing complex in which Stephanie lived were infamous for squeezing elegant and well-kept gardens into the small green space in front of their apartment buildings. Yet, because of housing restrictions, the upcoming spring was to be the year during which these families were to abandon their gardens and watch as their plants were mowed over and only the grass was planted in its place. As she explained it "we will not be happy if we have no land. Gardening is a piece of who we are." At this time, I could not possibly understand the depth and true significance of the problem Stephanie was speaking to, but as she looked to me to help her find a solution, I was compelled. As we sat and discussed the possibility of creating a community space for gardening, there began a partnership that has since inspired a community wide effort and culminated last spring with the construction of a community garden for more than 34 refugee families.

Due to her proximity to the nuclear reactant explosion at Chernobyl in 1986 and the ensuing radiation of the soil, air, and water, at 72 years of age Stephanie became a refugee and left her home country of Belarus to resettle in the United States. Like many other refugees who resettled in the United States, farming has always been an integral part of Stephanie's cultural identity. Unlike many other aspects of her culture which have not transferred, gardening is a pastime rich with tradition that can be preserved in the United States. Accordingly, gardening is an activity that provides her and her community with a great sense of accomplishment which has become increasingly important recently because most of her neighbors are elderly men and women who are no longer able to hold paying jobs outside the home.

Despite her age, Stephanie is a steadfast community organizer and works diligently to represent the needs of Russian speaking refugees in both public and private spheres through her work as a medical interpreter, as the community liaison between her community and local government offices, and as an active member in her religious community. With Stephanie, or the mayor as some now call her, at forefront of the community garden effort, families were eager to get involved with the community garden project. As I helped manage the project and, with the help of professors and advisors at my college, secured the funds for the construction of the garden through various grants and donations, the garden participants kept the project alive through regular community meetings. Through the use of as many as three interpreters for the Russian, Bosnian, and Somali speaking participants, the garden members learned how to work together, despite the obvious cultural and linguistic barriers. The enthusiasm and commitment to the success of the project was palatable, as gardeners developed lasting working relationships with each other and people outside of the apartment complex got involved.

In August, we entered the construction phase of the garden project. Through a joint effort by garden participants and their families and the surrounding community, within one week, we transformed an empty lot of grass in the center of the apartment complex to a place where families of different backgrounds with different agricultural traditions and experiences could garden side-by-side. More than a hundred volunteers from the surrounding community came to construct 34 individual plots for families of Bosnian, Russian, Ukrainian, and Somali decent. A garden fence with locks and keys was also installed as well as a water tank and garden benches.

The community garden in Utica, in which I was privileged to be a part, serves as a unique and valuable way for refugees or immigrants who moved from a rural homeland to a new city to maintain their own culture and connect with one another in meaningful ways. As the garden residents prepare for their second growing season, I am confident that the community garden will continue to serve as a place in which refugees are able to express their culture, their heritage, and their creativity as they help build a new future for their families in America. The garden has had a profound impact in a variety of ways. Not only does it enable more food security, but it also benefits the participants on personal and community levels, including reduced isolation for older gardeners; relationship and connection across cultures and ages; improved physical and mental health; reduced money spent on groceries for families; and an increase in economic activity when gardeners sell their surplus vegetables at local farmers' markets.

The U.S. government admits refugees escaping violence, religious and ethnic persecution from countries around the world. My community, like many of yours, has in recent years received an influx of refugees from countries such as the former Soviet Union, Bosnia, Somalia, the Sudan, Iraq, Burma, and Iraq. As refugees adjust to a new life in cities in the United States of America, many find it difficult to become integrated members of their new community. Beyond the most obvious linguistic and cultural differences, many refugees have come to the United States without family members and are thus simultaneously confronting the isolating nature of refugee status in America and yearning for the sense of belonging and companionship they felt in their homeland. Women are particularly challenged by the refugee resettlement process in the sense that they are often less likely to find stable employment, less educated than their male counterparts, and because of culturally specific notions of gender, limited to undervalued household work such as childbearing and rearing.

Refugees often face a great number of challenges upon resettling in the United States and it is our responsibility to first become conscious of these challenges and furthermore, create an environment that welcomes, empowers, and supports refugees' self-expression. The community garden in Utica has had a profound impact on both personal and community levels and thus I encourage you to consider supporting urban gardens initiatives in your local community.

Want to know what you can you do in your community to help support your new neighbors? Contact your local refugee center.

BETTER EARTH GIRLS

Anya Finley and Laura Finley

One evening when we were at the pool, Anya asked, "Mom, why don't you like the Bratz dolls?" I said I don't even like the name—it glorifies bad, bratty, behavior as if it is something cute. She suggested we should create a line of dolls that could teach peace instead. What a totally butt-kicking idea! So we got cooking on it, and came up with the BE girls. Below is a brief description of our plan that, with hope, will someday hit the market!

The BE Girls (Better Earth Girls) is a line of dolls intended to provide young girls ages 4–8 with inspiration and positive modeling for a better earth. The vision is to counteract the many negative images young girls see that emphasize violence, self-destructive behavior, negativity, and apathy. There will be 26 dolls—one for each letter of the alphabet—who demonstrate characteristics of peace, social justice, and environmental consciousness. Sample doll names, which reflect the world's many cultures, are described below.

The dolls would be made using fair trade labor and of the most environmentally friendly materials possible. Each doll would be dressed in an outfit that reflects her name—for example, Earth Emily might wear a shirt with a globe on it, a batik or tie dye skirt, and some sandals. Additionally, each doll would be packaged in a reusable backpack made of environmentally friendly materials.

Each doll would also come with a story detailing how the doll got her name. The stories will all be written in fun, rhyming fashion and will be appropriate for girls ages 4–8. The books will feature bright, colorful pictures with girls making a difference in their world. Similar book ideas are those coauthored by Jamie Lee Curtis and Laura Cornell (see www.jamieleecurtisbooks.com). Each book will end with a list of ideas for how girls can be more like their dolls, i.e., tips for being more like "Earth Emily."

SAMPLE DOLLS:

- Animal-Loving Anya
- Brainy Bela
- Creative Carolina
- Daring Denise
- Earth Emily
- Freedom Fran
- Generous Geneva
- Hopeful Hannah
- Ingenious Isabella
- Joyful Julianna
- Kind Katarina
- Loyal Lea
- Musical Maria
- Nice Nora
- Optimistic Olivia
- Peaceful Petra
- Sensitive Sophie
- Unique Uma
- Exciting Xo

EARTH EMILY

Emily and her mom were on the beach
Skipping and holding hands
When they looked down and were shocked to see
Something horrible in the sand

There were bottles, bags, and papers
Scattered everywhere
Emily threw her hands up,
"Doesn't anybody care?

These things will kill the fish,
They can make the seagulls die."
Her mom said, "Let's clean it up"
And Emily said, "I'll try."

So they got two bags from their car
One for recycling, one for trash
And they set about cleaning the beach
More came with each wave's crash.

So many people dumped their stuff
While they boated and jet-skied
That Emily and her mother
Had a very big job indeed.

But they worked and worked all day long
Until the sun went down
And when they gave it one last look
They saw no more trash around.

Emily and her mom felt good
About the difference they had made
But Emily said as they walked home
"There's more to do, I'm afraid.

We need to keep the earth clean,
But I've only got two hands.
We need the entire community
To pick up trash—on beaches and on land."

Right then and there she decided
She would spread the word around
So everyone in the town would help,
Until there was no more trash to be found.

She started talking and soon people joined her
In cleaning up their mess
They'd bring recycling bags when they walked around
And trash bags for the rest.

And better yet they decided
They could simply make less waste
Using less is better for the environment
And for the entire human race.

"One kid can make a difference!"
Emily told everyone she'd see
"And it feels really good
To be known as Earth Emily!"

How Can You Be More Like Earth Emily?

- Get a trash bag, a recycling bag, and some gloves and pick up wherever you go! Have your friends join you!
- Adopt a park or area in your town, and commit to keeping it clean. Take turns, if you need to!
- Participate in a beach cleanup or some other organized cleanup effort.
- Next time you want to make some cool art, do it out of recyclables! Or reuse something you already made to make a new, cool project!
- Make sure your school recycles. If they don't, try to get them to do it!
- Commit to making less trash! See if you and your family can put out fewer bags of trash next month . . . and the month after . . . and after that!!

ANIMAL-LOVING ANYA

Anya was walking home from the library
Excited to read her new book
When she heard a strange noise in the woods
And decided to take a look

She could hardly believe her eyes
What she saw made her feel so sad
A little puppy was whimpering awfully
His front paw hurt very bad

So Anya got a little bit closer
To see what had hurt the pup
She saw he had stepped on a rusty old wire
And gotten all tangled up

Anya rubbed the pup's head and said
In her most soothing tone
"I'm going to help you, little cutie,
Let me take you to my home

In her arms Anya carried
The little puppy all the way there
She showed her mom what was wrong
And said "I don't think that it's fair.

Someone left that rusty wire out
Instead of putting it in their trash can
No living thing deserves to be treated this way
Not animal, children, woman or man."

Anya and her mom called the Humane Society
And their staff members came right out
They told Anya what a great thing she did
"You're a hero, without a doubt.

Anya you just showed us
How animals should be treated.
Please keep helping animals,
Do not ever get defeated.

One kid can make a difference,
Can help animals be healthy.
It doesn't take a lot of work
And you don't have to be wealthy."

Anya's parents were very proud
Of their animal-loving girl.
"I'm animal-loving Anya," she cried
"And I'm ready to help the world!"

Chapter Ten

Creating a World We Love: Feminist Arts-Based Activism

Women today are increasingly using the arts to make social change. Since the 1960s, feminists have encouraged changes in the way women are portrayed on television, as they recognize the power and influence these images have.[1] Although by no means perfect, the mass media provides more positive role models for girls than ever before. This is particularly true of children's television, where characters like Dora the Explorer are popular with both girls and boys. Still, the female characters are more likely to show affection and boy characters still tend to be more aggressive. In his book *Alpha Girls*, Dan Kindlon cited movies with female stars like Angelina Jolie as Lara Croft or Lucy Lawless as Xena as examples of what feminists want to see in female characters—strong, powerful, and independent. Yet still these characters are powerful in a way that is sexualized, "a Hollywood version of the male sexual fantasy of the dominatrix."[2] This was true of earlier women characters as well. The original Wonder Woman was created by William Moulton Marston, a Harvard-trained psychologist who wanted to create a positive model for girls during World War II. Yet clearly the outfit Linda Carter wore as Wonder Woman—the skimpy, tight, spangly red and blue number—was intended at least in part to titillate.

Third-wave feminists create their own media like Web sites, blogs, zines, and radio shows. They form all-female bands that sing about women's issues, and host spoken-word contests. For instance, the Riot Grrl bands and the entire grrl culture of the 1990s took back the often-derogatory term "girl" and added the growling "rr" to emphasize women's strength and power. Feminists—both men and women—have long been concerned about the stereotypical images of women in pop culture and are taking huge steps to create broader awareness and to demand change.[3]

Rap music is often denounced for its sexism, and rightly so. But it has also been a vehicle for change. Feminist hip hop scholar Joan Morgan explained, "Any feminism that fails to acknowledge that black folks in

America are living and trying to love in a war zone is useless to our struggle against sexism. Though it's often portrayed as part of the problem, rap music is essential to that struggle because it takes us straight to the battlefield."[4]

Advertisements have long portrayed women in stereotypical ways. Jean Kilbourne has written and created documentaries about the ways advertisers depict women as nothing more than objects. Kilbourne explained that advertisements present women as "the other"—they dehumanize them. When a group has been dehumanized, it becomes far easier for others to take advantage of them and to victimize them. The United States has never censored this type of advertisements, but Canada has. The Canadian public prompted their government to implement Gender Portrayal Guidelines, which help prevent offensive depictions of women in advertising. New types of advertising campaigns are being released to counteract some of the unrealistic depictions of women. In 2005, Nike introduced a campaign presenting women who had "big butts, thunder thighs, and tomboy knees." Commentary focused on the fact that they liked their bodies. Feminists generally reacted positively, although some argued these were still not "thunder thighs." Rather, Nike was simply selling a different fantasy—that of the super fit, muscular athlete. Advertisers are increasingly using the discourse of empowerment to promote products to women, something that has been called "power feminism." This incorporation of feminist concepts is viewed by some as progress and by others as cooptation.

Groups like the Guerilla Girls have drawn attention to the denigration of women through other forms of art, asking "When sexism & racism are no longer fashionable, what will your art collection be worth?"

Women have also taken the power back from the fashion industry in some ways. When Laurel Thatcher-Ulrich coined the phrase, "Well-behaved women seldom make history" in 1976, she had no idea it would become a slogan for so many and in such diverse ways. She initially used the phrase in a scholarly article about Puritan funeral sermons. It was picked up and slightly altered, to read "Well-behaved women rarely make history," by journalist Kay Mills, who used it in 1995 in her informal history of American women, *From Pocahontas to Power Suits*. In 1996, Thatcher-Ulrich authorized Jill Portugal to use the quote on a t-shirt (in exchange for a free shirt). Portugal's shirt soon became a best seller and helped her launch her company, One Angry Girl Designs, which fights against rape, sexual harassment, pornography, and what she describes as "fascist beauty standards."[5] The quote has also been adopted by Girl Press, which publishes "slightly dangerous books for mavericks," including *Cool Women: The Thinking Girls' Guide to the Hippest Women in History.*[6]

Thatcher-Ulrich explained why the quote became so popular:

So how does a woman make history? Obviously, Marie Curie didn't win two Nobel Prizes by throwing tantrums in the lab. True, after her husband's death French tabloids pilloried her for having an affair with a married collaborator. But she isn't remembered today because she was "bad" but because she was "very, very good" at what she did. So why doesn't high achievement in science qualify a woman as well-behaved? Could it be because some people still assume women aren't supposed to stand out in a crowd? The "well-behaved women" quote works because it plays into long-standing stereotypes about the invisibility and the innate decorum of the female sex.[7]

The entries in this chapter demonstrate the many ways feminists use the arts. From painting to film, music to live events, activists have channeled the power of popular culture and the arts to draw attention to gender inequalities.

CREATING A PLANET

Emily Reynolds Stringer

In small villages around the world are people with big hearts yearning to be heard. I see these people in my dreams and my wish is for a world where they all can have a voice. I believe the world is a place where all people really want to be known, touched, and loved. That no matter what our differences may be that within our souls we all want to connect. Within the depths of my soul I believe we all wish for a ride on a peace train, yet we are continuously stopped by the roadblocks to get us there. The arts are one way to connect to something outside of our differences and unify a collective vision of a peaceful planet.

It is within this vision of a peaceful world that the creating a planet art show began. The foundation of the project is the idea that people themselves could collectively create their own "planet" where the arts are the spoken voice that all can be heard and no one is left behind. The idea is that small groups of people have a large blank canvas and a theme such as peace, friendship, love or unity, and so on and from there they dive in and create a collective piece of art. From here the art is collected and showcased for others to enjoy and become inspired.

When I first had a vision to connect people around the globe through art it scared me to tears. I thought how can I, a 24-year-old social work grad student, be a source for others to have peace—isn't that someone else's job? I saw this vision of people connecting through art, being inspired through color, and unifying on a deeper level through conversations, and chills ran down my spine at the thought of this actually happening in our world. It was in the moment that there was urgency for me to enroll other people to create art in small groups. I didn't have any resources or any idea how I was going to do it but I followed my husband's advice and jumped into the abyss.

I began by bringing a large canvas and some old paint to a friend's house with the idea for everyone at the party to paint and create the images of "friendship" and what it meant to them. It was amazing! A few people dove right in and drew peace signs, hands holding mother earth, hearts, and other symbols. Then something amazing happened; people began to get out of their heads and really capture what was within their souls. People painted colors, unique shapes, lines, shades of greens and blues, and the painting took on a new life form. It was unique and only recognizable to everyone at the party as to what it meant, but as a work of art it was beautiful because it spoke of what people were feeling and yearning for. It was from that point on that I had a stock of blank canvases in my car as well as a stash of crusty paintbrushes, paper plates, plastic cups, and various unique colors of paint.

The idea traveled from my car to the foster care homes I was interning at. I was working with young girls ages 13–18. I asked them to think about peace and what it meant to them. The young girls were a bit hesitant at first, some of them even saying, "peace, what is that?" "Why would I want to draw that, I've never seen peace?" In the midst of my almost broken heart at these words, I encouraged them to imagine what peace might be. They did and began to slowly paint things such as a dollar sign, a flag, and a hand, and then I encouraged them to step out of their heads and into their hearts. The transformation took place again! Gradually they began to get the hang of it and draw colors, unique symbols, lines, and so on. It was remarkable and at the end of the day they were hugging me and thanking me for being in their life. It was amazing to see such openness develop. I eagerly began sharing the idea of creating a collection of themed paintings with my fellow social work students and other people I knew who were working with underserved populations around the globe. From these conversations grew an art exhibit that showcased the artwork, conversations, connections, and peace that would not have happened had I not had the courage to put my vision out into the world.

The art show Creating a Planet showcased pieces of collective community art canvases. Underserved members of communities around the globe created the artwork that was inspired through the vision of peace. The artwork came to life in places such as homeless shelters, woman's shelters, foster care homes, schools in impoverished parts of Guatemala, people oppressed communities in Thailand, and in my own friends and families homes. These paintings represent that vision of peace we all yearn for. Please enjoy these few samples and hopefully you are left to inspire your own communities with a blank canvas.

Create Your Own Community Canvas

MATERIALS

Canvas (Any size, preferably large enough for each member of your group to have a place, you can also use: paper bags taped together, blank paper, walls or streets (with permission)—get creative!!!)

Paints, markers, crayons, or any form of color

People, any and all types

A theme, peace, friendship, unity, family, all coming from a
vision of a peaceful planet from your heart

Peace Meditation for Those Who Need Some Inspiration

If you close your eyes and imagine a peaceful world what does it
look like?

Imagine a place where the soft sun is shining on your face.
Your eyes are closed and your face is warm; maybe you are at
the ocean or on a mountain top, or in the midst of people who
enthuse you most. The air is warm and you hear the sounds of
blissful music tickling your ear. People are expressing themselves
in this world through music, dance, and written words, and art is
the spoken language amusing your tongue. People are all bonded
through what makes their spirits sing, and it is shared at the dinner
table. Children are encouraged to be different and express their
imaginations as the main lesson within their school days. You hear
the sound of laughter filling the air as if it were a constant song
playing in the streets. The trees, plants, and grass grow as green
as sparkling emeralds and water is so pure it can be drunk from
any trickling streams. This world is a vision of where our hearts really ache to be, it is where are spirits yearn to be set free, it is
where each of us dream to live. It is a planet that we collectively
choose to create in each and every action that you do.

Now open your eyes and discuss, collaborate, and create
this vision on your blank canvas. If you hear the voice of doubt
come over you like, "I'm not an artist or I can't do this," hear it,
let it go, and know within your heart that you really do have the
power to create.

I PREMIERED MY FIRST FILM IN AN INACCESSIBLE
CINEMA: CHANGING THE SOCIAL LANDSCAPE THROUGH
DISABILITY FEMINIST ACTIVISM AND FILM

Katie Ellis

In high school, my English teacher introduced me to feminism—I
felt strong, empowered, and relevant. Then, when I was 18 I had
a massive stroke and all I wanted to do was fit in. Although I lived
in the able world, I was constantly reminded that I was *other*
when people stared at my foot at the shops and when people I
just met asked my friends why I limped. But I didn't really see

my experiences as having any sort of feminist potential although I now believe disability can enrich feminist activism, as both seek equality through recognition of difference.

I went back to university the next year to study film and media and in my final unit I stood up at the beginning of the semester and pitched a film about my having had a stroke a few years before. Most of my class mates had no idea, I had successfully passed. My class voted to make this film and I began my process of "coming out" by talking about what I had experienced rather than silencing myself. My "passing" had deprived people of experiencing the diversity of society, although it took me a while to embrace my illness and disability as a feminist issue and to realize illness autobiography and honor in disease are possible because of feminists taking pride in stigmatized identities.

During my research I read about someone with a similar impairment to my own who started wearing their leg brace again, even though they hadn't worn it for years, for "political reasons." The politics: a social model of disability. I didn't understand; my whole identity was based on refusing to identify as disabled, believing empowerment lied in trying to fit back into non-disabled society as best I could. I even premiered the film about my disability in a cinema accessible only by a staircase, effectively preventing anyone in a wheelchair (as I had been fairly recently) from attending. But after a while this model started to resonate with me.

Once I took this new approach, I began noticing socially disabling aspects of life everywhere, from the things people said to and about me to the practical aspects of undertaking a research degree (I'd just enrolled in a disability studies Ph.D.). I joined the student association and approached university administration on several occasions to answer for what were disabling situations.

- Disability studies books being on the top shelf of the library (I never received a response although they were moved two years after I enquired.)
- People with disability/medical conditions were not covered under the university's universal insurance policy for overseas research travel (we were too expensive!)
- Delivery trucks parking in the disabled parking bays (They were too big for the loading zone.)

While I didn't receive an adequate response to any of these situations, by speaking up I was changing the social landscape in the way disability is understood. I was drawing on a history of

feminist activism that sought to establish that it was social structures that needed to change rather than the individual.

My activism eventually led me to a community project for
people with disability interested in making films. Although the
project was basically recreation, not advocacy, recreation often
turned to advocacy as we were a subjugated group. I encouraged the students to use self-reflection as the basis for their
storytelling and asked them to think about:

- If they had thought of something to say after a confrontation
  but it was too late?
- What frustrated them about everyday life?
- Things everyone accepts as normal but really aren't?
- Their different perspectives on life as a result of having a
  disability

Disability and feminist activism intersect as both strive to
change the social landscape. This intersection was most clear in
two films conceived by men. These films highlighted that gender
is an oppressive social construct for men as well.

One male student wanted to shake up cultural categories by
making a film about ANGER. He wanted non-disabled people to
see just how hard they were making life for disabled people "like
us." The basic premise was that people treat people with disabil-
ities terribly and then just walk away, while the person with disability may feel bad about it for weeks. The film did all those
things "positive" representations of disability, with their smiling
token cripples, don't do. It was in black and white, he spoke
directly to the camera, swore, and he got angry. Anger is rarely
seen in films which address disability. Normally people with dis-
abilities are constructed as helpless things who deserve pity, or
"super cripples" fighting to overcome insurmountable odds.
Behind these constructions is the mind-set that it is horrible to
be disabled and disabled people can, if they try hard enough,
look almost "normal."

This critique of the representational system so ubiquitous in our
image driven society enriches feminist inquiry because, like feminist activism, it changes the social landscape. This participant tried
to encourage the others to embrace disability activism like he had
by interviewing them in the hope that he'd be able to put a film
together about their anger. Unfortunately he found that many of
his colleagues would not identify as disabled and so as a group
we discovered there is no essential experience of disability.

Another film produced as a result of the project was a profound experimental documentary about speech, memory, and disability in which an emerging filmmaker in his early 20s put the focus on society by making the audience think about how they would react if confronted by him:

> It's hard to speak with others so I'm left out of conversations all the time. So everyone speaks for me and I find that really annoying [. . .] I can talk for myself, just hear me sometime and don't be so obnoxious.

In order for social change to occur we need a shift in the way we think about disability. These films re-imagine disability from the perspective of people with disability, and they comment on disabling society, lived experiences of disability, and the importance of acknowledging the effect of impairments. They change the social landscape and promote equality. An inclusion of disability into feminist activism also allows a space for men to articulate their experiences of social oppression. Like radical feminist filmmaking, these films expose the workings of oppression, examine subject formation, and offer a counter-narrative.

A note on sources: The argument that feminist activism is "changing the social landscape" and that disability has the potential to expand feminist activism is derived from the work of Rosemary Garland Thompson, in particular her chapter in *Gendering Disability* (2004). I have also been greatly influenced by Arthur Frank's work on illness narratives, autobiography and social change available online http:/www.ucalgary.ca/~frank/Dauto.html.

Final Tip for Making Films about Disability or Illness by Reflecting on Your Own Life

Stories of triumph over adversary aren't the only way to represent disability but they may help you to come to terms with the world of "health" and your position in it—try to include aspects of chaos and anger to destabilize cultural assumptions of body stability, illness, and disability.

DRAG IT OUT

Tabatha Mudra

Drag it Out is a multicultural grassroots project that creates a fun, free, self-expressed environment that supports and educates the community. Through workshops, fundraising, and mentoring, DIO aims to transform the ideas of gender stereotypes.

The workshops are designed to mentor the volunteers into full self-expression. DIO creates fundraising opportunities to benefit local charities supporting "the kids, the queers, and the animals!" Raising awareness and educating through entertainment.

What we are currently doing in Phase 2 of DIO is conducting weekly workshops for three classes, training in the art of "drag." By getting the word out on the web and via word of mouth we have over 15 attendees and 4 coaches.

Our successes range from the surprisingly diverse public attendance at our FUNdraising shows, to the adrenaline gifted at the time of performance for those with stage fright that cannot wait to get back on stage to drag it out again.

Our challenges have been anywhere from publicity on a commercial level to public harassments or hate crimes. There is a slight resistance to such stigmatic provocation. We are attempting to eradicate that stigma.

The impacts to date have been remarkable. I am so excited to read and share with the team what we cause in the world by participating in Drag it Out. By benefitting Animal Aid we helped fund a much needed operation for a furry canine friend in the shelter. We provided funds for such organizations as Safe Schools South Florida, which helps create a safe space for gay, lesbian, bisexual, transgender, and questioning youth to have a voice.

How does DIO and feminist activism relate? I am female and proud to be. I believe that supporting women and men in gender exploration provides a space to explore both sides of our DNA, get comfortable, and walk away with something larger than thought possible. Supporting our communities is wonderful, and creating one is empowering. The testimonials are a sure way of measuring the results, one below:

> For so long, I have defined myself through my femininity; my cat-like actions and gestures, my makeup, heels, and all things "girly." I felt that was the only way I would get attention or love. When I joined Drag It Out, I was nervous, felt as if I would look ugly and unattractive. How crazy that my idea of

ugly was looking like a man! I dealt with so many internal dia-
logues of insecurity while I was in drag that ultimately it led
me to let it all go, have fun, and embrace my masculine side.
I loved it! It gave me confidence, freedom, and a sense of
empowerment I had never felt. This was the best exercise of
the self, a view into your ideas of gender, beauty and societal
norms. I was to be free. My best tips for activating modern
feminist movement: Listen to your guide and continue full
speed ahead, in the face of all disagreement and resistance
à persevere! Continue in the process of making HER story.

"IF I CAN'T DANCE I DON'T WANT TO BE PART OF YOUR REVOLUTION"

Laura Finley

Sometimes, we get the chance to enjoy the arts when we least
expect it. That is how I met, and came to be a huge fan of, Pat
Humphries and Sandy Opatow, also known as Emma's Revolution. I was attending the American Society of Criminology annual
meeting in Toronto in fall 2005, enjoying learning at the sessions,
presenting myself, and hanging out with old friends and mentors
from graduate school. We were discussing what we should do
one of the evenings when a friend told us there was a free concert
that night. Free of course always sits well, and when he mentioned the bonus beverages we were definitely in!

I had never heard of Emma's Revolution prior, but they had
quite a following. Before joining with Sandy, Pat Humphries had
a very successful solo career. I did not know what I was in for,
but I found myself immediately engaged and excited. Emma's
Revolution performs songs to inform and inspire, amuse and provoke. I particularly enjoyed their song "Vote," a take on Donald
Trump's expression "You're Fired!" applied to the Bush
administration. The crowd screamed out all the names of people
who we felt had no place leading our country, and you could feel
the energy in the room. More than just their thoughtful lyrics and
their beautiful voices and instrumentality, Pat and Sandy use their
concerts to educate the crowd about social and political issues.
They tell the stories behind their music, whether they be sad, like
the story of Pat visiting Kent State to see her sisters and her
shock at the national guard shootings, or they be comical, like
Sandy's rendition of "Unsustainable" and the need to take action

to protect the environment. They have been called "bold, pro-found, moving, transformative, and hilarious."

I make it to whatever Emma's Revolution concerts are in my area (and fortunately, they come to town at least once a year), and Pat and Sandy have become friends. I even hosted a benefit concert for Women in Distress, the local domestic violence agency. They know my husband and daughter, and despite meeting people all across the world, Pat and Sandy always remember their names.

The duo has happily performed at a number of different types of venues across the globe. They have performed at universities, churches, and religious groups of all kinds, festivals, conferences (like the one I attended), and the inaugural peace ball in January 2009. They have traveled to the Middle East, Asia, and elsewhere to spread the word and help empower women. Pat's "Keep On Moving Forward" opened the NGO Forum at the United Nation's Fourth World Conference on Women in Beijing and has been called the conference's unofficial anthem. Their song "If I Give Your Name," about undocumented workers who died in the September 11 terrorist attacks but who receive no recognition due to their status, won the Grand Prize in the John Lennon Songwriting Contest. In addition to their music, they made Pat's song "Peace, Salaam, Shalom" into a t-shirt with the words translated into Arabic and Hebrew. My daughter Anya had her first shirt when she was two, and now has gone through two others as she grew. The song has been called "the anthem of the anti-war movement."

For more information, to listen, or to see a schedule of concerts, see www.emmasrevolution.com.

EXPANDING THE ROLES FOR WOMEN

Lián Amaris

During the spring of 2007, as an assistant professor of drama, I participated in a process we in our department called "student reviews" where the faculty discussed the progress of majors and minors as they got closer to graduation and gave them an opportunity to make requests of the faculty. One of the most heard requests from female students was "more and better roles for women." As the only resident female director in the department, I immediately took notice; I responded by directing Ellen McLaughlin's adaptation of Euripides' *Trojan Women* during the following semester. The cast featured an ensemble of twelve women and two men playing the epic characters adapted from Euripides. While I was concerned that the roles might be impossibly epic (for example, Helen as the most beautiful in all of history), I believed that McLaughlin's adaptation would offer new feminist perspectives on the complex relations between women in crisis.

McLaughlin suggested that Euripides' *Trojan Women* " ... is perhaps the greatest antiwar play ever written, certainly one of the oldest, and contains some of the most extraordinary roles for women in theatrical literature ... the Trojan War owes its mythic status as the quintessentially tragic war to the staggering waste it represents for both sides of the conflict." McLaughlin's text updated Euripides' language and the scenarios presented between the Trojan women who were left on the beach to be taken as slaves by the Greeks. Additionally, McLaughlin's complex characterizations of Helen (sex-object/sex-slave), Hecuba (powerful queen), and Andromache (mourning mother) presented very different kinds of women, and as I saw it, different embodiments of feminism. I also saw the potential for the play to act as an opportunity for race-blind casting and as an ostensible war protest. Additionally, I had the pleasure of working with a female costume designer and a female lighting and scenic designer who both assisted my vision as a feminist director.

At the time, we in the United States were in a war where "victory" was an elusive concept used to motivate, placate, and terrorize, and it seemed that part of my responsibility as a peace-seeking feminist was to use my art as an opportunity to address the war. The play itself narrates the very specific experiences of women during and after war—especially highlighting a culture where men are the majority of fighters, and therefore the majority of casualties. The experiences described by these women after the Trojan War were complicated—filled with honoring sons and husbands, anger at being left behind, and fear at what the future would bring as the women were enslaved by the victors.

While the play beautifully articulated these themes, it was far more than just a play about such a war. Our version of *The Trojan Women* was about the rich lives of mothers, daughters, and lovers, seen through their own memories and their fears about the future. It was about monumental loss, enduring strength, and the profound wounds that only women can inflict on one another. McLaughlin had written complex women characters who were always both victim and perpetrator, both saint and sinner, embodying different aspects of women, but also different feminisms. With the help of McLaughlin's adaptation, part of my feminist project was for the ensemble not only to perform the "legendary" (or the impossibly epic as I addressed earlier) but to also perform the "humanness" of these women—with all its inconsistencies, hypocrisies, failings, and vulnerabilities.

Because feminism addresses the intersections of gender, race, and class, my choice to cast a black woman as Queen Hecuba and a white woman as her daughter Cassandra were also strategic. The interracial family spoke to a more contemporary arrangement of family, and casting a black woman as the Queen of Troy made a very strong statement to a campus that had been struggling with issues of diversity among the student body. As the actress playing Hecuba moved across the stage, embodying power, pride, strength, and care for the other women on stage, the color of her skin was as much of a statement as the words she spoke.

Because of the content of the original play, the thoughtful adaptation by a feminist author, the casting choices and the holistic feminist vision I worked to produce, our performance of *The Trojan Women* put a compelling face on feminism. In many ways, the title brought an audience who wouldn't otherwise be interested in feminism—and packaged feminism and feminist perspectives in a live event. By viewing a theater piece, audience members are given access to actual people embodying concepts they may otherwise only read about (or as is often the case with feminist perspectives, they might be completely avoided). The show was a great success, as it was an entirely sold-out run.

After the performance, I spoke with many of the actresses in the show, and they were grateful for the opportunity to perform strong, complicated, compelling female roles under the direction of a woman, with a female design team. Additionally, many audience members were moved by the complexities of the characters that they saw on stage, and felt that the performance gave them new insight into the experiences of women in war.

As is the nature of the theater, both performing the roles and seeing the roles embodied perpetuates the vision of the performance—in this case the feminist vision. While our production had a reasonable budget, live theater can utilize very little (in terms of props, costumes, or design) to produce—but can inform new perspectives in engaging ways unlike any other medium.

OUTLET: PLUGGING YOUNG WOMEN INTO THE ARTS!

Laura Finley

Outlet is the brainchild of De Palazzo, a Ft. Lauderdale-based educator, trainer, humanitarian, activist, and kindred spirit. In 2008, she helped write a grant to the Aqua Foundation to sponsor a unique event targeted at young women and involving the arts. The grant was approved with some room for development, and De spread the word to get a diverse group of young women (and Laura Finley—not so young) involved in the planning process. The group is eclectic, but all committed to supporting young women through art and education. Outlet is what was birthed from that nine-month process.

Early on, the group met to brainstorm and settle on a vision and mission. Below is what we created:

Vision Statement

To inspire, empower, support and encourage young women of our LGBTQ (lesbian, gay, bisexual, transgender, queer and questioning) community through the arts and education, for and by women!

Mission Statement

The Mission of *OUTlet. Plugging Young Women into the Arts —A Conference for and by Young Lesbian, Bisexual, Transgender and Queer Women and our Allies!* is to unify as a community and encourage young women's personal growth by providing a safe space for artistic expression, education and networking that acknowledges our challenges and achievements. Through the stigma associated with the identity of being a young woman who does not conform to gender stereotypes, participants will elevate their consciousness, realize their full potential and interact as a growing support group for one another.

The event was held Saturday, April 18 at a gay-friendly location called Sunserve in Ft. Lauderdale. It was a tremendous success, with approximately 55 attendees benefitting from the 16 workshops and the keynote presentation by Dani Campbell of MTV's "Shot at Love." Eleven area agencies and philanthropists sponsored the event, and the group was able to provide $550 to area Gay Straight Alliances as seed money for projects they are planning in the upcoming year.

The ladies involved in planning all had unique perspectives on the event. Some of their comments in the week after include:

Natasha Abdin: "Outlet was an especially unique and challenging conference to organize, based on the fact that it was the first of its kind that catered to Straight, Lesbian, Gay, Bisexual, Transgendered, and Questioning Women in the CommUNITY.

The reason we decided to name the conference OUTlet was because we realized that all women need to have a way of escaping from the peer pressure or prejudice that they might experience in life, especially for those women who do not conform to the typical stereotype of 'what a women should be.'

Our goal was to create a supportive and education environment in which all women could freely express who they are as person without fear or being forced to portray a false identity.

We realized that young women especially suffer from lower self-esteem and lack of confidence in today's world and we wanted to change this! So we created a series of all day workshops to help empower women on their journey of life, particularly focused in the genre of art."

Tabatha Mudra: "Planning Outlet was nine months of bonding with some powerful female leaders that I otherwise wouldn't have had the opportunity to create such magic and miracles with! A learning experience that provided insight and gifts beyond expectation.

When the day finally came, there was such an electric buzz in the air, a collective creation of workshops that were so rewarding to witness and participate in. As I went around lightly photo-documenting each workshop, I became present to the beauty and relatedness that was naturally unfolding. The diversity and creativity of each breakout room was something to be OUT and PROUD about!

Thank you to all the generous women of OUTLET!

CONFESSIONS OF A FEMINIST CYBORG

Posted by Cyberthread [Rebecca Mushtare]

Early 1990s. Middle School. *Posted by Cyberthread.*
I'm totally a geek. I'm in the Young Astronauts club. Apparently my math and science skills have convinced my guidance counselor that I should be an engineer. She had the PTA send me to a summer engineering program (for girls) full of fractals, rockets, and wind tunnels.

Late 1990s. High School. *Posted by Cyberthread*.
This feels like an eternal struggle. I'm pushed into honors classes; I'm the only freshman and only one of two girls in the engineering class. I just want to take an art class. Where is my voice in these decisions?

Early 2000s. College. *Posted by Cyberthread*.
No engineering for me. I've met an incredible teacher. She is an art historian and director of the women's studies program (although I am not entirely sure I understand what that is). She has challenged me to be critical—to question and to seek answers. She has become my heroine.

Fall 2002. Graduate Application. *Posted by Cyberthread*.
I have graphic design credentials, but I don't want to advertise your product. I don't want to be at your service. I want to find purpose. I need more time.

August 2003. Graduate school. *Posted by Cyberthread*.
There are no tenured female faculty members here, just a sea of male faces. The undergraduate population matches. The grad students are different but few. This is a climate I have never experienced before.

September 2003. Graduate school. *Posted by Cyberthread*.
As a student in the computer art program I am learning how to sew (and to solder). Did you know the first computer was a loom? I've been discovering the writings of Sadie Plant, Donna Haraway, Sherry Turkle and Brenda Laurel . . . that hopefully will lead to others . . .

December 2003. Graduate school. *Posted by Cyberthread*.
The first exhibition of my combination of computer technology and quilting is official. The piece is called "Feminizing Technology." The viewer is confronted by pixilated images projected onto the handmade paper screens that were sewn into the quilt and three sewing machine pedals on the floor in front of it. Stepping on the first pedal the viewer sees images of cross-stitched letters reading "I am a quilt" come into focus on the small screens. The middle pedal plays the familiar sound of a sewing machine. The final pedal reveals video clips of the quilt being created on the larger screens.

May 2004. Graduate School. *Posted by Cyberthread*.
Not everyone "gets" my work. Apparently mixing quilting with the latest microcontroller isn't normal. "Sewing is antiquated and unimportant" is grumbled at me. I don't care. I'm frustrated. I'm tired.

Tears flow. Why do you think I am a radical?

Chapter Eleven

Feel Good: Feminist Activism for Empowerment

One definition of empowerment is "increasing the political, social, or economic strength of individuals and communities." Another definition calls it "the process of supporting another person or persons to discover and claim personal power."

While the first wavers were most concerned with political power and the second wavers with social and economic power, the third wavers tend to emphasis personal power. That is, feminists today take action that allows both men and women to control their own lives.

Empowerment happens when people are allowed to make choices. It is the rejection of confining stereotypes and the opening of opportunity to create new, powerful lives. Empowerment involves a woman's choice not to be a mother. Although this decision clearly involves her body, it is also an emotional one. Motherhood is thought to be an innate, biologically programmed behavior. Women are expected to be mothers and to take primary responsibility for their children's care. Women during the second and third waves in particular have been empowered to reject this notion and make their own choice about having offspring.[1]

Women have long been considered to be weaker than men, both physically and emotionally. Psychologist Sigmund Freud popularized this notion, arguing that during childhood boys go through a process of separation from the parents but girls do not. Consequently, Freud argued, women never develop the same degree of autonomy and thus have less ego strength and are prone to hysteria.[2] Empowerment means the rejection of this stereotype that women are weak. Feminist activists have pushed for greater inclusion of and support for women in sports, for instance. Feminists challenged unequal pay for female tennis players at the 1970 Wimbledon tournament, and throughout the next generation, feminists like Billie Jean King and Martina Navratilova inspired female athletes and helped paved the way for more media attention and better conditions. Opportunities in professional basketball have expanded as well. Women's participation in international amateur sports increased from 15 percent of Olympic athletes in 1972 to 40 percent in 2000.[3]

Feminists have held events like Eve Ensler's *The Vagina Monologues*, which debuted in 1998 (and the one described in this chapter called Look At Me Now), written music and poetry (like Maya Angelou's poem *Phenomenal Woman*), and utilized spiritual techniques to show women are indeed strong in many diverse ways. In 1990, Camille Paglia pointed to Madonna as "the future of feminism," arguing that her sexually explicit videos taught young women to be sexual and yet maintain control of their lives.

Many feminist activists have drawn attention to the ways our gender is socially constructed. They maintain that, as a society, we create narrow descriptions of what it means to be a man or a woman, and that these can then be adjusted to be less restrictive. In fact, some, like one of the authors in this chapter, refuse to overtly identify with the binary male/female.

Empowerment occurs, in part, through education. Feminist educators allow both men and women to hear new ideas, to see new things, and to question what they know as "the norm." In 1994, Peggy Orenstein wrote of the "hidden curriculum" in which boys flailed around until they received the attention of their teachers, regardless of whether they knew the answers, while girls politely waited their turns and, consequently, received less attention. Feminist educators try to reduce the typical power differentials that occur in traditional classrooms—where the professor or teacher is the "sage on the stage" and the students are merely passive recipients. Feminist educators generally allow everyone to learn from each other. Student's point of view and experience is an important element in feminist classroom. The goal is to effect both personal and social change—to get students to speak up, and out, about social injustices and to take action to remedy them. As Audre Lord once famously said, "silence will not protect you."[4]

Empowerment requires support. Activists can do a lot to help a man or a woman who is seeking greater power in his or her life. This support can come from family and friends, institutions or agencies, and the government. Historically, laws have not empowered women as they have not offered enough support or assistance. For instance, Hillary Clinton's proposed changes in health care and child care in the 1990s were criticized and thus not implemented, even though they would have offered women a lot of support in regard to child care and far greater access to health care. The plan included a $7.5 billion increase for child care block grants to states, with an additional $5.2 billion for dependent care tax credit to subsidize child care centers. Employers were to receive $500 million in tax credits, $800 million to professionalize daycare workers, and $6.8 billion was devoted to early childhood education. This raised the ire of conservatives, who argued that plans like these encourage women to leave their children in daycare to pursue some radical agenda of personal empowerment when they should be at home raising their own kids.[5]

Ultimately, empowerment is about letting people live the way they wish. Essays in this chapter discuss the power one feels when shunning traditional gender identity, how feminism and spirituality combine, the importance of having amazing relationships, how bringing a feminist perspective can enhance any career, and creating groups and events that build powerful connections among women.

LETTING WOMEN (AND OTHERS) LIVE THEIR LIVES
Gary Grizzle

My initial approach to feminist activism, which started in the mid-1970s, was fairly straightforward. I assumed that the goal of the feminist movement was to allow women to participate in mainstream American society on an equal footing with men. I also assumed that the best means for achieving that goal was through legislation. After all, that is what I was taught in school: in America equality is the goal and equal protection under the law is the means whereby we ensure equality. Plus, it was working for the Civil Rights Movement, wasn't it? In addition, that seemed to be what the National Organization for Women was about—ensuring equality for women largely (but not solely) through the legislative process. Thus, NOW's emphasis on the Equal Rights Amendment, affirmative action legislation, and laws to protect the rights and interests of women.

Armed with this agenda, I spent many years doing what I thought a male supporter of feminism should do: trying to vote for the right candidates and supporting legislation that would ensure that women are provided equal protection under the law. For a long time I considered myself to be a relatively effective advocate for the liberation of women. This sense of satisfaction came to an abrupt halt, however, when I started reading the works of the late nineteenth- and early twentieth-century social activist Emma Goldman. Reading these works convinced me that I was mistaken regarding both what women's liberation should be about and how it might be achieved. The following paragraphs introduce two important insights that I acquired from reading Goldman and discuss how they changed my approach to feminist activism.

The first insight that I acquired from my reading was that the emancipation of women requires something more than simply allowing women to participate in mainstream American society on an equal footing with men. After all, she argued, active participation in mainstream American society does not guarantee that someone will be liberated in any meaningful sense. In fact, there is much about life in mainstream American society that is the antithesis of freedom—dull jobs, long work weeks, constant stress, and the ever-present requirement to conform to the dictates of others—to mention just a few of the challenges faced by most participants in mainstream American society. A better goal for the women's movement, Goldman posited, would be to create an environment in which a woman is free to become anything she chooses: which might involve becoming a more active member of mainstream American society, but might just as well involve remaining on the sidelines of that society. Or, more importantly, it might even involve completely rejecting mainstream American society and its values. The more choices, the more liberation.

The second insight that I acquired from my reading of Goldman was that legislation is not a particularly effective tool for promoting the feminist agenda (especially not the agenda that she was proposing and I was accepting). The fact is, she claimed, historically legislation has done very little to improve the conditions of the disadvantaged. In fact, legislation has typically been a key component of the oppression of such parties—as a long list of discriminatory and suppressive laws will attest. In addition, she argued, even the best of legislation cannot be a source of true liberation because all legislation requires submission to the dictates of others, however reasonable such dictates might seem and however democratically they might be arrived at. A better approach to advancing any form of liberation, Goldman suggested, would be to work for the freedom of everyone to live as they see fit and in accordance with their needs and desires, unencumbered by laws and regulations. That is how you achieve true liberation.

Based on these two insights, I became convinced that the liberation of women can only be achieved by creating a society in which women (and others) are truly free to live their lives. I also became convinced that we can create such a society by incorporating some relatively simple practices into our everyday activities. The most important such practices are as follows.

Rejecting laws to a means to achieve social order. In order to create a society in which women (and others) are free to live their lives, we need to avoid relying on laws and regulations to create social order. Rather, we must seek to achieve such order through moral persuasion while ultimately allowing people to behave as they deem appropriate. To be sure, this approach is based on the belief that most people will behave reasonably well without legal coercion. However, I think that this belief is warranted. After all, the rule of law is a relatively recent phenomenon in human history with most societies having created social order simply through norms and customs. While this strategy might not always get the results we hope for, it doesn't seem likely that it will be any less successful at creating social order than legislation has been —as a quick glance at the morning paper will demonstrate.

Speaking up for our social goals. If we want to achieve social order through moral persuasion rather than legal coercion, we need to be daily advocates for our visions of such order. That is, we need to make others aware of the fact that we want a society characterized by peace, justice, economic prosperity for all, social equality, mutual respect, and freedom. We need to make this known to businesses and other organizations through our patronage (or lack thereof). We also need to make this known to the members of our communities, our colleagues, our friends, and our family members through the things that we say and do. (While such advocacy is a part of every feminist agenda that I know of, it is typically looked upon as something that is done in conjunction with promoting women-friendly legislation, not instead of promoting such legislation.) Again, this strategy might not always get the results we hope for, but it doesn't seem likely that it will be any less successful at creating our desired social order than legislation has been—as another quick glance at the morning paper will demonstrate.

Respecting the lifestyle choices of others. If we want to live in a society in which women (and others) are free to live their lives, it is essential that we be accepting of the lifestyle choices of those around us *provided they do not impinge on the freedom and prosperity of others.* That is, we should leave it to others to decide such things as what kind of work they do; how they spend their leisure time; who they fall in love with; what they eat; how they dress; etc. While this might result in a lot of people being personally offensive to us, if they aren't hurting anyone it really isn't any of our business.

In sum, through my reading of Goldman I became convinced that feminist activism does not consist of episodic political action, rather it consists of rejecting such action and pursuing a lifestyle that fosters a society in which people are truly free to become whatever they choose. Specifically, I became convinced that only by (on an everyday basis) avoiding the temptation to dictate through laws and regulations how people live their lives, engaging in moral persuasion for a just society, and accepting the lifestyles of others can we offer women the hope for true liberation. Liberation in the sense that women will be free to become whatever they choose, be that a doctor, firefighter, construction worker, nurse, teacher, fashion model, homemaker, or vagabond; a wife, life-partner, or single woman; heterosexual, homosexual, bisexual, or asexual; a fitness fanatic, weekend warrior, or couch potato; a women who wears business attire, pink leotards, or who dresses like I do; a conservative, moderate, liberal, or even a revolutionary—like Emma Goldman.

FINDING LIBERATION IN THE GENDER CHASM: A CALL FOR PRO-FEMINIST PHILOSOPHY AND ACTIVISM AMONG "MEN"

Gerald Walton, PhD

I do not know who I am, and I no longer feel a compulsion to find out. It is not that I have not felt angst and turmoil about my identities. I certainly have. But I have settled in with some aspects of my identity and have let others fade away, more or less comfortable with not defining myself in particular ways.

Let me explain.

Physiologically speaking, I am a typical male. I have all of the expected body parts. Unlike most other males, I do not consider myself to be a "man." I do not describe myself that way. In saying so, I do not want to give readers the impression that I am somehow self-loathing or that I view myself as wretchedly less than manly. I neither desperately attempt to masculinize myself so that I am perceived as a socially acceptable man, nor perpetually anguish about my manhood. Contravening dominant gender norms, I am openly gay, a fact that results in demerit points against me in the hierarchy of masculinity. Masculinity is hegemonic, meaning it exerts social control through practices that disguise such control and reframe it as "normal." My gayness (and thus my gender) positions me as "Other"—often despised "Other"—in the eyes of most men who identify as straight and who perform manhood through contemporary notions of masculinity. For instance, I do not follow organized sports. I do not watch *Jackass* or *Ultimate Fight Challenge*. I do not read *Sports Illustrated*, not even the swimsuit issue. I wear clothing of colors other than blue, green, black, brown, and gray. Rather than mere stereotypes to be dismissed, these characteristics constitute examples of gendered practices of contemporary masculinity that are regulated and imposed upon those born with a penis. What I refer to as *adolescent male stupidity* is pervasive among men of all ages.

I have been told that I have a gay-sounding voice, meaning that my voice is feminine. My gender performance apparently matches my voice, both of which reveal my difference. I have become comfortable with being perceived as different; the process has been protracted and anguished but ultimately liberating.

During my teens and twenties, my difference was highly problematic for other boys and for me. It was a problem for other boys because I represented what they could become if they were to fail to express themselves as "real" boys. That I was not properly gendered as a boy (as indicated by my interests, mannerisms, vocal quality, and long hair) meant that I was routinely and necessarily the target of other boys' discomfort. I say "necessarily" because I became the mirror by which other boys measured their own masculinity. As long as they were not like me, they could feel a degree of security in their boyhoods, in their own budding masculinity.

It was a problem for me because I came to believe what boys my age said about me: that I was a fairy and a sissy who deserved to be bullied and socially excluded. I was a failed boy. I skipped rope with girls rather than played baseball with boys. Girls were my companions, yet I was not one of them, either. I represented a chasm between two gendered worlds that did not seem to overlap. I did not proudly stand up or fight back against bullying and other forms of exclusion that were so pervasive in my life. I wish I had. Instead, I came to believe that I deserved them. In academic parlance, I had internalized the very oppression that marginalized me.

I tried for years to be a man. In my early twenties, my attempts landed me squarely in the middle of fundamentalist Christianity. Having internalized my own oppression, I was vulnerable and desperate for the "healing" of my gender identity crisis and homosexuality, as *fundies* promised God would do. That I would become a "normal" heterosexual man was an assurance that hooked me and reeled me in, without my resistance.

But years of private despair covered by a public face of Christian joy took its toll. I had not become a "normal" man after all, nor were my desires for men quelled. I eventually abandoned the *fundy* ship, and turned toward activism against it.

As I had done when I was a child, I align myself with women, even though I am not a woman. But neither am I a man. I continue to stand in the gender chasm. I am highly critical of manhood, which I see as a hoax and as an injustice.

In the documentary film *Tough Guise: Violence, Media, and the Crisis in Masculinity*, pro-feminist, antiviolence educator Jackson Katz illustrates the injustice of manhood. He points out that men are responsible for the overwhelming majority of violence in the world, and that hegemonic manhood is a common theme in violence against women, violence between and among men, violence in war and political conflicts, and violence expressed as extreme bursts such as school shootings. Men desperately trying to be men perpetrate such forms of violence. Furthermore, manhood is never stable, but instead requires constant validation, especially from other men. Men are vigilant about their own manhood and those of other men. Disparaging men and boys who breach the prescribed norms of masculinity as fairies, sissies, faggots, or queers is a powerful way by which to police the boundaries of gender.

Many men would defensively point out that not all men beat up and rape women, or open fire in schools and offices. They would be correct. They might also say that many women, too, perpetuate the hegemonic masculinization of men and boys. Correct again. However, the pervasive pattern of men-perpetrated violence cannot be refuted. It is boys and men, not girls and women or generic "people," who are responsible for most of the violence that corrodes society and destroys people, families, and communities around the world. The social script to be in control, to hide one's emotions, and to be aggressive are ingredients that, combined with social and political contexts that serve to validate men's violence and aggression, lead to horrific forms of men's control over and violence toward women, other men, children, and the earth.

I have come to renounce manhood as a strategy for gaining my own freedom from enforced masculinity. I know that this does not mean that I get off scot-free. I am perceived as being a man regardless of my disavowal. Being perceived as a man means that I am a recipient of social privilege, despite also being gay. With privilege comes responsibility. It is the responsibility of men (and those like me who are perceived as such) to teach men about men's violence, sexism, and patriarchy. Such work is feminist work.

Challenging feminist men to reach beyond the restrictions of the personal, bell hooks critiques the focus on individuals as the sole agents of change. For hooks, men must also embrace feminist struggle as political work. Doing so is "potentially the most powerful contribution men can make in feminist movement" (p. 112). To her assertion I would add: as would renouncing manhood as a strategy for the liberation of women, men, and those of us in the gender chasm.

FEMINISM FROM A SPIRITUAL PERSPECTIVE

Ilene Gottlieb

You know how children communicate volumes by what they choose for a Halloween costume? Well, I was the child that wore the little white nurse's costume and carried the stethoscope, thermometer, colorful candy medicine, and the little black bag (which

I think was actually more for a doctor's costume but, it came with mine, so of course, I used it). I never wanted to BE anything else. And what I've learned through the years is that being a nurse is to be a person whose service is to facilitate other human beings in their journey of healing. This is who I've been my entire life. And you know what? I see all my life experiences as "good," although I will admit, at times it hasn't felt good. Ah, to be human!

In the 1970s, I started out in a BSN program at American University in Washington, D.C., and after two years transferred to a diploma program at the Hospital of the University of Pennsylvania School of Nursing. The reason being, I wanted to actually "do the work," not the paperwork. We were trained in team nursing and this team approach expanded to include physicians, social workers, nutritionists, etc. Each member of the team had a purpose, and when we all worked together, the process worked and good patient care was the result. Nursing was a female-dominated profession and medicine was male-dominated at that time, with some wonderful changes since then. But the way I was trained, one's gender did not affect one's position of respect as a member of the team. I was always taught, by my parents and my nursing training, that mutual respect for a team member's role brought the best of the team approach to not only patient care but to all relationships, and that was my experience. I always received respect from other team members largely because that was the way I treated them. Looking back on it, my training was so amazing in how it prepared me for much of what I've experienced in my life.

Today, I tend to look at everything in life from the energetic and spiritual perspective. I believe and trust that everything in life occurs in perfect and divine order and that we are the cocreators of our reality, which is a core tenet for self-empowerment. And, I believe with every fiber of my being that we are all here on this dear planet, Mother Earth, at this most amazing time, to learn how to live our human journey from the place of conscious heart connection. Simply put, if it doesn't feel good, then we're not in our hearts. To solve the problem, no matter what it is, and to be at peace, to be in our joy, all we need to do is approach the situation from the place of conscious heart connection and wisdom. Certainly sounds easy enough, right? And it is when we have the simple tools to "do the work."

In spite of never having children of my own, I have been blessed with nurturing many, through simple tools of empowerment, to walk this journey of life with more grace and ease and joy. And so, what I've learned as a woman, as a human being, is that to heal our differences is to honor our differences and treat each other with mutual respect as we walk this journey of life.

We, as women, are in a unique position of teaching our children, whether we have birthed them into this realm or not, how to view other human beings in a way that is loving and that sees each person as an individual, rather as a gender. If we choose to empower our children in their journey of life, then we must choose to listen to *their* wisdom and assist and guide them by fostering a consciousness that is global and that honors that we are all one in our sharing of this planet. But most importantly, we are powerful in our ability to assist humanity in healing our differences by doing what we do best—loving from the heart and seeing everyone as perfect and whole just as they are. From my heart to yours, I wish for you joy, peace, and expansive love as you enjoy your moments, one breath at a time. Namasté.

SISTERHOOD

Carmen Ramirez

Sister. Sisterhood. Dictionary.com defines sister as a congenial relationship or companionship among women; mutual female esteem, concern, support, etc. Webster's dictionary defines it as the community of women who participate in or support feminism. Awesome! Sign me up! Sadly, I never belonged to a sisterhood growing up. I have sisters. However, I am only really close to one of them. Since I can remember, I have yearned to belong to a larger, more worldly sisterhood. A sisterhood not bound by blood but by choice. I have experienced that most interactions among women are defined by envy, competition, gossip, jealousy, and betrayal. In college, I joined my first sisterhood, National Organization for Women. These were my humble beginnings where I started learning the power of the group, the power of a sisterhood.

Currently, I am an advocate for victims and survivors of domestic violence. I cofacilitate a self-esteem group with Fran Asaro, an amazing volunteer. Together we created an environment where women lift and empower each other. We motivate and coach these women to use dialogue and feedback in our discussions. The dialogue used is always positive, encouraging, and nurturing. The self-esteem group is diverse and multicultural, and it centers around the creation of a sisterhood among women.

In the beginning, I experimented. I showed up to group with positive insight, focused the women's energy on their self-development and mutual encouragement. My theory was that when women and girls spend time in an environment that is positive, nurturing, and inspiring, the women will follow. I experimented with reading, exercises, dancing, dvds, group activities, and projects, anything that would bring the women together as a team.

Through all of these shared experiences, the group was what held us together. Hence, the sisterhood was born. Through the joys, tears, fears, failures, success, loss, laughter, hate, and love, it was the sisterhood that supported all of us. I am often asked why my group is so successful. The answer is simple: I use powerful, feminist language. The rest is up to them. Today, the self-esteem sisterhood continues to grow. The sisterhood is no longer bound by the walls of our center. It now runs free in our community helping other girls and women. One of the biggest lessons I have learned from working with the self-esteem group is that everyday feminism is simple. The most powerful way to express and spread feminism everyday is a choice. Choose to empower, nurture, support, lift, guide, encourage, coach, and accept every girl and woman in your life.

THE POWER OF DATE NIGHT

Kristen Manieri

I'm not sure of the exact figure, but it's safe to say that the majority of adult Americans are married. It's also safe (and sad) to say that, at some point in time, more than half of these couples will divorce. The way back to the courthouse, this time to end the marriage, surely isn't a pretty one. There's bound to be a lot of unhappiness and anger involved and not just for the couple in question either. Unhappy couples share their misery with their kids, families, coworkers, and fellow citizens in general.

Imagine a world where marriages lasted, not just because people saw their commitment through, but because they were happy to continue to share their lives with their spouse. Imagine a world where the joy couples created at home overflowed into every aspect of their lives. I do.

Call me a hopeless romantic but I believe that the only thing most relationships are lacking is quality time. During courtship, couples carve out hours, even days, to simply hang out, connect, and talk. Strangely, the more committed we become, the less time we put in. Add jobs, kids, parents, bills, and a myriad of modern technological distractions and it's no wonder that the average couple is spending less than 10 minutes each day experiencing "quality time" together.

While it's easy to let our quality time as couples slide to the bottom of our "to do" lists, there are few things more important to a marriage and family. Quality time allows couples to reconnect, tune in, and nurture their friendship. It gives them the opportunity to actually talk versus the quick exchanges that help families coordinate who's picking up whom and whose turn it is to take out the trash.

Like coming up for air, date night is the lifeline of my marriage, especially since the birth of our baby girl. After Elizabeth was born, I was amazed at how much time could pass without Marc and I even making eye contact, never mind having a meaningful conversation that didn't involve the words milk or diaper. Days drifted into weeks, weeks melted into months. Overtired and underfed, neither of us was on our best behavior and the normal niceties we exchanged went out the window.

After about six weeks, we reenacted our weekly date night ritual again and watched as the love in our marriage slowly, but surely, returned. While I've always been a believer in date nights, this experience made me a true convert.

When Marc and I moved to Orlando in 2006, we were both excited about discovering a bevy of new date night activities in our new town. Every so often, we'd share our discoveries with other couples who always reacted with surprise. Most people we knew had never heard of all the fun things we were doing. So, I decided to write a book called *Great Dates Orlando* which gave couples more than 50 fantastic date night ideas. Soon after, I started my blog at www.greatdatesorlando.com, and ever since I've been posting a weekly date night idea plus maintaining a Couple's Calendar filled with fabulous events suitable for quality time. I've been asked to speak on television and I'm a frequent guest on a local talk radio show, plus I've written numerous articles for local publications.

My goal is to encourage as many people as possible to set aside quality time for the people they love. Every so often, someone will e-mail to thank me for giving them so many great date night ideas. They tell me that their relationship was getting stale and stagnant and that their renewed commitment to date night had relit their flame.

I know there's a lot of hardship in this world—world hunger to solve, children to save, and the planet to rescue. Those are all really important issues and I try to support them in my own way. I'm trying to make a difference in the lives of couples because maybe, just maybe, if all these millions of married people were just a little happier, if their hearts were just a little more open, maybe they'd give back to the world in bigger ways too. The Beatles weren't kidding when they sang "All You Need Is Love." It all starts with more love.

LOOK AT ME NOW

Fran Asaro

When I was asked to write a piece on feminist activism, my first thought was "Who Me, I'm a pacifist!" In my mind, an activist is radical and political. I thought about it for a bit and then realized that while I don't consider myself an activist specifically, I take an active stand for the empowerment of others, especially women. One of the reasons I became a life coach was to support women in living a life of empowerment. It all began when I was inspired to apply for a volunteer position at our local center for domestic violence. Again I thought "why me?" After all, I had not been a victim in my life. I applied anyway and through a series of events trying to find my place in the organization, I found myself co-facilitating the self-esteem support group with Laura Finley. I immediately knew I was "home." For me, this was something I could sink my teeth into and support the women in growing themselves. Eventually, Laura left the group and Carmen came as my new co-facilitator. Carmen, in a new and unique way, had a passion for this group, and together we partnered in something huge. As the group evolved, we saw a need for "more" when it came to the women in the group. After all, they came week after week, working diligently on themselves. Stretching and breaking out of old molds and creating their lives anew.

We decided to put on an event that would celebrate the women of the self-esteem support group. We called it the Look At Me Now event. It was designed to acknowledge and showcase the women in ways they had not been presented in years if ever. Celebrating a new time in their lives, a new person to look at and see differently.

The women have complete makeovers, new outfits and hairdos as well as having a glamour shot taken. They are presented with flowers and gift bags. Each woman walks down a red carpet before an audience of the centers' volunteers, employees, and other participants. Each is announced in a way that emphasizes her strengths and accomplishments. Each woman chooses a song of empowerment as it is played in the background during the event. Slides of powerful women and empowerment quotes chosen by the women are displayed on stage. Once the women are seated, one by one those that choose to perform before the audience will come up. They sing, they dance, they recite poetry, and some just come up to say words of gratitude. The tears are flowing. They say they feel like this is a fairy tale. For them, being a victim is over and from today on, they are victors in their lives.

The evening is symbolic. It represents a shift in consciousness for them and those around them. Often women stay victims because that's how they are perceived. After this evening all predispositions about them have disappeared. Many of them come to a place where they thank their domestic violence situation for providing them with the awareness and tools that afford them this powerful life they would never have known otherwise.

The audience is equally celebrated on this evening as the employees get to see a woman go from broken to whole, the volunteers who get to see the fruits of their labor, and the newer participants who get to see what is possible for them and their future.

Wouldn't life be more palatable if we could take a stand in moving forward, releasing the past, and seeing the future and what it can hold? I don't want to negate the horrible experience that domestic violence or any crime is. I believe that any methods of healing supporting forward thinking are most effective. This was a clear demonstration of that.

REFLECTIONS OF A FEMINIST LIBRARIAN

Marie Jones

I'm a librarian. Although I am technically adept and comfortable in the world of digital information, I do not call myself an information scientist. I am a librarian because that title brings with it a rich history of women providing service (not subservience) and fulfilling a vital educational and social mission. Librarianship is a profession based in community, regardless of the community served.

The very idea of a library is a bit radical. Long before file-sharing systems evolved on the Internet, librarians were building collections that large numbers of individuals shared, almost always for free. Imagine if communities provided all kinds of non-consumables this way: bicycles, cars, lawn mowers, etc. What would the world look like if we shared more than we do now? Would the environment be less polluted because fewer items would be produced? Would the United States be less consumption obsessed?

Librarians do not maintain their professionalism by setting themselves up as experts who know better. Unlike doctors and lawyers, librarians empower people to be self-sufficient. We hand over the keys to the kingdom of finding, accessing, and evaluating information. Libraries put their most credentialed professionals on the front lines so that you don't have to work your way through layers of bureaucracy to get to the expert. When you walk into most libraries or use the phone, e-mail, text, Facebook, or whatever the technology-of-the-moment is to ask a question, you usually get an answer from someone with a master's degree. The librarian interviews you to find out what you need and offers alternatives for delivering that information in formats to suit your needs.

In most library settings, the librarian also teaches you how to find what you need and how to do the same thing the next time you need something similar. Most of the time, you didn't have to make an appointment to do this. You were able to contact the library at the time of your information need. In fact, you could contact some libraries electronically at any time of the day or night. Compare this to other models: When you go to a lawyer for an uncontested divorce, the lawyer doesn't teach you how to find the appropriate forms and fill them out yourself. Instead, you must contact the lawyer's office manager to make an appointment at a time convenient for the lawyer and rely on his or her expertise to complete the process. If you get divorced a second or third time, you must go to the lawyer again and pay him/her again—unless you decide to go to your local public or law library and ask if they can help you find do-it-yourself divorce information.

Libraries are not only community centers and information gateways, they are also workplaces for librarians and library staff. For me, work has never been a world of disembodied workers boxed into bureaucratic niches. My coworkers menstruate, juggle child care and eldercare, experience menopause, fight with their partners and, most of all, help each other through both life and work. It is not assumed that my coworkers have someone else at home to pick up the dry cleaning or wait for the plumber. I've talked with older librarians who had to fight to get maternity leave, and I honor those feminist librarians who broke all kinds of institutional barriers for the rest of us. Those were huge and important battles. Yet while those major external struggles were going on, women in libraries were practicing feminism every day: talking about bodily functions and children in ways that weren't considered appropriate in other workplaces; making decisions consensually in small or large groups; subtly subverting the masculine models that controlled their lives.

A strong feminist undercurrent can be present in academic libraries like the ones I've worked and studied in because they are, in many ways, autonomous agents within the larger bureaucracy of the university. Libraries are very different from academic departments or administrative or student services units. Managing a library includes a large budget, building, server and other infrastructure issues, and planning, organizing, and maintaining collections and services. It is a very complex operation that serves not only students, but also faculty, staff, community, and researchers from other institutions.

In my own personal experience and in the course of my research, I've found that collaboration and consensus, two elements at the root of consciously feminist organizations, also underlie the library as workplace. Libraries share resources with one another through interlibrary loan and consortia, increasing the materials available to their communities and cooperating rather than competing with other libraries. In addition, within libraries, librarians tend to make decisions through cooperative and collaborative means. My own library functions in a style of decision-making free-for-all, with faculty meetings encompassing topics ranging from someone's new shoes to the selection and acquisition of a particular database. The feminist element here is that individuals are allowed equal voice in the meetings with no overt influence of position or hierarchy. Decisions are often made in a spirit of collaboration and cooperation, and while each of us is an expert in our own niche, we don't hesitate to help wherever and whenever help is needed. I have seen library directors replace light bulbs when a custodian is not available, and library clerical staff adeptly handle difficult faculty when the director is out of the office. That kind of egalitarian functioning at all levels creates an environment where it is possible to be egalitarian in meetings and in decision-making. When everyone respects each others' skills, library workers at all levels can come together on an even footing to make decisions that steer the direction of the libraries in which they work. Library directors, in some instances, become budget managers and organizational facilitators more than hierarchical leaders. In the end, librarians value the outcomes of this collaborative and consensual decision-making, as summed up by a librarian in a college I recently visited, "We have collectively reached much better decisions than any one of us would have reached alone."

The sense of community, sharing, empowerment, and egalitarianism that permeates librarianship is an everyday feminism that seldom receives the "F word" as its label, but is nonetheless feminist in its very essence. Feminism strives to even the playing field for women and men, to build community and respect. I'm lucky enough to work in a place that understands the importance of these elements at its very core and to have my own personal ethics enacted in my chosen profession.

Chapter Twelve

Our Future: Feminist Activism by and for Youth

Girls and young women today have it both good and bad. On the good side, many teenagers live enthusiastically in a world of entitlement. They believe that all their mothers and grandmothers fought for, like the right to choose, the right to control their own bodies, the right to be free of violence and harassment, and the right to work where and when they want, has been accomplished. Essentially, they have undergone a complete psychological overhaul. "They assume they'll have equal access to education and employment opportunities, and that they are just as capable as their male peers (if not more so) of achieving success. They're competing in sports with as much vitality and drive as men, and entering the job market—including the military, police and fire departments, and the political sphere—in unprecedented numbers."[1] In his book *Alpha Girls*, Dan Kindlon argued that these girls are confident and are neither anxious nor defensive. He calls these girls "Alpha Girls." An Alpha Girl has a GPA of 3.8 or higher, holds at least one leadership position (such as in band, a sport, a club, etc.), participates in extracurricular activities, scores high on achievement motivation assessments, and has high self-ratings of dependability.[2]

Some critics have argued that the feminist movement has been unfair to boys. Kate O'Beirne offered a lengthy indictment of how feminists have let girls take over:

We parents of boys have meekly allowed gender warriors to treat our sons like unindicted coconspirators in history's gender crimes, while parents of girls permit their daughters to be patronized as helpless victims of a phantom, crippling sex bias in America's schools. Classrooms have been turned into feminist re-education camps to stamp out all sex differences and smother the natural attributes and aspirations of boys and girls. When Gloria Steinem, who has raised neither, declared "we badly need to raise boys more like we raise girls," she summed up the feminist conviction that boys' gender identity had to be radically reformed. And the feminist re-education project in our schools is determined to "free" young girls from their natural feminine traits. Our schools and universities are battlefields in a determined feminist campaign of indoctrination and intimidation, and students and scholarship have been the casualties.[3]

Yet, at the same time that some girls are experiencing unprecedented opportunity and confidence, other girls and young women experience something dramatically different. Some girls fall prey to self-mutilation, binge drinking, and other problems. Mary Pipher said girls' confidence goes down in crash during adolescence, like the mysterious Bermuda Triangle. In adolescence, girls are told what they are and what they are supposed to be by their peers, by the media, by popular culture, by adults—by everyone. She is neither a child nor an adult. America does not know how to treat adolescent girls. For some purposes they are children. This is typically when legal issues are involved. For other purposes, generally those that make money or provide pleasure, girls are considered women.[4] "The adolescent lives of girls are a Caliban stew of conflicting laws, twisted social policy, and bent cultural interpretations that can wreak havoc on their developing psyches. It is a schizophrenic time made that much more inconsistent by traditional expectations, power politics, and a public persona threatening to undo it all."[5]

Michael Kimmel attributed these largely to pressures exerted by the "culture of Guyland." Guyland is his term for the culture of hypermasculinity that young men—particularly those who have graduated from high school—are increasingly immersed in. They play video games, drink excessively, and above all, denigrate and use women. He explained that how a girl navigates Guyland will impact not just her self-esteem, but it can determine her life chances.

> Much of a girls' social status is determined by her relationship with guys even today. To achieve high standing with guys, and thus with other girls, a girl must conform to Guyland's notions of what a girl should be. . . . Girls live in Guyland, not the other way around. Whereas guys are permanent citizens, girls are legal aliens at best. As second-class inhabitants, they are relegated to being party buddies, sex objects, or a means of access to other girls. While guys spend their time posturing for the validation of other guys, the girls who live in Guyland spend their time working tirelessly for the validation and approval of *those same guys*. Guys have the parties, supply the alcohol, and set the terms for social life. If a girl wants to play, she has to play by their rules. Even those they may have been raised by forward-thinking mothers, many of these young women don't seem to be able to

envision an alternative to Guyland, and without a different reality in mind, they can't critically analyze what is happening.[6]

Another example is the "Circle of Fat" exercise, described by Margaret Soos, who wrote as a would-be sorority pledge at a California college. It is recounted by Alexandra Robbins in *Pledged*. The entire pledge class is led downstairs into the living room of the sorority house. They are dressed only in their underwear and are met by their sisters, who wear white robes. Large bed sheets cover the windows. The sisters hand the pledges strips of white sheets and instruct them to blindfold themselves and lie facedown on the cold hardwood floor. Here's what happens next:

> and that's when the men entered the room, whistling and howling . . . . The men circled us . . . I as becoming disoriented and felt nauseated. Something smelled toxic. Then something cold came into contact with my thigh. I gasped. "It's okay, baby," said one of the men. "I'm just helping to make you look good." The cold moved to my inner thigh. The men had drawn circles and x's in permanent marker on areas of their bodies that "needed work."[7]

Kimmel has explained that girls in "Guyland" can either be "bitches" or "babes." Bitches are self-confident and independent. They are the ones who do not buy into the stereotypical gender roles and are thus ridiculed, denounced as lesbians, excluded, or shunned. "Babes" conform with the guys' vision of what a girl should be—physically fit, but definitely not muscular, sexy but not so much that she is slutty, naturally pretty, not too smart but not dumb either, adoring of guys but not needy, a drinker but not a drunken slob. Basically, "an unachievable fantasy."[8]

Although women today are beginning to see that this dichotomy is false, it is still difficult to completely reject it. They want to be successful in school and careers but also want to be sexy enough to attract the right mate. "This leaves many of them feeling like they have to live up to two impossible standards—they're expected to 'act like a lady' while also acting 'like a man.' They have to be thin, pretty, and well-dressed, even after they stay up all night studying for a final or writing a term paper. They have to be tough and competitive, but they can't appear too eager in their assertiveness or it might be mistaken for aggression."[9] Young women definitely need some help navigating these difficult waters. Thankfully, help is available. For instance, in 2000, Donna Shalala's U.S. Department of Health and Human Services announced its "Girl Power" kits were available for communities to address the self-esteem gap. Social services and organizations provide education and assistance to young girls (and guys) grappling with the difficulties of adolescence.

Despite all this, young men and women have become powerful feminist activists. They have integrated feminist principles into their lives, regardless of whether they adopt the label.[10] The entries in this chapter show the tremendous range of activity young people engage in. They are powerful thinkers, they speak out, and they take action that helps reduce gender inequalities.

FINDING FEMINISM

Cori Lynne Fleser

Many people hold feminist beliefs within them and they don't even know it. There are many people who act or live or think in a way that is feminist but will not identify with the term if their lives depend on it. It is too true that during the second and third waves of feminism, the term became an ugly word with an even uglier connotation that apparently no person in his or her right mind would want to claim. When I think of that sentiment, I think of my mother. From an early age, my mother recognized that a disparity existed between her and her brother for the simple reason that he was a boy and she was a girl. She tells me stories of her childhood, playing baseball with all the boys in the suburbs of Detroit and getting yelled at by her mother for wearing jeans and not "acting like a lady." When Title IX mandated the equality of men's and women's athletic programs, she played on her college's first women's softball team. She raised my brother and me to understand that men and women are equal and I vividly remember her repeatedly telling me that I could do anything a man does. Despite all of this, my mom will swear to you, to this day, that *she* is not a feminist.

Few things make me happier than to hear people talking about feminism, claiming feminism, or openly identifying with feminism and not freaking out about the word for sake of reputation or social stigma. Truthfully though, I don't think people just wake up one morning and decide they're going to call themselves a feminist. It is an evolution and exploration of oneself and one's beliefs which can become quite frightening. My feminist journey is a long one and I have learned some very valuable information along the way that may be helpful to those of you who are also currently embarking on or beginning your path to feminist enlightenment.

1. Feminism is an evolution and a journey unique to each person. It is always developing and is never stagnate. One of the first indicators that you are progressing on your personal journey will be when someone calls you a feminist and you feel proud or even honored. Many of these journeys are similar and different at the same time. It is probably one of its most beautiful and confusing characteristics but it is the primary reason feminists have been able to accomplish so much over the last century. It has been stated time and time again, and I will say it again here, that one of feminism's greatest strengths and greatest weaknesses is that it includes everyone. Everyone gets to create their own idea of

what feminism means to them and it means different things to different people. The great thing about this characteristic is that we can always learn something from another feminist. We will always encounter new perspectives, ideas, and creative ways to live out our own embodiment of the term. So when the day comes that you don't think you're a good enough feminist because someone else had a "better" or a more "enlightened" definition than yours, take a deep breath and ask them how or why they got there. Engage a discussion. Discourse is how we evolve our personal journeys and our movement as a whole.

2. Feminism will shock you. I think sometimes there can be hurdles when being introduced to feminism. The word itself sounds and feels shocking. And then there's overcoming the look of question on people's faces when you tell them you're a feminist. Work with it; it comes with the territory. One of feminism's introductory perspectives includes a complete revision of how we view gender in our society. Having been socialized to behave and believe one way, it can be difficult (or liberating) to think or become aware of an alternative. When you learn that during your life there have been systems in place to keep certain groups at a disadvantage, it may make you infuriated or upset or you may just shrug your shoulders. But that you were offered an alternative perspective and the option of how you wanted to react to it is the essence of feminism. Every now and then feminism can provide answers to questions you may not have been able to answer before. It's like trying to solve for X in a math problem. I had lots of X's that I was trying to figure out and then a light bulb went off in my head in my first sociology class. I questioned. Feminism answered. Be prepared.

3. Feminism has a slippery slope. In recent decades many women have been exhibiting "acts of feminism" by exploiting their bodies as a demonstration of their status as women. Blatant examples of this would be women flashing their bare breasts at cameras, dancing on bars, making out with other women in public or on camera for the satisfaction of the audience (think *Girls Gone Wild*). Many argue it is empowering because they are exercising their own agency in a culture where they can get away with it because women and men are more equal nowadays. I'll tell you right now that our foremothers did not fight this hard to elevate the status of women just so we could throw it right back into the hands of the system they were fighting against. Like I said, anyone can be a feminist; however, it is a slippery definition when one's "feminist" actions play right into the patriarchal hands feminists have been combating for decades. What I'm talking about here is a female bravado that has developed during my

generation; women using their bodies as a way to control not just men but other women and essentially whatever they want. I'm not talking about strippers or prostitutes—that's another conversation. I am talking about your average everyday woman who uses her body as her main tool of achieving power and/or control. The system that has been ruling us for centuries also evolved with the times and tricked us into thinking that we actually possess this power. Where some argue that the ability of women to use their bodies in this way is a result of the feminist movement, I argue that their actions are setting us back decades. We have been in a constant battle over our bodies and rights to them. We have fought hard so that our bodies were not the only currency afforded to us. Yet today there are some who are misinterpreting the very rudimentary facets of feminism and driving us into another bodily financial crisis.

4. Feminism is not only about women's rights. Feminism did essentially start as a movement to increase the status of women and that is still at its core today. However, there are so many other issues that are attached to it. Because women are also part of different cultures, classes, races, ages, religions, sexual orientations, etc., feminism is intrinsically linked with many other movements and it is almost impossible to separate them. To be feminist is not just to believe that men and women are equal. At its most basic principle, feminism is to believe that humans are equal. Too often we join a movement and suddenly get tunnel vision where all we can focus on is the end goal for our specific issue. We lose sight of other important resources around us and alienate those who try to "steal our thunder." But we are not fighting against each other. It is not an "us" versus "them" thing. We need to remain inclusive rather than exclusive. No one cause is more important than the next. Remember that feminism and other movements opposing the status quo are linked together, collaborating and helping one another and working as a team. Power with, not power over. My solution for people whose only problem with feminism is the word itself is to find a cause with a word they do like. That's feminism too.

5. Knowledge doesn't always come from a book. Practice and experience is at the core of feminism. There have been many books, essays, theories, and articles written about feminism. You can read all of them that you want until you have a complete understanding of feminist theory from all over the world, but until you put some of that knowledge into practice it can only be considered extensive research. Reading about feminism is intriguing, but experiencing its application is mind opening and life changing. Feminism in this sense is kind of like a lot of other things;

once you've learned about it, apply it, and tell others. Since one of the ultimate goals of feminism is to spark some level of change, it is critical that once you've developed your own interpretation of word, go out and experience it. This not only is very reaffirming to your beliefs but it perpetuates the evolution of them and maintains that beautiful fluidity within feminism. My suggestion is to pick a feminist issue that you are very passionate about and work with it in some way. It can be anything, big or small, whatever you can think of that will utilize your feminist beliefs. For me, it was domestic violence; for my friends it was sexual violence, immigration, reproductive rights, etc. We each had knowledge of feminism, we each had our passion within it and we each went out and explored it. It is OK that our initial views have since changed; like I said, that is what's supposed to happen. What is even better is that we were able on some small level to contribute to a greater movement which is something you will never experience by only reading books. Feminism is one of the greatest secrets you will never have to keep to yourself.

These five attributes are simply some of the things that I have discovered over and over again during my exploration of feminism. It is important to realize that everyone's journey is different, some happening faster or slower than others. It never ceases to amaze me all that has resulted from embracing that word. Feminism for me personally was a search for a truth that I could believe in. Before I even discovered feminist beliefs I had questions that needed to be answered and a void that needed to be filled. My first introduction to feminism was a feminist literary theory class in college. On a personal note, I recommend that you ease into feminism in some other way. This class was sink or swim feminism and I sunk initially in feminist theory but swam in feminist identity. I love that my journey discovering my own interpretation of the word has been rocky and confusing with its own ups and downs. It has become my lifestyle, dictating my interactions and life pursuits. I feel most comfortable in it and I believe it started with my mother. She may not consider herself a feminist, but the spark she ignited in her daughter grew into something powerful. I now know, after my journey, it was feminism.

I CAN DO ANYTHING

LuElla Putnam

I wear high heels every day to work. I go tanning, get pedicures, and I'm a bit of a shop-a-holic. In short, I'm probably not what you'd expect when encountering a feminist. And I won't lie. When my purple car that I'd named "Princess" got a flat tire just two weeks after purchasing "her," I had no idea what to do. I lived in Charleston, South Carolina, at the time, and it was the middle of summer. I was stuck on the side of the road, hot, sweaty, and overall pretty disgusting. I scanned through my cell phone and searched for any male name I felt could help me. I finally got a hold of my friend's husband, Matt, to come and change the tire for me. Matt's a nice guy, but he couldn't help but to make a few jokes about how I needed a "man" around when I experienced these problems, and he offered to set me up on a date with one of his friends. I felt helpless, standing there and watching him as the cars whizzed past me.

When I finally got home, I got online and searched for "how to change a flat tire." Within just a few minutes, I printed out instructions. After embarrassing myself by sending my hubcaps rolling all over my driveway (and after having my neighbor asking me if I needed help multiple times), I finally figured out how to work a tire jack and what exactly lug nuts are. It took me most of the afternoon, but I made sure to try it over and over again until I knew I could do it myself without any help.

A few months ago, I moved to Oklahoma from South Carolina. During my move—about 45 minutes from my destination—my back left tire picked up a nail. Rather than sifting through my phone and feeling miserable, I felt empowered as I pulled over on the side of the road and knew exactly what to do to take care of myself. I flagged on motorists who tried to help me, and I couldn't help but smile as I saw a few looks of surprise from some of them as I took out a pipe for leverage from my trunk and bent down by the tire in my dress and heels. I realize plenty of women can change flat tires. This isn't anything new or groundbreaking. But for me at least, I felt this moment marked an important step in my life. Rather than stereotyping myself in certain roles as I'd been used to before, I learned it doesn't matter what others may expect from me, simply because I'm a woman. I can change a flat tire, and I can accomplish anything else I set my mind to as well.

ROLE MODELS, LIKE IT OR NOT

Sade Brooks

Over winter break, my boyfriend and I spent a lot of time with my younger cousins, Kayla, who is eight years old, and Omari, who is five. The kids' mother purchased a boxing set for Omari's fifth birthday, and Paul, my boyfriend, was really excited to teach Omari how to use it. He viewed it as "guy-bonding time."

On one occasion, I was sitting in the living room with Paul and Omari while they were playing with the boxing set and I heard Paul say, "Don't punch like a girl." This really bothered me, and I questioned Paul about what he meant. I don't want Omari growing up with the impression that girls are wimps. This is a closed-minded perspective. I believe both boys and girls are much more dynamic than this type of stereotype implies. I also wanted Paul to realize what he was saying and that little comments like this teach children values that we should be concerned about.

Initially, Paul said I was "attacking him" and even accused me of being sexist. But my goal was to make him more aware that what he says has an impact on children. We are role models, like it or not. So I wouldn't back down. Eventually, Paul was able to understand where I was coming from and why I was bothered. He admitted that he could have said something different to get Omari to hit the punching bag harder. I feel good that I said something, even if the fact that we argued about something like this is sort of comical.

STUPIDITY IS A DISEASE

Julia Gonzalez

His name was Julio Cecilio Santiago and he died a week before I was born. The only memory I have of him was the teddy bear he gave my mother to give to me. Strangely enough, he knew he would not see the day I was born. In his honor, my mother named me after him. As I came to age, my mother told me stories of the man that I was named after. She told me of the great smile that he always wore and how every time he laughed it brought an air of happiness. She also stressed how he never hesitated to help someone who was in desperate need. This man was my uncle and he was gay. At the age of 26, he was diagnosed with AIDS.

I was never ashamed to tell people that my uncle was gay, especially when I reached high school. In high school, I didn't know too many closed-minded people. Many students in my school were open about their sexuality and so the idea of having a gay uncle was seen as relatively normal. I was never offended when a person said that they did not like the idea of gay relationships. Everyone has the right to their own opinion.

When someone said that "the idea of being with someone of your own same was outright disgusting," I just casually shrugged my shoulders because of course everyone is different. I knew that my uncle was different, but it did not bother me enough to comment back when people made this type of remark. However, there was one incident when I just could not stay quiet.

In my last year of high school. I decided to take contemporary literature. The idea of expressing yourself through writing and poetry fascinated me. My teacher decided to have us read a poem that was written by a man who was also gay. She did not tell us he was gay until after we read the poem, though. After hearing that the author was gay, a girl in class commented that she would never have guessed it, since he spoke with such male superiority. While my teacher was addressing that comment, a boy who sat two seats behind me said very loudly, " I would never be gay because I wouldn't want to die from AIDS."

As soon as I heard his comment, my face flushed. I became really upset with this immature comment. I took long deep breaths to calm down, but it didn't work. I must have looked annoyed, because my teacher asked me if I was okay. Without hesitating, I turned to the back of the room where he sat and said, "AIDS is a sexually transmitted disease that can come from any type of relationship, whether you are straight or gay. If a person is gay it doesn't mean that they are going to get AIDS. So before you open that pathetic, uneducated mouth again, you might want to get your facts straight. And the only person I see spreading any type of disease is you. That disease is plain stupidity."

I turned back around in my seat and let out a loud sigh of satisfaction. As the entire class sat in complete silence and my teacher was hiding a smile behind her podium, I knew I had made my uncle proud. The only thing I cannot tolerate is when a person makes it seem that all gay people are walking diseases. I think Martin Luther King Jr. said it best when he stated, "We must learn to live together as brothers or perish together as fools."

TEACHING EVERYDAY FEMINIST ACTIVISM: HOW TAKING IT TO THE STREETS HELPS STUDENTS BECOME EVERYDAY ACTIVISTS

Carmen D. Siering

Teaching the introductory course in the women's studies program at a mid-sized Midwestern university is a blessing and a burden. I often find myself approaching the upcoming semester with both anticipation and trepidation. After four years, I find the class often begins the same way. Twenty-five students come into the course, most of them having either no idea what feminism is or having some pretty negative ideas about the word. Yet relatively soon, the uninformed, confused, or even hostile students I encounter the first weeks of class become incredulous and then curious as they read about the inequities in women's lives, both past and present. As the semester progresses, these same students become more and more anxious to do something to change what they recognize as the injustices perpetuated by a patriarchal culture. They often ask for direction: "How can I get involved? Where can I find more information?" My standard response has been to direct them to a variety of organizations—on campus, online, or elsewhere. And then I trust that they follow through. But I always wonder if that fire dies once they leave the classroom and the camaraderie of like-minded others who are as passionate about making change in the world as they are.

Because of that concern, I have recently chosen a different approach with not only the students in my introductory course, but all my women's studies courses. Because women's studies grows out of the decidedly activist feminist movement, I decided that students in my courses would be required to participate in what I term activist projects. The projects can take a variety of forms, but the goal is always the same: to extend what the students have learned in the classroom to the larger campus and/ or local community in some way.

I was initially unsure how the students would take to the project, unsure what sort of response I would receive. And while there are some students who do the minimal work to get credit for what they see as just another assignment, others take up the challenge and go far beyond what is required for the course. These students become activists in their own right; their projects become something much more than an assignment or a way to get a grade. Reading about activism and being an activist are very different things. What my students learn from this activity is something I could never teach them in the classroom. Through a variety of different activities, my students have learned how to become feminist activists on their own terms.

One group of students chose to defy a campus ordinance against drawing on sidewalks with chalk and taping handmade signs to structures, spending a Sunday night doing just that. Each sign or chalk drawing tried to clear up a misconception about feminists and feminism. As they proceeded to "tag" the campus, they had a chance to talk to several students about what they were doing, which gave them an opportunity to explain their project and their feminist philosophy. By Monday morning, many of the flyers had already been ripped down by campus workers, and I actually had the chance to witness their chalk drawings being power-washed off a highly trafficked intersection. Still, when I talked to them about their project, they were upbeat. They felt their message had been seen and heard, and were excited that at least a few of their signs were still flying a week later.

Several students chose to create informational brochures, flyers, cards, or buttons to hand out at busy spots on campus. The reactions they received varied from mild interest to outright hostility. What seemed to receive the most unfriendly reaction was the use of the word "feminist" or "feminism" on any printed material. One student reported having her flyer wadded up and thrown at her feet. The flyer in question contained information on Gloria Steinem and her work as a feminist activist. During the autumn political campaign season, another student reported having a male student take a brochure only to return some time later and shove the brochure back into her hands with an expletive-filled diatribe on how disgusting it was. The brochure contained information on the political candidates' views on issues of concern to women, information on maternity leave in the United States, and several quotes from prominent feminists both past and present.

The Internet provided a great opportunity for activism. Creating a Web site or blog is a way to reach out to many people in many places without having to go anywhere. Several students chose this option, with varying degrees of success. Marketing their online presence was one of the obstacles to gaining an audience, and those who worked to market themselves were usually the most successful. However, one blog that attracted a rather large following, especially considering its rather narrow scope, was one created by Jackie DiSarro. Her blog, "The Mirena Mishap," was one of the projects that had the most impact, both on a student and on an issue. Writing about a medical ordeal involving a migrating IUD and her subsequent surgery, Jackie's blog attracted the attention of women from all over the country. She soon found that what she thought was a rather unusual experience was, unfortunately, all too common. And while she first used her blog as a vehicle for venting her anger and frustration at a medical establishment that had failed her, and as a way to connect with women who had had similar experiences, she soon realized she wanted more out of this project. As she became aware of her growing desire to begin a movement against the false claims made by the manufacturers of dysfunctional birth control, Jackie began transforming the blog into an activist vehicle, one that could be used as a way of connecting those interested in sharing information and getting involved in this emerging activist movement.

Whether they stood in the rain and tried to hand out flyers or sat at a table and tried to engage passers by in dialogue, each of my students learned something from their activist projects. One of the most important things they learned was that being an activist is hard work. Being an activist requires physical and mental stamina, as well as courage and good will. Being out in public, talking to people about topics that are near to your heart but may go against everything someone else stands for, can take a toll on the best of us. Having your efforts denigrated, or your flyers wadded up and thrown at your feet, can be disheartening. Being an activist can be, at times, a very thankless effort.

The activist project taught us all many things. It taught us to be more appreciative of those who have fought, and continue to fight, for equality and justice. It taught us not to take the battles won by our feminist foremothers for granted. Most importantly, it taught me that my students learn more when they take on a cause they care about and share it with others than when they read about it in a textbook. Because no matter that their work was torn down or thrown at their feet or rejected, most of my students say they will keep on being activists. By taking their projects to the streets, they discovered their actions can make a change in the world. And that is a lesson I could never have taught them in the classroom.

TIPS FOR TEACHING THE ACTIVIST PROJECTS

- Allow students to pick their own subjects for the project. No topic is too small. For many students in my introductory courses, simply telling others about feminism is a big step.
- Encourage students to work in groups. My students realized early on that there really is safety in numbers. Their enthusiasm and courage were bolstered by working the streets together.
- Take pictures or capture their efforts on video. Sharing these images in class after all the projects are done is a great way to celebrate the successes and share the tough moments. It helps confirm the reality of their experiences as activists.
- Encourage them to contact the press, to write letters to the editor, and otherwise promote their activities. The more

attention they can garner, the more they will realize the kind of impact their activism can have on the world.

- Make the project meaningful, but don't grade too harshly. If effort was expended, if the student was engaged, and if learning occurred, then the project was a success. Most students will work very hard on their projects because it is something about which they care very much.

"SECRET"

Natasha Abdin

Let me let you in on a little secret
Everybody has secrets, some have more than others
Everybody has problems, some more serious than people let on
Some of us keep our problems a secret
And why you may ask?
Maybe it's because society tells us it's wrong
Maybe it's because we suppress our feelings and emotions, so that others won't feel uncomfortable
Maybe it's because if we truly speak from the heart, no one would think that we could possibly share similar feelings
Maybe it's because we are scared
But then who scared us?
Really the question should be who stands by us
Not against us

But in a country that lets people openly discriminate
Since when was it OK to threaten us or treat us like second class citizens?
Why is it OK for us to be treated worse than our enemies?
At least our enemies smile to our face
Let's talk about family values
Who are you to say that I don't have any?
Since when did discrimination and prejudice become a core value of family values?
And when did hate become something taught and not said?

General Pace said that gays are immoral
That their behavior is equivalent to fatality, which is a sin
What about the "Don't Ask, Don't Tell" policy enacted by former U.S. President Bill Clinton, isn't that a form of discrimination?
Some people can talk about their families and great loves of their life, especially in times of crisis

But this is just another secret that we must keep or risk being dishonorably discharged

Never before have we had a president go on national television and say that marriage is between a man and a woman
And then push to have it defined in the Constitution as such
Well, our Constitution states a lie, because it says that all men are created equal
But then the pledge also consists of a lie, because it says with liberty and justice for all
And that most certainly isn't the case

Let's talk about former New Jersey Governor Jim McGreevey who had an affair and resigned from office
The only thing different about his affair, is that he was cheating with another man and it cost him his career.

In a place where popular stars can be a target for homophobic remarks
And sport stars can say they don't like gay people, don't want to have them on their team, or that they shouldn't be living in this country

It's no wonder why we all have problems and secrets
Society isn't ready
People are not ready
To listen to my secrets and my problems
But it is our job, our duty to help educate and speak up for ourselves.
Yes, we have a right to belong.
And it is up to you and me to help make a path for us, and all other people who don't fit inside of a neat little box.

IT'S MY RELIGION, TOO

Nicole Patouhas

My father was born and raised in a small village in central Greece. I have a home there and feel almost as much a part of that community as I feel a part of my community in the United States. I believe the Greek culture definitely places a higher value on males than it does females. Most Greeks, especially the older ones, believe males are superior to females.

This inequality rears its ugly head often in Greek culture. When a Greek couple becomes engaged, most people utter the expression "Ena Yo." This translates into a wish for a male child, as it is generally considered more desirable to produce male off-spring. It is still common for marriages to be arranged and for the family of the bride to pay "preeka," or a monetary gift to the groom. Women in that culture are not only prohibited from serving in the priesthood but are considered unwelcome in certain areas of the church. I had a personal experience with not feeling wel-come in a Greek sanctuary.

Two summers ago, my family made plans to visit one of the most renowned, beautiful monasteries in central Greece, located in a town called Metera. I was extremely excited about the visit, so much that I made the effort to purchase a travel guide and spent the week prior reading about the monastery's history. When we finally arrived at the monastery, however, I was told that I would not be able to enter it. I was not even permitted to stand within 20 feet of the entrance. This was devastating, as I had hoped to be able to take the ride to the top of the monastery in an ancient basket and light a candle in the highest sanctuary. The reason I was prohibited? Because I am a female. My brother, a hyper 10-year-old at the time, was not only welcomed, but encouraged to go up.

I complained to my father, who told me I was being disre-spectful. I tried to talk to him again and he put the palm of his hand up, meaning I was not permitted to speak further about the sub-ject. I then turned to my mother, who agreed to accompany me to speak to a priest. I explained to him how much it meant to me to be able to light a candle, as I had planned. After some deliber-ation, he agreed to allow me to enter the bottom sanctuary, although I still was not allowed to ride to the top. I know this might seem like a minor accomplishment, but to me, my persistence was important. I feel proud that perhaps I opened the door for other females. And, more importantly, that I challenged this dis-criminatory practice and practiced my religion as I wished.

TEACHING ENGLISH IN CHILE: A FEMINIST APPROACH

Sheena Vega

I am a 23-year-old, liberal, female, college graduate. Most of my friends are people of my age, many of them female, many of them liberal, college graduates. Until recently, I have spent my entire life living in the United States of America. I have traveled to other countries but I never stayed anywhere long enough to really understand the culture or the people that gave those places life.

These simple facts may be part of the reason that while I have always been aware of the social inequalities that women face on a daily basis, I never believed that I was personally affected by them. That is, until I moved here, to Santiago, Chile.

I have been living in Santiago for seven months. I teach English as a foreign language to adults who work in large companies. Most of my students are male. To be perfectly honest, I didn't notice the noteworthy difference of male to female students until I had quite a few classes. Eventually, I realized that on average, for every eight men that I teach, I teach one female.

Coincidence? Well, I wasn't sure myself so I began asking questions. What I found was that most of the employees in large companies here are men, and most men request female English teachers. When I asked the men in my classes why they preferred female instructors over male instructors, they were surprisingly direct. As a native speaker of English, I am clearly more advanced in the language than my students are. Some of my male students told me without hesitation that they feel less threatened intellectually by a female instructor. With a man they feel that they have to compete, but with a woman there is no competition. Women are soft, I have heard. Women are more compassionate than men, women are less severe, women are easier to listen to, women have voices that sooth, women are less likely to be critical. Women are more interesting to watch. These are all reasons I have been given by my male students for why they request female instructors.

As a young woman, the belittling rationale of my male students was disturbing to me. What was I to do? Financially, it would be impossible for me to stop teaching men. Because they make up a majority of my classes, they unfortunately make up a majority of my paycheck as well. So, I decided that I would simply have to make sure to contradict their common beliefs about women. That is to say, I am a difficult teacher. I challenge them constantly in my classes, I don't cut them any kind of slack. I speak with confidence, in a strong voice, that would not under any circumstances lull them to sleep. I don't respond with coy expressions to their compliments. I don't laugh at their sexist jokes, that despite my strict teaching, are sometimes told anyway. Many of my students have made comments about my "style" of womanhood so to speak. I have heard from a few of the men in my classes that I am "not like most women." To which I have replied, "No, most women are not the way you believe them to be."

I deal with inequality on a daily basis here and I am completely aware of it. Whether it's the uncountable whistles, grunts, and whispers that I and other women receive while walking down the street, or the offensive sexist jokes my students continue to share with each other in my classes, it exists and I feel it. Sometimes, however, inequality comes in a prettier package, one that is more difficult to recognize and perhaps easier to participate in. For example, men often give up their seats on the bus for women. After a long day of teaching and standing it is extremely tempting to accept such an offer. However, I am perfectly capable of standing, just as capable as he is. And so while it's a nice gesture, I simply respond with a "no thank you" because by sitting down, I feel that I would only solidify his belief that as a woman I'm somehow weaker than he is. And, if showing our strength and capability is the only thing I can do, I must do it.

We must do it.

RESISTING MILITARISM

Nancy Cruz

As students, we are constantly being targeted by the military, whether it's through recruiters at our schools, calls at our homes, or even through our educational curriculum.

Toward the end of our high school years, we find ourselves deciding whether or not to pursue higher education or to choose what seems to be "the easy way out" (the military, in some cases). Sometimes raised by immigrants or by a single parent, we struggle with the reality that we do not all receive equal access to resources to prepare us for college. What should be our right is only a privilege for a few.

In most urban schools like Mission Bay High School, in San Diego, California, students dream of being lawyers, probation officers, teachers, doctors, and psychologists. But counselors who are overwhelmed or uncaring neglect to provide the information we need to satisfy our dreams. Instead, counselors push students to take classes like Junior Reserve Officer's Training Corps (JROTC), a military science course, to fill up spaces.

When going back to Mission Bay High School to speak with students about the importance of continuing their education, I have asked, time after time, what they want to do with their lives. All but a few respond "go to college." The ones that respond that they do not want to go say it is because they do not see themselves there. It is hard to dream when we are told we are not good enough. Looking back, during high school I gave up on my "dream school," UCLA, because I thought I would not be able to make it, because in my mind only the best go to UCLA.

The military knows our vulnerabilities, insecurity, and fears, seeking us everywhere we go—at home, at the malls, and at school—and by every communication channel—mail, phone calls, e-mail, radio, and television. In my high school we have a career center. Its function should be to provide information about various careers, but while I was there I never saw anyone except military recruiters come to speak to us. The U.S. Air Force, Navy, and Army were present week after week and the Marines had no need to go, since they were already there. Our principal took it upon herself to establish a Marine JROTC at our school during my senior year. It was and continues to be a daily reminder that there is a need for soldiers.

While I was in high school (only two years ago), we were constantly bombarded. For example:

- The school organized a "carnival" to reward students who raised their state test scores. Navy recruiters were placed at the entrance, giving out t-shirts in exchange for our personal information.
- Several times during the year military recruiters came and organized competitions in our quad.
- In promoting the ASVAB (military entrance exam), a teacher decided to excuse a test grade if we took it.
- Students were told that there was no room in other classes and that the ONLY option is JROTC.
- The last week of school recruiters came several times.

There are great disparities in San Diego schools between wealthier neighborhoods, which are not exposed to the military, and schools like mine, where the majority of students are minorities and where the military is ever present. The academic rigor was and is withheld for less than 10 percent of the student body. At Mission Bay, like in many other schools, the education that most students receive is insufficient to be able to succeed in higher education. With a lack of academic support programs, such as Advancement Via Individual Determination, a college preparatory program, and with the implementation of other programs such as JROTC, the priorities of our administration were clearly laid out. With the academic achievement gap increasing and a shooting range being built on campus for the JROTC class, I realized there was a need to organize within schools. Not only educate my peers but mobilize them.

Perhaps the most difficult task of all has been appealing to my peers and getting them involved in impeding the militarization of our schools.

I have been organizing since the beginning of my sophomore year in high school around multiple social justice issues. When I began confronting militarism at Mission Bay High School, I was alone. I had the knowledge but not the numbers. I realized that the best way to spread word about what was happening was to dialogue with my peers. I shared what I knew and some of them became interested. Then one great teacher supported this movement along with me. We reached out to parents because we knew that if anybody had power, it was them. Parents were surprised to hear about the JROTC shooting ranges and all of the exposure to the military that their children where receiving.

As students, we have taken it upon ourselves to do what is right and let our principal, administration, parents, school board, and nation know what we think. We have petitioned, protested, walked out, leafleted, spoken to the school board, been interviewed by TV and radio stations, networked with other schools such as Lincoln High School, and helped found the Education Not Arms Coalition (ENAC).

Although we struggled for two years, our campaign to remove shooting ranges from high school campuses was successful. A multigenerational coalition made it possible. The integration of parents, teachers, students, and community members into one cohesive struggle was fundamental. We serve as a model for organizations around the country which face similar issues. While participating in the National Network Opposing the Militarization of Our Youth Conference I realized the amount of impact our campaign had. San Diego is one of the most militarized cities and yet we were able to protect ourselves and other youth.

Since my devoted participation during my senior year, I have worked around prevalent labor issues in Los Angeles while attending UCLA. I continue to work with ENAC and youth. Considering myself to be privileged in many ways by the knowledge I hold, I strive to share it.

Conclusion

What principles should guide feminist activists as we move forward? Susan Shaw and Janet Lee posit seven precepts essential to our shaping a just future in which feminism is activated and activism is feminized:

1. Setting feminist-inspired priorities and keeping them;
2. Balancing personal freedom and identity with public and collective responsibility;
3. Presenting a critique of corporate capitalism;
4. Utilizing technology to make social change, while recognizing its limitations;
5. Advocating for a sustainable physical environment;
6. Recognizing everyone's human dignity and working toward equality of access and equality of outcome; and
7. Doing it all with a sense of humor and taking time to play and celebrate. As Emma Goldman famously said, "If I can't dance, I don't want to be part of your revolution."[1]

It is the authors' hope that this book contributes to the development of just such a world. The inspiring stories that we have assembled reinforce our conviction that feminist activism is not just one road but as many paths as the human brain and heart can devise, that we can all make a difference, and that it is our responsibility as human beings to work for the betterment of all.

Appendix One

Ideas for Feminist Activism

- Create a number of cards with professions or categories written on them, all of which often elicit stereotypes (i.e., blonde woman, elementary teacher, NFL linebackers, plumber, etc.). Have a volunteer come up and hold the card above his/her head so the individual cannot see what it says but the audience can. Ask the audience to provide one word adjectives that describe the category/profession, and remind them not to be so obvious they give it away (no examples, just adjectives) and that they do not need to worry about being offensive. See what list of adjectives emerges, and if the volunteer can guess what the card says. Discuss the activity.
- Get together a group of guys and a group of girls. Ask each to discuss what they do to prevent rape (most likely, the girls will generate a long list and the guys will say little, if anything). Discuss with both groups why the responsibility to prevent rape lies with women, and the implications of that.
- Review films that feature gender-related issues. Have a viewing party and discussion! Some interesting selections include:

But I'm a Cheerleader
The Stepford Wives
North Country
G. I. Jane
Thelma and Louise
The Joy Luck Club
Real Women Have Curves
Tough Guise
Wrestling with Manhood
Beauty Mark

Boys to Men

Dreamworlds 3

Generation M

Killing Us Softly (I, II, and III)

Hip Hop: Beyond Beats and Rhythms

Milk

Born into Brothels

The Price of Pleasure

Erin Brockovich

Interesting short clips are available at:
  www.mediathatmattersfest.org/

- Listen to music that discusses gender-related issues. Discuss the meanings of the lyrics. If there are local groups who perform this type of music, host a house party or sponsor a concert. Some great feminist groups include:

Emma's Revolution (www.emmasrevolution.com)

Holly Near (www.hollynear.com)

Ani DiFranco

Indigo Girls

Dar Williams

Tori Amos

Tracy Chapman

- Conduct an analysis of the depiction of men and women in children's films or children's books. What images are presented to young people? If they bother you, call or write to the authors, publishers, or filmmakers!
- Violate a gender norm publicly, such as the article included herein by Victor Romano, and note the responses.
- Try for one day to engage in only gender-neutral language. How difficult was this? What were the conversations or topics that were most difficult? Why?
- Take a test of your implicit biases. See www.understandingpre judice.org/ to take several tests related to gender and racial bias.
- Get involved in a local women's group or organization.
- Inventory your home, dorm room, workplace, school, etc., for gender equality. What do you notice?
- Pay close attention for a specific stretch of time to the advertisements you see on television, in magazines, etc. What messages are

presented about women? About men? Check out some of Jean Kilbourne's great work on the subject at www.jeankilbourne.com.

- Host an awareness event about some women's issue, like domestic violence, human trafficking, the wage gap, etc.
- Start a book club devoted to gender issues.
- Write letters to the editor to bring awareness about gender issues in your community.
- Start or contribute to a feminist blog.
- Celebrate historical achievements, events, and holidays related to gender issues, like the ratification of the Nineteenth Amendment, International Women's Day, etc.
- Look up and discuss great quotes on men, women, and feminism.
- Conduct interviews with diverse groups about what it means to be a feminist.
- Analyze textbooks for the fair inclusion of both genders.
- Engage in structured community debates about controversial topics related to gender.
- For classes: Tell students or a group of people they are to pretend they are from another planet and have no idea how men and women are supposed to look like or act. Then pass out a bunch of magazines (for instance, *Glamour, Cosmopolitan, Men's Health, Maxim*) and ask them to use the pictures and articles to find their answers and report out.

  Gather a bunch of magazines (*Maxim* and *Cosmopolitan/Glamour/ Elle* work well).

  I randomly passed them out to my class as they entered the room. At the beginning of class I told them to pretend that they were coming to this planet for the first time (I know that sounds a bit weird). I asked them to use the magazine they were holding as a good "reference" for learning what men and women were supposed to act/be like in our culture. I had them jot down some notes, and then we had a really neat discussion afterward about the media's portrayal of gender. It was a nice setup for a number of things (gender roles, body image, careers, personality, etc.).

- Write a journal or letter to your son, daughter, niece, nephew, or child you are close to about your vision of equality, perhaps something for them to read and think about when they are a bit older. The idea is to set up a foundation of support for them to be able to lean on when questions may arise for them in school, with peers, on television, etc.
- Bring a blank canvas to your next social event, birthday party, pot-luck, dinner party with friends, and ask them to paint their visions of peace, equality, or an issue that rings in your heart.

- Journal about your own personal issues around being a man or a woman and what issues you have faced within your life.
- Exchange household chores with your partner, spouse, or roommate for one week.
- Volunteer! Find a group that you may not be familiar with, perhaps a gay rights group, domestic violence support, homeless support, and ask about volunteer opportunities.
- Interview your friends about gender issues they have faced.
- Get out of your own box! Try something new and different even if it feels uncomfortable.

Appendix Two

Recommended Resources

BOOKS

Essay Compilations

Ellison, Sheila, and Wilson, Marie. *If Women Ruled the World: How to Create the World We Want to Live In*. Novato, CA: New World Library, 2004.
  A compilation of essays that inform and inspire feminist activism.
Rothenberg, Paula. *Race, Class, and Gender in the United States: An Integrated Study*. 6th ed. New York: Worth Publishers, 2003.
  A collection of facts, news reports, and academic articles about race, class, and gender.
Woolf, Virginia. *A Room of One's Own*. Richmond, VA: Hogarth Press, 1929.
  Essays examining females as literary forces.

Work/Economics

Clift, Eleanor, and Brazaitis, Tom. *Madam President: Shattering the Last Glass Ceiling*. New York: Scribner, 2000.
  Insider's view of Washington, D.C. as an "old boys' network."
Ehrenreich, Barbara. *Nickel and Dimed: On (Not) Getting by in America*. New York: Holt, 2002.
  Chronicles Ehrenreich's research involving the working poor in the United States.
Hays, Sharon. *Flat Broke with Children: Women in the Age of Welfare Reform*. New York: Oxford University Press, 2004.
  Presents research demonstrating the ineffectiveness of 1990s welfare reform.
Hochschild, Arlie, and Machung, Anne. *The Second Shift*. New York: Viking, 1989.
  Important book examining women's work at home.

Historical

Collins, Gail. *American Women*. New York: Harper Perennial, 2003.
Collins, Patricia Hill. *Black Feminist Thought: Knowledge, Consciousness, and the Politics of Empowerment*. Sydney, Australia: Allan and Unwin, 1990.

Critical academic contribution about the contributions of black feminist activists.

Coontz, Stephanie. *The Way We Never Were: American Families and the Nostalgia Trap*. New York: Basic, 1993.

Historical review debunking misconceptions about families.

Coontz, Stephanie. *The Way We Really Are: Coming to Terms with America's Changing Families*. New York: Basic, 1997.

Coontz's followup examines the reality of modern families in the United States.

Dicker, Rory. *A History of U.S. Feminisms*. Berkeley, CA: Seal, 2008.

Excellent review of first, second, and third waves.

Eisler, Riane. *The Chalice and the Blade: Our History, Our Future*. Gloucester, MA: Peter Smith Publishers, 1994.

Historical examination of patriarchy, adds important historical contributions by women.

Faludi, Susan. *Backlash: The Undeclared War against American Women*. New York: Crown, 1991.

Excellent review of the backlash against second-wave feminism.

Faludi, Susan. *Stiffed: The Betrayal of the American Man*. New York: Harper Perennial, 2000.

Faludi's follow up to *Backlash* focusing on how American men feel a crisis in masculinity.

Freedman, Estelle. *No Turning Back: The History of Feminism and the Future of Women*. New York: Ballantine, 2002.

Friedan, Betty. *The Feminine Mystique*. New York: Dell, 1964.

Classic, kicked off the second wave.

Friedan, Betty. *The Second Stage: With a New Introduction*. Cambridge, MA: Harvard University Press, 1998.

Friedan's follow up to *The Feminine Mystique*, cautions against factionalism in the movement and invites male *participants*.

Fiction

Gilman, Charlotte. *Herland*. Mineola, NY: Dover, 1998.

A classic, Charlotte Perkins Gilman presents a hilarious vision of a women's utopia.

Violence

Allison, Dorothy. *Bastard Out of Carolina*. New York: Dutton, 1994.

Compelling story of sexual violence and its legacy.

Ensler, Eve. *The Vagina Monologues*. New York: Villard, 2007.

Ensler's book and play is a world phenomenon that takes the private and makes it public.

Katz, Jackson. *The Macho Paradox: Why Some Men Hurt Women and How All Men Can Help*. Naperville, IL: Sourcebooks, Inc., 2006.

Calls men to action to help end violence against women.

Sebold, Alice. *Lucky: A Memoir*. New York: Back Bay, 2002.

Tells the story of the author's rape as a college freshman.

Third Wave

Adams, Carol. *The Sexual Politics of Meat: A Feminist Vegetarian Critical Theory*. London: Continuum International Publishing, 1999.

Baumgardner, Jennifer, and Richards, Amy. *Manifesta: Young Women, Feminism, and the Future*. New York: Farrar, Straus, and Giroux, 2000.
  Directed at young women, incites enthusiasm for third-wave feminist activism.

Findlen, Barbara. *Listen Up! Voices from the Next Feminist Generation*. Berkeley, CA: Seal Press, 2001.

Hernandez, Daisy, Rehman, Bushra, and Moraga, Cherrie. *Colonize This! Young Women of Color on Today's Feminism*. Berkeley, CA: Seal, 2002.
  A compilation of multicultural third-wave feminists.

hooks, bell. *Feminism Is for Everybody: Passionate Politics*. Boston: South End, 2000.
  hooks examines challenges facing feminists today.

Muscio, Inga. *Cunt: A Declaration of Independence*. Berkeley, CA: Seal, 2002.
  Examines the history of the insulting term as well as a third-wave analysis of how women can reclaim their bodies.

Valenti, Jessica. *Full Frontal Feminism: A Young Woman's Guide to Why Feminism Matters*. Berkeley, CA: Seal, 2007.
  Valenti passionately asserts the need for continued feminist activism.

Walker, Rebecca (Ed.). *To Be Real: Telling the Truth and Changing the Face of Feminism*. New York: Anchor, 2005.

Adolescents

Kindlon, Dan. *Alpha Girls: Understanding the New American Girl and How She is Changing the World*. New York: Rodale, 2007.
  Offers an interesting rebuttal to the argument that all adolescent girls suffer self-esteem losses.

Pipher, Mary, and Ross, Ruth. *Reviving Ophelia: Saving the Souls of Adolescent Girls*. New York: Riverhead Trade, 2005.
  Examines psychological issues faced by girls during adolescence.

Sadker, Myra, and Sadker, David. *Failing at Fairness: How Our Schools Cheat Girls*. New York: Scribner, 1995.
  Addresses gender bias in schooling.

Gender Roles

Adams, Rachel, and Savran, David. *The Masculinity Studies Reader*. New York: Wiley-Blackwell, 2002.
  Essays on many different aspects of and issues related to masculinity.

Bornstein, Kate. *Gender Outlaw: On Men, Women, and the Rest of Us*. New York: Vintage, 1995.
  Bornstein describes the process of becoming transsexual.

Connell, Robert. *Gender*. Cambridge, UK: Polity, 2002.
  Offers a sociological analysis of gender and gender roles.

Dowd, Maureen. *Are Men Necessary? When Sexes Collide*. New York: Berkley Trade Press, 2006.

New York Times columnist Dowd's scathing indictment of the utility of men today.

Gilligan, Carol. *In a Different Voice: Psychological Theory and Women's Development.* Cambridge, MA: Harvard University Press, 1993.

Seminal work on how women view the world.

Tannen, Deborah. *You Just Don't Understand: Women and Men in Conversation.* New York: Harper, 2001.

Highlights the ways men and women are socialized to communicate differently and the impact of these differences.

Williams, Joan. *Unbending Gender: Why Family and Work Conflict and What to Do About It.* New York: Oxford University Press, 2001.

Emphasizes the need for flexible work policies for women balancing employment and motherhood.

Global

Kristof, Nicholas, and WuDunn, Sheryl. *Half the Sky: Turning Oppression into Opportunity for Women Worldwide.* New York: Knopf, 2009.

Amazing examination of global violence against women, maternal health, and education.

Murray, Anne Firth. *From Outrage to Courage: Women Taking Action for Health and Justice.* Monroe, ME: Common Courage, 2008.

Discusses global health issues impacting women, including stories of resilience and activism.

Bodies

Ehrenreich, Barbara, and English, Deirdre. *For Her Own Good: Two Centuries of the Experts' Advice to Women.* New York: Anchor, 2005.

Explores the increasing roles of "experts" in women's lives, especially in regard to medical issues.

Kilbourne, Jean. *Can't Buy My Love: How Advertising Changes the Way We Think and Feel.* New York: Free Press, 2000.

Informative review of advertising's impact.

Wolf, Naomi. *The Beauty Myth: How Images of Beauty Are Used against Women.* New York: Harper Perennial, 2002.

Thorough review of media images of beauty and how they harm women.

Parenting

Burkett, Elinor. *The Baby Boon: How Family-Friendly America Cheats the Childless.* New York: Free Press, 2002.

Draws needed to attention to discrimination against those who do not elect to reproduce.

Crittenden, Ann. *The Price of Motherhood: Why the Most Important Job in the World Is Still the Least Valued.* New York: Holt, 2002.

Global examination of how women's work at home is undervalued.

Drew, Naomi. *Peaceful Parents, Peaceful Kids: Practical Ways to Create a Calm and Happy Home.* New York: Kensington, 2000.

Offers great tips on peaceful parenting.

Evans, Elrena, and Grant, Caroline. *Mama, Ph.D: Women Write about Motherhood and Academic Life*. New Brunswick, NJ: Rutgers University Press, 2009.
Compilation of entries examining barriers for women in higher education.
Fessler, Ann. *The Girls Who Went Away: The Hidden History of Women Who Surrendered Children for Adoption in the Decades Before Roe v. Wade*. New York: Penguin, 2006.
Illuminating review of women who were coerced to give up their babies.
O'Reilly, Andrea. *Feminist Mothering*. Albany: State University of New York Press, 2008.
Highlights how feminist mothering is empowering and can lead to social change.
Moving and informative examination of issues faced by mothers today.
Peskowitz, Miriam. *The Truth behind the Mommy Wars: Who Decides What Makes a Good Mother?* Berkeley, CA: Seal, 2005.
Important contribution to the debate about working versus stay-at-home mothers.
Rowe-Finkbeiner, Kristen, and Blades, Joan. *The Motherhood Manifesto: What American Moms Want—and What to Do about It*. New York: Nation Books, 2006.
Roy, Denise. *Momfulness: Mothering with Mindfulness, Compassion, and Grace*. San Francisco: Jossey-Bass, 2007.
Offers useful tips and activities for mothers.
Strong, Shari. *The Maternal Is Political: Women Writers at the Intersection of Motherhood and Social Change*. Berkeley, CA: Seal, 2008.
Compilation of personal reflections on feminist mothering.
Tannen, Deborah. *You're Wearing That? Understanding Mothers and Daughters in Conversation*. New York: Ballantine, 2006.
Interesting examination of the love-hate conversations between mothers and daughters.

WEB SITES

Work/Economy

She Source: www.shesource.org.
Devoted to "closing the gender gap in news media."
National Association of Working Women: www.9to5.org.
Advocates changes in the workplace.

General Feminist Sites

American Association of University Women: www.aauw.org.
National organization promoting gender equality, in particular in education.
Feminist: www.feminist.com.
Clearinghouse site for information, events, links, shopping, and more.
Feminist Campus: www.feministcampus.org/default.asp.
Provides information and resources for making higher education more feminist.
Ms. Foundation for Women: www.ms.foundation.org.

Access the magazine plus a lot more.
National Organization for Women: www.now.org.
  Articles, events, and much more!
National Partnership for Women and Families: www.nationalpartnership.org.
  Information and advocacy for women.
Strong Women, Strong Girls: www.swsg.org.
  Devoted to building communities of strong women.
The Women's Mosiac: www.thewomensmosaic.org.
  Nonprofit organization providing "education, inspiration, and motivation for
  women to rise up and rock the world!"

Bodies/Health

Adios Barbie: www.adiosbarbie.com.
  Focuses on encouraging women and girls to love their bodies.
Feminist Women's Health Center: www.fwhc.org/index.htm.
  Hub of information about health issues for women and teens.

Third Wave

Guerrilla Girls: www.guerrillagirls.com.
  Offers information, books, and speakers about third-wave feminism.
Third Wave Foundation: www.thirdwavefoundation.org.
  Feminist activist organization supporting young women and transgender
  youth.

Parenting

Hip Mama: www.hipmama.com.
  Political commentary and stories by and for mothers.
Moms Rising: www.momsrising.org.
  National and state campaigns focusing on gender equality and mother's
  empowerment.
Mothers Acting Up: www.mothersactingup.org.
  Offers information, events, and actions, including "girlcotts."
Mothers and More: www.mothersandmore.org.
  A nonprofit devoted to "improving the lives of mothers through support, edu-
  cation, and advocacy."
Mothers Movement: www.mothersmovement.org.
  "Resources and reporting for mothers and others who think about social
  change."
Mothers Ought to Have Equal Rights: www.mothersoughttohaveequalrights.org.
  A grassroots coalition providing support to mothers and other caregivers.

Global

Amnesty International: www.amnesty.org.
  Information and actions relevant to human rights, including violence against
  women.

Association for Women's Rights in Development: www.awid.org.
  "Strengthening movements to advance women's rights and gender equality
  worldwide."
Global Fund for Women: www.globalfundforwomen.org/cms/.
  Information and grants for programs helping women and girls, largely in
  developing countries.
Human Rights Watch: www.hrw.org.
  Global human rights monitor. Great reports on the status of human rights.
International Center for Research on Women: www.icrw.org.
  Promoting a world free of poverty for all people through insight and action.
Madre: www.madre.org.
  "Demanding rights, resources, and results for women worldwide."
Nobel Women's Initiative: www.nobelwomensinitiative.org.
  Established by six women Nobel peace laureates with goal to bring people
  together for peace and justice.
Peace X Peace: www.peacexpeace.org.
  Global network devoted to women's peace-building.
Sisterhood Is Global Institute: www.sigi.org.
  Helps bring together women from around the globe.
The Global Peace Initiative of Women: www.gpiw.org.
  Provides a global platform for fostering unity, peace-building, and develop-
  ment.
United Nations Development Fund for Women: www.unifem.org.
  Information on global gender issues.
Women's E-News: www.womensenews.org.
  News source with complete coverage of issues and events impacting women.
Women's Environment and Development Organization: www.wedo.org.
  Working for a peaceful and just world for everyone.
Women for Women International: www.womenforwomen.org.
  Dedicated to helping female survivors of war rebuild and transform their
  lives.

Violence

Code Pink: www.codepink4peace.org.
  Female-led activism for peace.
Equality Now: www.equalitynow.org/english/index.html.
  Works to end violence and discrimination against women and girls, world-
  wide.
Men Can Stop Rape: www.mencanstoprape.org.
  Calls on men and boys to engage in efforts to stop sexual assault.
National Coalition Against Domestic Violence: www.ncadv.org.
  Information and resources for victims, advocates, and the general public.
National Organization for Men Against Sexism: www.nomas.org.
  Information and activism by and for men.
Rape, Abuse, and Incest National Network: www.rainn.org.
  The nation's largest antisexual assault organization.
White Ribbon Campaign: www.whiteribbon.ca.
  Male-led activism to end violence against women.

Girls

Free the Children: www.freethechildren.com.
   Empowers children to help children, worldwide.
Girls in the Game: www.girlsinthegame.org.
   Promotes sport, fitness, and nutrition for young girls.
Girls, Inc.: www.girlsinc.org/index.html.
   Information and education for smart, strong, and bold girls.
New Moon Girls: www.newmoon.com.
   Online community for young girls.
Teen Voices: www.teenvoices.com.
   Resources and online community for teens and tweens.

Media

Girls, Media, and Women Project: www.mediaandwomen.org.
   Helps increase awareness of how popular culture and media depict women.

Environment

Eco Mom Alliance: www.ecomomalliance.org.
   "Because one of nature's strongest forces is a network of women."
Women's Voices for the Earth: www.womenandenvironment.org.
   Women-led campaign for ecological sustainability.

Bodies

NARAL Pro Choice: www.prochoiceamerica.org.
   Wealth of information related to pro-choice efforts across the United States.
National Latina Institute for Reproductive Health: www.latinainstitute.org.
   Devoted to ensuring reproductive health and rights for Latina women.

Politics/Government

American Civil Liberties Union: www.aclu.org.
   Protects civil liberties for all.
Institute for Women's Policy Research: www.iwpr.org.
   Conducts research and disseminates findings relevant to women and girls.
League of Women Voters: www.lwv.org.
   Works to promote government and impact policies.
The White House Project: www.thewhitehouseproject.org.
   Aims to advance women's leadership in all areas, including the White House.
U.S. Department of State Office of Global Women's Issues: www.state.gov/g/wi/.
   Working for the political, economic, and social empowerment of women.

Gay and Lesbian

Gay and Lesbian Alliance Against Defamation: www.glaad.org.
  Devoted to fighting defamation of gays and lesbians and changing hearts and minds.

Diversity

Teaching Tolerance: www.tolerance.org.
  Information on teaching K–12 students acceptance of all peoples.
Women of Color Resource Center: www.coloredgirls.org.
  Organization devoted to promoting the well-being of women and girls of color.

JOURNALS AND MAGAZINES

Magazines

Bitch Magazine: Provides commentary on our media-driven world from a feminist perspective.
Bust Magazine: The magazine for women with something to get off their chests.
Ms.: The landmark journal for feminist viewpoints.

Journals

Differences: A Journal of Feminist Cultural Studies: A critical forum for exploring differences.
Feminist Journal: Online, user-friendly journal featuring articles, blog, and advice.
Feminist Review: Devoted to writing reviews from a feminist perspective that explore the world through an anti-oppression lens.
Feminist Studies: Academic source featuring articles on issues relevant to all classes of feminists.
Feminist Teacher: Provides a medium for educators to discuss curricula and teaching methods from a feminist lens.
FemTAP: A Journal of Feminist Theory and Practice: Investigates the intersection of feminist theory and practice.
Gender & Society: Academic journal examining a variety of issues relevant to gender.
Hypatia: A Journal of Feminist Philosophy: A forum for cutting edge work in philosophy.
Journal of International Women's Studies: Academic journal focusing on international women's issues.
MP: An Online Feminist Journal: An online, peer-reviewed, international feminist journal.
Off Our Backs: The Feminist Newsjournal: News journal collectively produced by and for women.
Thirdspace: An academic journal of feminist theory and culture.

Violence Against Women: Academic journal addressing all facets of violence against
    women.
Women's Studies: Provides a forum for scholarship and criticism about women in
    various fields.
Women's Studies Quarterly: Academic journal publishing research and essays rel-
    evant to women's studies.

Notes

CHAPTER 1

1. Freedman, Estelle, *No Turning Back: The History of Feminism and the Future of Women* (New York: Ballantine, 2002).
2. Freedman 2002, 7.
3. Kimmel, Michael, *Guyland: The Perilous World Where Boys Become Men* (New York: HarperCollins, 2008), 264.
4. Morgan, Robin, *The Demon Lover: The Roots of Terrorism* (New York: Washington Square Press, 2000).
5. Johnson, Allan, *The Forest and the Trees: Sociology as Life, Practice, and Promise* (Philadelphia, PA: Temple University Press, 1997).
6. Freedman, 2002.
7. Eisler, Riane, *The Chalice and the Blade* (New York: HarperOne, 1988).
8. Freedman, 2002, 1–2.
9. Mays, Dorothy. *Women in Early America: Struggles, Survival, and Freedom in a New World* (Santa Barbara, CA: ABC-CLIO, 2004).
10. Collins, Gail, *America's Women: 400 Years of Dolls, Drudges, Heroines, and Helpmates* (New York: Harper Perennial, 2003), 49.
11. Collins, 2003.
12. Collins, 2003.
13. Collins, 2003.
14. Collins, 2003.
15. Angstar, Kelli, "Rule of Thumb and the Folklaw of the Husband's Stick," *Journal of Legal Education* 44 (1994): 341–65.
16. Collins, 2003.
17. Collins, 2003.
18. Collins, 2003.
19. Mays, 2004.
20. Collins, 2003.
21. Kendall, 2001.
22. Thatcher-Ulrich, Laurel, *Well-Behaved Women Seldom Make History* (New York: Alfred A. Knopf, 2007), 125.
23. Rowe-Finkbeiner, Kristen, *The F Word: Feminism in Jeopardy* (Berkeley, CA: Seal, 2004).
24. Thatcher-Ulrich, 2007, 125.

25. Rowland, Debran, *The Boundaries of Her Body: The Troubling History of Women's Rights in America* (Naperville: Sphinx, 2004), xxv.

26. Hunt, L., *Inventing Human Rights: A History Rights* (New York: W.W. Norton, 2007).

27. Hunt, 2007.

28. Freedman, 2002.

29. Freedman, 2002, 37.

30. Freedman, 2002.

31. Freedman, 2002, 52.

32. Freedman, 2002.

33. Collins, 2003.

34. Collins, 2003.

35. Collins, 2003, 128.

36. Collins, 2003, 123.

37. Collins, 2003, 88.

38. Collins, 2003.

39. Collins, 2003, 98.

40. Collins, 2003.

41. Freedman, 2002.

42. Freedman, 2002.

43. Freedman, 2002, 21–22.

44. Freedman, 2002.

45. Freedman, 2002.

46. Collins, 2003.

47. Collins, 2003.

48. "Elizabeth Blackwell." *National Library of Medicine*, January 10, 2008, www.nlm.nih.gov/hmd/blackwell (accessed October 14, 2009).

49. Rowland, 2004.

50. Collins, 2003.

51. Collins, 2003.

52. Collins, 2003.

53. Collins, 2003, 240.

54. Collins, 2003.

55. Rowland, 2004.

56. Collins, 2003, 242.

57. Collins, 2003.

58. Collins, 2003, 247.

59. Bernikow, Louise, "Women Demanded Their 4th of July Discordant Note," *Womensenews*, July 4, 2006, www.womensenews.org/story/our-story/060704/women-demanded-their-4th-july-discordant-note (accessed October 14, 2009).

60. Rowland, 2004.

61. Rowland, 2004.

62. Freedman, 2002.

63. Collins, 2003, 320.

64. Collins, 2003.

65. Collins, 2003.

66. Collins, 2003.

67. Collins, 2003, 280.

68. Freedman, 2002, 64.

69. Rowland, 2004.
70. Cited in Rowland, 2004, 39.
71. Rowland, 2004.
72. Collins, 2003.
73. Collins, 2003.
74. Collins, 2003.
75. Collins, 2003, 336.
76. Collins, 2003, 337.
77. Collins, 2003, 327.
78. Collins, 2003.
79. Collins, 2003.
80. Rowland, 2004, 42.
81. Freedman, 2002.
82. Freedman, 2002.
83. Freedman, 2002, 83.
84. Freedman, 2002, 83.
85. Rowland, 2004.
86. Collins, 2003, 367.
87. Collins, 2003.
88. Collins, 2003, 376.
89. Collins, 2003.
90. Rowland, 2004, 85.
91. Rowe-Finkbeiner, 2004, 23.

CHAPTER 2

1. Shaw, Susan, and Janet Lee, *Women's Voices, Feminist Visions* (New York: McGraw Hill, 2007), 10.
2. Shaw and Lee, 2007.
3. Collins, Gail, *America's Women: 400 Years of Dolls, Drudges, Heroines, and Helpmates* (New York: Harper Perennial, 2003).
4. Rowland, Debran, *The Boundaries of Her Body: The Troubling History of Women's Rights in America* (Naperville: Sphinx, 2004).
5. Collins, 2003.
6. Collins, 2003.
7. Collins, 2003.
8. O'Beirne, Kate, *Women Who Make the World Worse and How Their Radical Feminist Assault Is Ruining Our Schools, Families, Military, and Sports* (New York: Sentinel, 2006).
9. Collins, 2003.
10. Thatcher-Ulrich, Laurel, *Well-Behaved Women Seldom Make History* (New York: Alfred A. Knopf, 2007).
11. Freedman, Estelle, *No Turning Back: The History of Feminism and the Future of Women* (New York: Ballantine, 2002).
12. Thatcher-Ulrich, 2007, 198–99.
13. Freedman, 2002, 88.
14. Thatcher-Ulrich, 2007, 203.
15. Thatcher-Ulrich, 2007.

16. Thatcher-Ulrich, 2007, 206–7.
17. Thatcher-Ulrich, 2007, 207.
18. Freedman, 2002.
19. Freedman, 2002.
20. Collins, 2003.
21. Freedman, 2002.
22. Shaw and Lee, 2007.
23. Thatcher-Ulrich, 2007, 205.
24. Collins, 2003, 444–45.
25. Freedman, 2002, 89.
26. Freedman, 2002.
27. Steinem, Gloria, "Foreward," in *To Be Real: Telling the Truth and Changing the Face of Feminism*, ed. Rebecca Walker (New York: Anchor, 1995), xv.
28. Steinem, 1995, xvii.
29. Faludi, Susan, *Backlash: The Undeclared War against American Women* (New York: Three Rivers Press, 2006).
30. Frye, Marilyn, "Opression," in *Women's Voices, Feminist Visions*, ed. Susan Shaw and Janet Lee (New York: McGraw-Hill, 2007), 84.
31. Freedman, 2002, 95.
32. Cited in Freedman, 2007, 51.
33. Rowe-Finkbeiner, Kristen, *The F Word: Feminism in Jeopardy* (Berkeley, CA: Seal, 2004).
34. Brownmiller, Susan, *Against Our Will: Men, Women, and Rape* (New York: Ballantine, 1993).
35. Rowe-Finkbeiner, 2004, 27.

CHAPTER 3

1. Pollitt, Katha, cited in Rowe-Finkbeiner, Kristen, *The F Word: Feminism in Jeopardy* (Berkeley, CA: Seal, 2004), 1.
2. Shaw, Susan, and Janet Lee, eds. *Women's Voices, Feminist Visions* (New York: McGraw-Hill, 2007).
3. Freedman, Estelle, *No Turning Back: The History of Feminism and the Future of Women* (New York: Ballantine, 2002).
4. Gillespie, M., "Equal Time," in *Feminism: Opposing Viewpoints*, ed. J. Hurley (San Diego, CA: Greenhaven, 1998 repr.), 119–21.
5. Freedman, 2002.
6. Kimmel, Michael, *Guyland: The Perilous World Where Boys Become Men* (New York: Harper, 2008), 263.
7. Bellafante, G., "Feminism: It's All about Me," in *Feminism: Opposing Viewpoints*, ed. J. Hurley (San Diego, CA: Greenhaven, 1998 repr.), 108–18.
8. Rowe-Finkbeiner, Kristen, *The F Word: Feminism in Jeopardy* (Berkeley, CA: Seal, 2004), 32.
9. Poe, A., "You Call This Progress?" in *Feminism: Opposing Viewpoints*, ed. J. Hurley (San Diego, CA: Greenhaven, 1998 repr.), 18–21.
10. Walker, Rebecca, ed., *To Be Real: Telling the Truth and Changing the Face of Feminism* (New York: Anchor, 1995), 209.
11. Rowe-Finkbeiner, 2004, 2.

12. Walker, 1995, xxxi.

13. Walker, 1995.

14. Rowe-Finkbeiner, 2004, p. 5.

15. Katz, Jackson, *The Macho Paradox: Why Some Men Hurt Women and How All Men Can Help* (New York: Sourcebooks Trade, 2006), 75.

16. Katz, 2006, 75.

17. Gillespie, 1998.

18. Findlen, Barbara, *Listen Up: Voices from the Next Feminist Generation* (Berkeley: Seal, 2001), xv.

19. Pharr, Suzanne, "Homophobia: A Weapon of Sexism," in *Women's Voices, Feminist Visons*, ed. Susan Shaw and Janet Lee (New York: McGraw-Hill, 2007).

20. Rowe-Finkbeiner, 2004, 5.

21. Walker, 1995, p. xxxii–xxxiii.

22. Walker, 1995, xxxiii.

23. Walker, 1995, xxxv–xxxvi.

24. Rowe-Finkbeiner, 2004.

25. Shaw and Lee, 2007.

26. Rowe-Finkbeiner, 2004.

27. Delombard, Jeannine, "Femmenism," in *To Be Real: Telling the Truth and Changing the Face of Feminism*, ed. Rebecca Walker (New York: Anchor, 1995), 21–22.

28. Findlen, 2001, xv.

29. Kirk, Gwyn, and Margo Okazawa-Rey, *Women's Lives, Multicultural Perspectives* (New York: McGraw-Hill, 2007).

30. Rowe-Finkbeiner, 2004.

31. Rowe-Finkbeiner, 2004.

32. Bellafante, 1998, 112.

33. Gillespie, 1998, 120.

34. Rowe-Finkbeiner, 2004.

35. Rowe-Finkbeiner, 2004, 90.

36. Rowe-Finkbeiner, 2004, 92.

37. Steinem, Gloria, "Foreward," in *To Be Real: Telling the Truth and Changing the Face of Feminism*, ed. Rebecca Walker (New York: Anchor, 1995), xiii.

38. Crittendon, D., "Back to the Future," in *Feminism: Opposing Viewpoints*, ed. J. Hurley (San Diego, CA: Greenhaven, 1999 repr.), 81–86.

39. McIntosh, Peggy, "White Privilege and Male Privilege," in *Women's Voices, Feminist Visions*, ed. Susan Shaw and Janet Lee (New York: McGraw-Hill, 2007).

40. Lorber, Judith, "The Social Construction of Gender," in *Women's Voices, Feminist Visions*, ed. Susan Shaw and Janet Lee (New York: McGraw-Hill, 2007), 141.

41. Flanders, L., ed. *The W Effect: Bush's War on Women* (New York: The Feminist Press, 2004).

42. Easton, N., "The Power and the Glory: Who Needs the Christian Coalition When You've Got the White House? The Religious Right's Covert Crusade." in *The W Effect: Bush's War on Women*, ed. L. Flanders (New York: The Feminist Press, 2004), 5–10.

43. Berkowitz, B., "Team Bush to Abused Women: Fuhgedaboutit!" in *The W Effect: Bush's War on Women*, ed. L. Flanders (New York: The Feminist Press, 2004), 11–14.

44. Bunch, C., "Whose Security?" in *The W Effect: Bush's War on Women*, ed. L. Flanders (New York: The Feminist Press, 2004), 58, 253–57.

45. Where Barack Stands (nd). *Women for Obama*, http://my.barackobama.com/page/content/womenissues (accessed March 5, 2009).

46. Where Barack Obama stands, nd.

47. Where Barack Obama Stands, nd.

48. Where Barack Obama Stands, nd.

49. Where Barack Obama Stands, nd.

50. Where Barack Obama Stands, nd.

51. Where Barack Obama Stands, nd.

52. Pollitt, Katha, "U.S. Feminism Lite: Claiming Independence, Asserting Personal Choice," in *The W Effect: Bush's War on Women*, ed. L. Flanders (New York: The Feminist Press, 2004), 280–84.

53. Jones, Elllis, Ross Haenfler, and Brett Johnson, *The Better World Handbook: Small Changes That Make a Big Difference* (Gabriola Island, British Columbia: New Society, 2007).

CHAPTER 4

1. Freedman, Estelle, *No Turning Back: The History of Feminism and the Future of Women* (New York: Ballantine, 2002).

2. Freedman, 2002.

3. Rowe-Finkbeiner, Kristen, *The F Word: Feminism in Jeopardy* (Berkeley, CA: Seal, 2004), 259.

CHAPTER 5

1. Freedman, Estelle, *No Turning Back: The History of Feminism and the Future of Women* (New York: Ballantine, 2002).

2. Kindlon, Dan, *Alpha Girls* (New York: Rodale, 2006).

3. Freedman, 2002.

4. Kindlon, 2006.

5. O'Beirne, Kate, *Women Who Make the World Worse and How Their Radical Feminist Assault Is Ruining Our Schools, Families, Military, and Sports* (New York: Sentinel, 2006), 119.

6. Kindlon, 2006.

7. Freedman, 2002.

8. Peskowitz, Miriam, *The Truth Behind the Mommy Wars: Who Decides What Makes a Good Mother?* (Berkeley, CA: Seal, 2005).

9. Freedman, 2002.

10. Rowland, Debran, *The Boundaries of Her Body: The Troubling History of Women's Rights in America* (Naperville: Sphinx, 2004).

11. Burk, Martha, "Power Plays: Six Ways the Male Corporate Elite Keeps Women Out," in *Women's Voices, Feminist Visions*, ed. Susan Shaw and Janet Lee, 3rd ed. (New York: McGraw-Hill, 2007), 483–86.

12. Freedman, 2002.

13. Shaw, Susan, and Janet Lee, *Women's Voices, Feminist Visions*, 3rd ed. (New York: McGraw-Hill, 2007).

14. O'Beirne, 2006, 67.

15. O'Beirne, 2006.

16. Rowland, 2004.

17. Freedman, 2002.

18. The names of people and places have been replaced with pseudonyms or omitted in order to protect the identities and jobs of the women I interviewed and spent time with.

CHAPTER 6

1. Freedman, Estelle, *No Turning Back: The History of Feminism and the Future of Women* (New York: Ballantine, 2002).

2. Freedman, 2002.

3. Solinger, Rickie, *Pregnancy and Power: A Short History of Reproductive Politics in America* (New York: New York University Press, 2005).

4. Freedman, 2002.

5. Freedman, 2002, 207.

6. Freedman, 2002, 209.

7. Freedman, 2002.

8. Solinger, 2005.

9. Rowland, Debran, *The Boundaries of Her Body: The Troubling History of Women's Rights in America* (Naperville: Sphinx, 2004).

10. Rowland, 2004, 271.

11. Baumgardner, J., "*Roe* in Rough Waters," in *The W Effect: Bush's War on Women*, ed. L. Flanders (New York: The Feminist Press, 2004), 65–69.

12. O'Beirne, Kate, *Women Who Make the World Worse and How Their Radical Feminist Assault Is Ruining Our Schools, Families, Military, and Sports* (New York: Sentinel, 2006), 159.

13. Rowland, 2004.

14. Rowland, 2004.

15. Freedman, 2002.

16. Freedman, 2002, 214–15.

17. Freedman, 2002.

18. Shaw, Susan, and Janet Lee, *Women's Voices, Feminist Visions* (New York: McGraw-Hill, 2007), 229.

19. Freedman, 2002.

CHAPTER 7

1. Ehrenreich, Barbara, and Deirdre English, *For Her Own Good: Two Centuries of the Experts' Advice to Women* (New York: Random House, 2005).

2. Kindlon, Dan, *Alpha Girls* (New York: Rodale, 2006).

3. Hochschild, Arlie, and Anne Machung, *The Second Shift: Working Parents and the Revolution at Home* (New York: Viking Penguin, 1989).

4. Olivella, Mary, Kristin Rowe-Finkbeiner, and Joan Blades, "Maternal Profiling: A *New York Times* Buzzword," *Mother and Family Matters*, www.feminist.com/activism/momsrising4.html (accessed May 5, 2009).

5. Rowe-Finkbeiner, Kristin. "Foreward," in *The Maternal Is Political*, ed. MacDonald Strong (Berkeley, CA: Seal, 2008), 1–4.

6. Rowe-Finkbeiner, 2008.

7. Krischer Goodman, Cindy, "With Income Drying Up, Moms to the Rescue," *Miami Herald*, May 6, 2009, 1-2A.

8. Carbone, 1999.

9. Coontz, Stephanie, *The Way We Never Were* (New York: Basic, 1992).

10. Maushart, Susan, *The Mask of Motherhood* (New York: Penguin, 1999).

11. Tiemann, Amy, "Peaceful Revolution Motherhood Awakens 'Naptime Activists'," *Mother and Family Matters*, www.feminist.com/activism/momsrising9 .html (accessed May 5, 2009).

12. Nelson, Amie, "Unleashed," in *The Moment: Mothers Acting Up 2009 Calendar* (Boulder, CO: Mothers Acting Up, 2009).

CHAPTER 8

1. Murray, Anne, *From Outrage to Courage* (Monroe, ME: Common Courage, 2008).

2. Murray, 2008

3. Freedman, Estelle, *No Turning Back: The History of Feminism and the Future of Women* (New York: Ballantine, 2002).

4. Freedman, 2002.

5. Katz, Jackson, *The Macho Paradox: Why Some Men Hurt Women and How All Men Can Help* (New York: Sourcebooks Trade, 2006), 67–68.

CHAPTER 9

1. Dekha, Maneesha, "Disturbing Images: PETA and the Feminist Ethics of Animal Advocacy," *Ethics and the Environment* 13, no. 2 (2008): 35–76.

2. Regan, Tom, *The Case for Animal Rights* (Berkeley: University of California Press, 2004).

CHAPTER 10

1. Kindlon, Dan, *Alpha Girls* (New York: Rodale, 2006).

2. Kindlon, 2006, 23.

3. Rowe-Finkbeiner, Kristen, *The F Word: Feminism in Jeopardy* (Berkeley, CA: Seal, 2004).

4. Morgan, Joan, "From Fly-Girls to Birches and Hos," in *Women's Voices, Feminist Visions*, ed. Susan Shaw and Janet Lee (New York: McGraw-Hill, 2007), 532.

5. Thatcher-Ulrich, Laurel, *Well-Behaved Women Seldom Make History* (New York: Alfred A. Knopf, 2007), xiv.

6. Thatcher-Ulrich, 2007, xx.

7. Thatcher-Ulrich, 2007, xxi.

CHAPTER 11

1. Shaw, Susan, and Janet Lee, eds. *Women's Voices, Feminist Visions* (New York: McGraw-Hill, 2007).

2. Kindlon, Dan, *Alpha Girls* (New York: Rodale, 2006).

3. Freedman, Estelle, *No Turning Back: The History of Feminism and the Future of Women* (New York: Ballantine, 2002).

4. Shaw and Lee, 2007.

5. O'Beirne, Kate, *Women Who Make the World Worse and How Their Radical Feminist Assault Is Ruining Our Schools, Families, Military, and Sports* (New York: Sentinel, 2006).

CHAPTER 12

1. Kimmel, Michael, *Guyland: The Perilous World Where Boys Become Men* (New York: HarperCollins, 2008), 142.

2. Kindlon, Dan, *Alpha Girls* (New York: Rodale, 2006).

3. O'Beirne, Kate, *Women Who Make the World Worse and How Their Radical Feminist Assault Is Ruining Our Schools, Families, Military, and Sports* (New York: Sentinel, 2006), 67.

4. Rowland, Debran, *The Boundaries of Her Body: The Troubling History of Women's Rights in America* (Naperville: Sphinx, 2004).

5. Rowland, 2004, 512.

6. Kimmel, 2008, 244–45.

7. Kimmel, 2008, 243–44.

8. Kimmel, 2008, 249.

9. Kimmel, 2008, 253.

10. Findlen, Barbara, *Listen Up: Voices from the Next Feminist Generation* (Berkeley: Seal, 2001).

CONCLUSION

1. Shaw, Susan and Janet Lee, eds. *Women's Voices, Feminist Visions* (New York: McGraw-Hill, 2007).

Index

About the Authors and Contributors

Natasha Abdin has been active in politics and community projects from a very young age. She is now 20 and focuses her energies on making the world a better for all people.

Rebecca Ajo graduated from Barry University in May 2009 with a degree in criminology. She plans to attend law school and become a lawyer.

Kimiko Akita is an assistant professor in the School of Communication at the University of Central Florida in Orlando. She teaches intercultural communication, international communication, gender communication, and research methods.

Kathlyn Albert is a certified nurse midwife and family nurse practitioner, primarily caring for women and children. She currently works for Pro Care Medical Group in Milwaukee, Wisconsin.

Lián Amaris is an interdisciplinary performance theorist and artist who focuses on media, pop culture, and gender.

Fran Asaro is the president of Thrive Any Way Personal and Business Coaching. She attributes much of her success to working with domestic violence survivors in a self esteem group.

Amy Barnickel is an ABD doctoral student in the texts and technologies program at the University of Central Florida.

Lydia Bartram, MSW, is the director of the Karen Slattery Educational Research Center for Child Development at Florida Atlantic University in Boca Raton, Florida.

Corinne Becker, RN, BSN is a nationally recognized professional speaker and Transformational Women's workshop leader.

Renee Bernett was a teacher for 15 years. She has contributed to and started numerous advocacy groups assisting those with breast cancer, childhood diabetes, and celiac disease.

Sade Brooks is currently a sophomore at Barry University, majoring in criminology. She plans on going to graduate school and upon completion aspires to be a youth advocate.

Khadija Charles is finishing her bachelor's degree at Florida International University and will be applying to graduate programs in social work.

Enbar Cohen is a student at Barry University in Miami, Florida. She is actively involved with Safe Schools South Florida, helping to provide workshops and training that ensure a safer school climate for lesbian, gay, bisexual, transgender, and questioning students.

Jacque Daugherty is program coordinator at the University of Cincinnati Graduate School, where she is also finishing her PhD.

Andrea Janelle Dickens teaches ancient and medival church history in Dayton, Ohio, at United Theological Seminary. She is also a published poet and a ceramicist.

Jackie Disarro is a graduate of Ball State University and plans to attend graduate school to earn a master's degree in psychology.

Craig Elliott, PhD, is assistant vice president of enrollment and student services at Samuel Merritt University in Oakland, California. He received his PhD in transformative learning and change at the California Institute of Integral Studies, where his doctoral research was on fathering as a feminist experience.

Katie Ellis is a disability support worker at Uniaccess: The University of Western Australia's Disability Office where she is developing an online community for students with disability as part of UWA's social network-ing and blogging site node.

Anya Finley is now six years old and in first grade. She loves animals and helping people, as well as art, music, and talking.

Laura Finley, PhD, is Assistant Professor of Sociology and Criminology at Barry University. She is also an author and community activist for peace, justice, and human rights.

Cori Lynne Fleser was, until recently, violence prevention coordinator at Women In Distress of Broward County.

Julia Gonzalez is majoring in pre-law at Barry University. Her dream is to be a justice in the U.S. Supreme Court. She is also a dedicated activist for animal rights.

Ilene Gottlieb is a registered nurse with 39 years of experience in different areas of nursing including pediatrics, maternal-child health, medical-surgical, and hospice.

Gary Grizzle is currently associate professor of sociology and chair of the department of sociology and criminology at Barry University in Miami, Florida.

Marie Jones is the assistant dean of libraries at East Tennessee State University in Johnson City, Tennessee. She recently completed a doctoral degree in educational leadership.

Marianna Leishman, L.L.B., is currently undertaking a master's in gender and cultural studies at the University of Sydney and is writing her thesis on political activism, gender subversion, and feminism in erotic performance.

Iwona Lepka graduated from University of Warmia and Mazury in Olsztyn in 2008. She is currently a PhD student at the faculty of languages, University of Gdańsk.

Nancy Leve graduated from West Virginia University in 1981 with a master's degree from the department of sociology focusing on marriage and family studies. She is currently self-employed.

Doreen Maller teaches therapeutic communications at John F. Kennedy University and runs a private practice in San Mateo California specializing in adolescents and their families. She is completing her PhD at the California Institute of Integral Studies.

Kristen Manieri is a freelance writer and author of the blog and the book, *Great Dates Orlando* and *Miami for Couples*.

Dianne McDonald is a national columnist known as "The Everyday Feminist," and she is a graduate from the University of Massachusetts in women's studies.

Tabatha Mudra is a graduate of the Art Institute of Fort Lauderdale. She is a photographer and community activist.

Rebecca Mushtare is a NYC-based digital media artist, and she is currently an assistant professor in the communications department at Marymount Manhattan College.

Jeff Nall is a writer, academic, speaker, and peace activist. Nall earned a master of liberal studies degree from Rollins College and is completing a PhD in comparative studies at Florida Atlantic University.

Jennifer Nardozzi, PsyD., is a psychologist who specializes in treating women with eating disorders. She is the national training manager of the Renfrew Center and she also has a private practice in Miami, Florida.

Rebecca Nicholson has her master's degree in conflict analysis and resolution. She lives an exciting, childless life in Fort Lauderdale, where she is working on her PhD.

Roslyn Parker is president of the SafeSpace Foundation in Miami, Florida.

Nicole Patouhas is a student at Barry University in Miami, Florida.

Lauren Pilnick serves as the sexual violence education coordinator in the Women's Center at MSU, Mankato. She has two bachelor's degrees in crime, law, justice, and women's studies from the Pennsylvania State University and a master's of women's studies from Florida Atlantic University.

LuElla Putnam received a master's degree in English from a joint program between the Citadel and the College of Charleston in South Carolina 2008. She is currently enrolled in the PhD program in literature at Oklahoma State University.

Carmen Ramirez has a bachelor's degree in anthropology and began doing advocacy work at the age of 16. She is currently an advocate at a domestic violence center.

Victor Romano is assistant professor of sociology and criminology at Barry University, where he teaches and coordinates departmental internships.

Li-Hsiang Lisa Rosenlee is an associate professor of philosophy at the University of Hawaii—West Oahu. Her areas of interest include Asian and comparative philosophy, feminism, and ethics.

Dvera Saxton received her bachelor's degree in anthropology from Hartwick College in 2004, and is currently pursuing a PhD in anthropology at the American University in Washington, D.C.

Carmen D. Siering teaches women's studies and English composition at Ball State University in Muncie, Indiana.

Emily Reynolds Stringer holds a master's degree from Florida Atlantic University.

Jenney Stringer received a bachelor of arts from Hamilton College with honors in women's studies. She is currently pursuing a degree in nurse midwifery.

Ellen H. Ullman, MSW, graduated from Pennsylvania State University with a bachelor's degree in anthropology and a certificate in Middle Eastern studies. She obtained her MSW in 2009.

Sheena Vega graduated from Florida Atlantic University in 2008 with a bachelor's degree in English literature. She currently works in Santiago, Chile, teaching English as a foreign language to adults.

Ariana E. Vigil is an assistant professor of English and ethnic studies at the University of Nebraska, Lincoln.

Gerald Walton, PhD, is assistant professor in the faculty of education at Lakehead University in Thunder Bay, Ontario. He teaches diversity and equity in education.

Annie Warshaw is a graduate student at Roosevelt University with a focus in women's history. She is very active with different women-based organizations.

Emily Yanez graduated from Barry University in May 2009 with a degree in communications.